THE COMPLETE NEW GUIDE
TO PREPARING BABY FOODS

is a book for the mother of the '80s: economy-minded, self-sufficient, and aware of the overwhelming importance of good nutrition during the baby's first years of life.

Whatever your reasons for desiring to prepare your own baby foods, the important thing is to get started. Decide for yourself which methods and foods fit most easily into your schedule. For the small amount of extra time or thought you may put in, you will receive great satisfaction in knowing that you are not taking chances with your baby's present or future health and that the food he eats is highly nutritious. He will also learn to enjoy the natural flavor of good foods that are simply and easily prepared. Where else can you get so much more while paying less!

"Sue Castle has written a book based on sound medical knowledge and her own experiences as a mother of two children. Use this book as a clear and easy guide in preparing nutritious meals for your child. All mothers will benefit from the many useful suggestions offered."

Charles H. Bauer, M.D.
Clinical Associate Professor of Pediatrics
at New York Hospital—Cornell Medical
Center; Attending Pediatrician,
Roosevelt Hospital

THE COMPLETE NEW GUIDE TO
PREPARING BABY FOODS

SUE CASTLE

BANTAM BOOKS

TORONTO • NEW YORK • LONDON • SYDNEY • AUCKLAND

THE COMPLETE NEW GUIDE TO
PREPARING BABY FOODS

A Bantam Book / published by arrangement with
Doubleday & Co., Inc.

PRINTING HISTORY
Doubleday edition published June 1981
Bantam edition / March 1983

ISBN 0-553-23042-5

Published simultaneously in the United States and Canada

Bantam Books are published by Bantam Books, Inc.
Its trademark, consisting of the words "Bantam Books"
and the portrayal of a rooster, is Registered in U.S.
Patent and Trademark Office and in other countries.
Marca Registrada. Bantam Books, Inc., 666 Fifth Avenue,
New York, New York 10103.

PRINTED IN THE UNITED STATES OF AMERICA

O   0 9 8 7 6 5 4 3

*To my mother, Jay, Jennifer, and Bethany
for their patience, understanding,
and aid—thank you!*

Contents

FOREWORD   xiii

INTRODUCTION   xvii

1. NUTRITION   1

   Calories 2

   Protein 3

   Carbohydrates 4

   Fats 6

   Vitamins 7

   Minerals 14

2. HOW TO SAVE MONEY   18

   "Nutritional Cost" 18

   Inexpensive Protein 19

   How to Read Labels 20

   U.S. Grades 21

   Inspection Shields 21

   Brand Names 22

   Weights, Measures, or Counts 22

Description of Food 23
"Natural Foods" 24
Dating Codes 25
"RDA" Nutritional Information 26
List of Ingredients 26
    Additives 27
    Fortifiers 30
A Shopping Checklist 31

3. FEEDING YOUR BABY   33
  Breast Feeding or Bottle Feeding 33
    How to Prepare a Formula 36
    Supplements 39
  Schedules 39
  Why, When, and How to Introduce Solid Food 41
    When to Introduce a Food Table 42
    How to Introduce New Foods 43
    How to Introduce Coarser Foods 44
  Planning a Balanced Menu 45
  Feeding Equipment 47
  When Your Baby Won't Eat 49
  Self-Feeding 50
  Digestive Difficulties 51
  Feeding Your Baby Away from Home 53

4. EQUIPMENT FOR EASY COOKING
  AND PURÉEING   55
  Cooking with Steam 55
  Microwave Ovens 59
  The Electric Blender 59
    Selecting a Blender 60
    Using Your Blender 61
    Repairing Your Blender 63

The Food Processor 64
 Selecting a Food Processor 65
 Using Your Processor 65
 Repairing a Food Processor 66
Other Ways to Purée 66
Miscellaneous Utensils 68
Recommended Equipment List 69

5. THE SAFE AND HEALTHY WAY
 TO STORE FOODS 70
 How Spoiled Food Can Affect Your Baby 70
 Signs of Spoilage 72
 General Rules of Handling and Storing Foods 72
 Purées Need Special Care 73
 Pantry Storage 74
 Refrigerator Storage 75
 Freezer Storage 78
 How to Check Your Freezer Temperature 78
 What and How to Freeze 79
 Refreezing Food 81
 Food Cubes 82
 Canned Foods 83
 Home Canning 84

6. THE BABY-FOOD SYSTEM 86
 How to Plan 86
 How to Save Time 87
 How to Use Leftovers 88
 How to Purée 89
 Thinning—Thickening 91
 Food-Combination Guide 92
 How to Use and Modify the Recipes 93
 Cooking Methods and Times 93

Salt 94
Fats and Oils 94
Sweeteners 95
Measurements 96
Substitutions 97

7. CEREAL GRAINS   99
Cereals 100
   Preparing Cereal 103
Flour, Pasta, Baked Goods 104
   Using Flour 105
   Using Pasta 106
Wheat Germ 108
   Using Wheat Germ 109
Rice 110
   Rice and Meat Dishes 113

8. FRUITS   115

9. VEGETABLES   142
General Vegetable Recipes 183

10. PROTEIN FOODS   188
Meats: Beef, Lamb, Veal, Pork 188
   Puréeing Meat 196
*Organ Meats: Liver, Kidney, Brains,
Sweetbreads* 197
Poultry 200
   Puréeing Poultry 203
Fish 204
   Puréeing Fish 208
Soybeans 208

    Eggs   210
        Using Eggs   212
    Yogurt   217
    Cheese   219
        Using Cheese   220
    Nonfat Dry Milk   221
    Protein Economy   222

11. **DESSERTS**   226

12. **BEVERAGES**   232
    Milk for Your Baby   232
        Skim Milk or Whole Milk?   235
        Milks Not for Your Baby   236
        How to Store Milk   237
        Homemade Fortified Milk   238
    Juices: Fruit and Vegetable   239

13. **INSTANT BABY FOOD: HOW TO
    LIVE OFF THE LAND**   247
    Cereal Grains   248
    Fruits   248
    Vegetables   250
    Protein Foods   251
        Eggs   251
        Liver   251
        Precooked Meat and Poultry Meals   252
        Dairy Foods   252

14. **FINGER FOODS**   255
    Some General Suggestions   256
    Cereal Grains   257

Fruits 262
Vegetables 264
Protein Foods 266
Eggs 266
Meats and Poultry 268
Fish 272
Cheese 273
Peanut Butter 274

APPENDIX A: NUTRITIVE VALUES
OF FOODS   275

APPENDIX B: PERSONAL FEEDING
CHART   301

BIBLIOGRAPHY   307

INDEX   310

Foreword

In the medical, especially pediatric, journals and textbooks, there are a number of specific articles with proper references that critically evaluate various commercial baby foods, or present research on infant nutrition. These articles, even if they were readily available, might not be helpful to the average mother. However, I feel very strongly that most mothers would like to receive guidance in feeding their babies. Most physicians caring for newborn babies attempt this, but have neither the time nor the inclination to go into any details. This book, used in conjunction with your physician, fills this vacuum.

As director of the Premature Institute at The New York Hospital—Cornell Medical Center for ten years, I taught and directed the education of physicians and nurses from all parts of the United States and the world in the latest techniques in the care and feeding of infants. Nearly all of these professional persons agreed with me that most mothers had little, if any, knowledge of the proper nutritional needs of their babies, and they needed assistance. In my own fifteen years of private practice of pediatrics, I have been aware of this same problem. The author frequently refers to Dr. Samuel Fomon. He is professor of pediatrics at the University of Iowa, and has participated in many conferences relating to nutrition of the child. He has written many scientific articles in the medical literature and is accepted by most pediatricians as an authority on this subject. The author must be complimented on her choice of such a valuable authority.

The first chapter, "Nutrition," contains information about the various ingredients of food as relevant to the specific nutritional needs of the infant. Many lists of nutritionally valuable, but inexpensive, foods are given and I find these extremely helpful. I also feel that the chapter on "Feeding Your Baby" is very important. The author keeps stressing the need of advice of a physician and that the information should not replace the advice of a specific doctor. No two children are alike and one cannot generalize, but it is nearly always true that rigid feeding schedules are mostly for a mother's convenience rather than the baby's needs.

It is also true that very few physicians agree as to when to introduce solid foods; the table in the text therefore is extremely valuable as a guide. All mothers will certainly benefit from the many useful suggestions offered in the section on "How to Introduce Solid Foods." There is no doubt that the mother's facial expression when offering a new food to her baby is extremely important. A mother should not show her own personal dislike of food to her baby.

When a baby is approximately one to three years of age, many mothers are extremely worried about their child's lack of appetite. They cannot understand "how baby survives," not to mention weight gain. The suggestions offered by the author are generally accepted by physicians and will be treasured by nearly all mothers.

As we now are a society which is no longer stationary but travels a great deal, the hints on feeding your baby away from home can simplify all efforts of feeding your baby.

If your baby develops digestive difficulties, you should always contact your doctor, as is stated in this book. Do not use medications on your own, but only under proper medical supervision.

I feel that the author's repeated statement that there is no need to add salt or sugar to the baby's food is correct. How true is the statement that "the last thing you want to do is to accustom your baby to the controversial adult preference for salted or sweetened foods."

Sue Castle has written a book based on sound medical knowledge and her own experiences of being a mother of two children. The new mother should use this book as a clear and easy guide in preparing nutritious meals for her own child.

Charles H. Bauer, M.D.
Clinical Associate Professor of Pediatrics at The New York Hospital—Cornell Medical Center; Attending Pediatrician, Roosevelt Hospital

Introduction

As a new or expectant mother you have, no doubt, been told by many older women, "It's so easy to feed a baby nowadays. I remember when I had to make everything myself." You become even more impressed and appreciative when you go to the supermarket and see the baby-food sections overflowing with a gourmet array of foods, attractively packaged and stamped with official-looking seals of approval. And, of course, you are more than willing to pay any cost for quality in your baby's diet.

But are you really giving your baby the best food for all the money you are spending?

In 1970, after hearing many mothers complain that their babies often refused to eat their high-priced meals, I became concerned about feeding my own new baby. When I began looking into this question, I found even more disturbing information.

There was growing criticism of the nutritional value and medical safety of commercial baby foods by Dr. Jean Mayer, Professor of Nutrition at Harvard and the President's consultant on nutrition; Dr. Samuel Fomon and Dr. Norman Kretchmer, pediatricians and authorities on infant nutrition; consumer advocate Ralph Nader; and many qualified and respected research scientists.

As a result of this criticism, the baby-food manufacturers first discontinued adding MSG (monosodium glutamate) as a flavor enhancer when it was shown capable of causing brain damage in infant mice. Then, in 1975, sodium nitrite was removed as a preservative in meat purées because of its cancer-causing potential. BHT, often used in cereals and baked goods, was also eliminated after it was banned in Britain from use in baby foods.

That still left sugar, salt, and starches as unnecessary and possibly harmful ingredients in almost every brand and variety of commercial baby food. Dr. Spock warns that sugars and starches are "nutritionally empty," that is, they are filling without providing nourishment.

Sugar and starches also contribute to overweight, which is now considered a major health problem in children and adults. Studies by Dr. Jules Hirsch, at Rockefeller University, have shown that an animal who becomes fat at infancy has an increased number of fat cells and tends to remain fat throughout life. Overweight adults have also been shown to have a high number of fat cells in their bodies. So, the image of a fat baby as a healthy baby is one that pediatricians are now trying to discourage.

Many mothers fight a constant battle with their children against eating sweets, for weight and dental reasons. It is highly possible that infants who become accustomed to the taste of sugar-laden baby food will crave sweets as they grow older. Dr. Fomon stated: "The influence of added sucrose in infant foods could be of significance with respect to dental caries and, possibly, obesity well beyond the period of infancy." Studies in England have also suggested that babies who are fed large amounts of sugar, or sucrose, will have a tendency to hardening of the arteries or heart trouble as adults.

Yet babies are not born with a taste for sweets—just give your baby a slice of lemon and watch him enjoy it!

Salt was another frequent ingredient in baby food that was included to please a mother's taste. However, Dr.

Fomon, of the University of Iowa, demonstrated in tests on infants up to seven months that there is no taste discrimination between salted and unsalted foods. The desire for salt is an acquired taste, one that is sometimes necessary to unlearn later in life. Dr. Louis K. Dahl, chief of staff at the Medical Research Center, Brookhaven National Laboratory, showed that the salt content of baby food was extremely high, in meats five to six times the amount in fresh meats, and in vegetables six to sixty times the amount in fresh vegetables. He suggested that a high intake of salt might be a contributing factor in the development of hypertension in adult life.

Water is a major ingredient of many strained and junior foods. This may be due to economic and processing requirements; however, the commercial foods often contain as much as 25 per cent *more* water than the same food prepared in the home. Then, modified food starch is added to give a more solid appearance or texture to the food. Have you ever fed your baby directly from a jar, then found that the remaining food has become useless liquid? This is caused by the saliva on the spoon, which breaks down the food starch added to solidify the food. Besides the money that you are spending, or wasting, on this added water and starch, you should consider the loss of nutrition. Your baby can eat only a limited amount, so why fill him up with water and starches?

In addition, research indicates that modified food starches may not be completely broken down by the baby's saliva, adding to the burden on the rest of the digestive tract.

In 1971, the controversy over the possible hazards and nutritional value of the commercial baby foods was just beginning, but a rapidly increasing number of mothers were not willing to take a chance during these crucial months of their infants' development. They turned to the same easy alternative I found: make your own baby food!

By 1977, the sales of commercial baby food had declined even though the birth rate had been rising. One company then attacked the obvious cause. In a letter sent to 760,000 new mothers, they warned that home-prepared baby foods were less nutritional and could even result in asphyxiation or food poisoning. There was an immediate and widely publicized denial by outraged pediatricians and nutritionists. They stated that *home-prepared baby foods were safe and preferable to the commercial foods!*

Consumers Union then did a comparison study that showed that the commercial foods—after being processed, heat-treated, sugared, salted, and starched—were indeed *less nutritious* than home-prepared baby foods. They even found some foods that contained enamel paint chips broken off from the undersides of the jar lids!

This nationwide publicity raised the consciousness of thousands of mothers who had never thought of questioning the contents of the commercial foods! It gave a tremendous boost to home preparation and caused even more of a decline in sales.

Finally, the manufacturers removed salt and sugar from many foods and introduced a new line of "natural" baby foods with the rather ironic advertising, "We know what is best for babies." So the situation is better than before, but they still have a way to go to merit that claim!

A recent trip through the baby-food shelves showed that many fruits, desserts, and dinners still have a high liquid content that has been thickened with the controversial tapioca starch or modified food starches. Sugar, in some form, is still present in desserts. If you do want to use some of the commercial foods, read the fine print in the list of ingredients and avoid any foods that contain sugars, starches, or unnecessary liquid.

The high heat processing still destroys nutrients and you are really buying "canned" foods—not as nutritious as raw or simply prepared fresh foods. The taste is also affected—as many mothers find out when they try to slip in some commercial food to a baby who has become accustomed to home-prepared food!

Another drawback of these "new" baby foods is their cost. While rising food prices are a serious problem that affects the entire family, the prices of the commercial baby foods have risen even more! They are *two to three times more expensive* than home-prepared baby foods!

HOME-PREPARED			COMMERCIAL
Egg Yolks	$ .70 lb.	vs.	$2.76 lb.
Liver	1.50 lb.	vs.	2.76 lb.
Squash	.27 lb.	vs.	.85 lb.
Peaches	.39 lb.	vs.	.80 lb.
Apple Juice	.65 qt.	vs.	1.90 qt.

Bananas, a staple baby food, are a striking example. A commercial jar contains water, bananas, and modified cornstarch. It costs $.81 a pound. A fresh banana, which only requires mashing with a fork and no thinning, usually can be bought for only $.30 a pound or less. How much actual banana is in that baby-food jar?

When you take advantage of sales, seasonal foods, and family meals you can save even more money—reason enough for preparing your own baby foods!

Women today are intelligent consumers concerned with value and nutrition. The only appeal of commercial baby food is its convenience. When the subjects of cost and nutritional value are discussed, most mothers agree with and are concerned about the criticisms, and often mention the struggle of getting their babies to eat the food. But they rationalize their use of the commercial products by saying: "I'm lazy," "It's so easy to open a jar," or "I'm too busy to bother with more cooking." On the other hand, many women who do make their own baby food say that there is nothing difficult involved and what is so special about the idea? It appears that thinking about preparing baby food is much more awesome than actually doing it.

I realized the reason for this attitude when I decided to make my own baby foods for my children. The little information or instruction I found was outdated by at least thirty years and did not take into account the advances in equipment (especially the blender and now the food processor), storage methods, or the variety and availability of new foods which can be readily used in baby-food preparation. I began preparing my own baby foods with the thought in mind that if it involved too much work and time, I would stop and resign myself to using the commercial variety. But, after some trial and error, I found that proper planning and using all the modern advances, together with the attitude that baby foods do not have to have gourmet seasoning, wide variety, or sterilization, made the process convenient, economical, and interesting. Over the last few years, many thousands of other mothers have also found that making their own baby foods is easy and economical!

I wrote this book as a complete guide to planning, preparing, and feeding your baby low-cost, high-nutrition meals until he is old enough to eat family table foods. I have revised it to include changes over the last ten years in feeding practices, use of new equipment (especially the food processor), and more information on how to get the most nutrition for the least money. I am also gratefully including the suggestions and comments that I received over the years from many mothers who used this book; thank you for your enthusiastic support!

- In chapter 1 you will find the latest facts on infant nutrition and specific nutritional information under each food and in the **Nutritive Values of Foods** table.
- Chapter 2, "How to Save Money," will help you to shop economically and to get the most nutrition for your money while avoiding additives.
- In chapter 3, "Feeding Your Baby," I have included suggestions from my experience in feeding my own two children; and the charts **Menu Planning Guide** and **When to Introduce a Food** as advised by several pediatricians.
- There are detailed recipes for almost any food that you may want to serve your baby—you can easily look up how and when to introduce it, and how to prepare it.
- The foods are also divided into chapters according to their main nutrition group, so you can easily plan balanced menus.
- "The Baby-Food System," chapter 6, contains the secrets of easy efficient baby-food preparation and shows you how to use or modify any recipe for *your* own convenience.

- The **Instant Foods** chapter, on the use of foods which require no cooking and little or no preparation, will be especially valuable if you are traveling, visiting, or just too busy.
- When your baby begins to feed himself, you will find the chapter on "Finger Foods" very useful.
- On the **Personal Feeding Chart** you will be able to keep a complete record of the foods your baby eats and his reactions to them. If your baby shows signs of allergies, this will be valuable for your own quick reference and for use by baby sitters.

Since the basic information on good nutrition, smart shopping, and storing and preparing food really applies to *any* simple meal—that *any* member of your family can enjoy—I'm sure that you will use this book long after your baby has graduated from his baby foods.

Whatever your reasons for desiring to prepare your own baby foods, the important thing is to get started. You will decide for yourself which methods and foods fit most easily into your everyday family cooking. For the small amount of extra time or thought that you may put in, you will receive great satisfaction in knowing that you are not taking chances with your baby's present or future health and that the food he eats is highly nutritious. He will also learn to enjoy the natural flavor of good foods that are simply and easily prepared. Where else can you get so much more while paying less!

1

Nutrition

There is a growing awareness that Americans, with a high standard of living and a large selection of food, are in many ways overfed but undernourished. This condition is not simply a result of low family income or the amount spent on food. In 1965, a government study showed that only 63 per cent of families with incomes of $10,000 or more were eating what were considered good diets.

We can only assume that the problem is one of not understanding the basics of nutrition. This subject is usually taught early in high school, when we are least interested or least likely to use this information. By the time we are buying and preparing food for our own families, we have forgotten the essentials and do not have time to catch up, especially with an infant in the house.

There are also very few sources of specific information on a baby's nutritional needs. Since your baby is eating a limited diet and is growing at a rapid rate, his needs are not the same as those of an adult. Good nutrition is even more important in a baby's first year, as research has shown that the earlier a nutritional deficiency occurs, the more serious and permanent the effect. Also, many deficiencies in infancy do not show up until later years, as in the case of rickets. So a good understanding of infant nutrition is essential and worth going into in some detail.

The specific advisable daily intake of various nutrients is based on information by Dr. Samuel Fomon and his research group at the University of Iowa, who are considered to be authorities on infant nutrition. I have included these amounts so that you can have some basis for interpreting the **Nutritive Values of Foods** tables and the amounts of nutrients that are often listed on product labels. You might also occasionally look at an average daily menu to see if you are supplying your baby with the advisable daily intakes. However, unless you happen to have a lot of spare time and enjoy arithmetic, you do not have to use these specific amounts in planning your baby's daily meals.

Please note that research has shown that it can be just as dangerous to consume very large amounts of any one food or vitamin and mineral supplements!

The easiest way to ensure your baby's good nutrition is to understand the general principles of good nutrition and to serve a balanced selection of the foods that supply the essential nutrients. These nutrients are calories, protein, carbohydrates, fat, vitamins, and minerals.

Calories

Calories are present in all foods, especially in high-carbohydrate and fat foods. A calorie is a measure of the energy value of the food. A certain amount of calories is necessary each day to maintain growth and good health and to give your baby energy. An excess of calories will accumulate as fat in the body tissues. An excess of fat, or overweight, can cause a variety of health problems for infants as well as adults. The recommended daily intake of calories is an average of 55 calories for each pound of the baby's weight. For example,

POUNDS	DAILY CALORIES
8	440
10	550
12	660
14	770
16	880
18	990
20	1100

A large portion of these calories will be supplied by *milk*. Even if your baby is drinking the minimum of three 8-ounce bottles a day, he will get 515 calories from reconstituted evaporated milk, 480 calories from whole milk, and 270 calories from skimmed or nonfat dry milk. If he drinks four 8-ounce bottles, the calories increase to 686 for evaporated milk, 640 for whole milk, and 360 for skimmed milk. A mixture of half skim, half whole milk will contain 500 calories. As you can see, if your baby is on skim milk, it is important to supply calories from other high-calorie foods such as *cereal grains*.

Protein

Protein is the main material for growth and development of many parts of the body—muscles, glands, blood, heart, nerves, brain, and skin. It also forms an important part of the enzymes that aid in the digestion and absorption of food. Protein is especially important in the rapid body-building that your baby will do in his first years. A lack of protein in infancy can cause serious problems such as mental retardation and physical impairment, during childhood and in adult life. Resistance to infection can also be lowered.

Since protein cannot be stored in the body, your baby should eat protein food through the day, including some complete protein foods. The recommended daily intake is at least 14–16 grams. This can be adequately supplied by as little as two 8-ounce bottles of whole or skim milk. Human milk contains only one-third the amount of protein as in cow's milk, but if nursing is the main source of food, a baby will still receive adequate amounts of protein. It is important, if your baby breast-feeds and also eats a good amount of solid food, that you select those foods which contain high amounts of complete protein.

Complete Protein. Some foods contain all the elements, called amino acids, that are contained in protein and are required by the body. The following foods are excellent sources of complete protein:

Milk	Fish	Yogurt
Meat	Eggs	Nonfat dry milk
Poultry	Cheese	Soybeans

Incomplete Protein. Other foods supply only some of the protein elements that are essential for nutrition and are considered incomplete protein foods. These foods are still an important source of protein, and since they are usually inexpensive, they are good to serve as a supplement:

Whole-grain cereals, bread
Dried peas, beans, lentils
Nuts, peanut butter
Enriched pastas
Brown and converted rice
Wheat germ

Carbohydrates

Carbohydrates, in the form of sugar and starch, provide at least one-half the total calories that an active baby needs for heat and energy. They are the main source of immediate energy and the only energy source for the central nervous system. If the daily carbohydrate intake is too low, valuable protein will be converted for energy instead of for growth and other necessary functions. If an excess of carbohydrates is eaten, they will be stored in the body as fat. A moderate amount of carbohydrates is necessary each day for an active, healthy baby.

Starch Sources. There are many natural sources of starches among foods that you will serve your baby:

Bananas	Potatoes	Dried beans, peas
Corn	Noodles	Winter squash
Peas	Cereals	

Sugar Sources. There are also many natural sources of sugar in fruits and vegetables:

Bananas	Peas	Orange juice
Apples	Beets	Grape juice
Carrots	Sweet potatoes	Grapes

Empty-Nutrition Sources. If your baby is eating a balanced daily diet which includes cereals, fruits, and vegetables, he will be receiving an adequate amount of carbohydrates. In view of the abundance of natural sugars and starches, the addition of refined sugar and starches to any food is unnecessary. (However, many commercial baby-food fruits and "dinners" contain modified food starch, tapioca starch, or flour. The "desserts," which many doctors advise against, contain refined sugar, flour, or starches.) Research indicates that infants may not properly digest these food starches.

An overabundance of these "empty-nutrition" carbohydrates can affect your baby in several ways. They can give him a false sense of being full, thus decreasing his appetite for other necessary foods. Since these sugars and starches are nutritionally "empty," your baby may become deficient in many vitamins and minerals while giving the appearance of being "fat" and "healthy." The extra fat will be produced because the baby is consuming more carbohydrates than he requires. Research now indicates that being fat during infancy leads to a tendency to become overweight as an adult. A major concern of many adults today is the problem of losing unnecessary weight because of the various health hazards. If your baby becomes accustomed to sweet food, he may also grow up with a craving for sweets that can result in nutritional deficiencies and tooth decay.

So, while carbohydrates are necessary in your baby's daily diet, you should serve them in moderation and choose those sources with the highest nutritional value.

Fats

Fat, usually thought of as a nasty word, is also a necessary element in nutrition. The calories in fat provide a concentrated source of energy and prevent the loss of protein being burned as energy. Fat helps in the absorption of the fat-soluble vitamins, A, D, E, and K, into the body. Stored fat protects the body from excessive loss of heat and supports and protects the vital organs. There are both liquid and solid sources of fat.

Oils are fats that are liquid at room temperature and are generally made from vegetable sources. These oils contain mostly polyunsaturated fatty acids which result in lower levels of cholesterol in the body. Coconut oil and palm oil are the exceptions and are high in saturated fats.

Some oils are *hydrogenated* in order to harden them for use as margarine and shortening. Research now suggests that this hydrogenation process can cause a nutritional imbalance in the body, so the hydrogenated or "hardened oils" should also be avoided. You should use a brand of shortening that lists *"liquid vegetable oil"* as the main ingredient.

Some polyunsaturated oils are:

Corn oil	Peanut oil
Soybean oil	Wheat-germ oil
Safflower oil	

Mineral oil is totally lacking in nutrients and is nondigestible. It absorbs the fat-soluble vitamins in the body and can cause deficiencies. **You should never give mineral oil to your baby.**

Do not use cottonseed oil or foods that contain cottonseed oil. Cotton is not considered a food crop and may be treated with many chemical sprays.

Solid fats are generally made from animal sources and

have a high amount of saturated fat, which can raise the level of cholesterol in the blood. Although this may be a concern for some adults, most doctors and nutritionists agree that a *moderate* amount of food cholesterol is necessary in an infant's early development. Unfortunately, the commercial formulas use vegetable oils, and so they are low in saturated fats. If your baby is drinking these formulas, or skim milk, you can serve the following foods, which are high in saturated fats:

Butter   Egg yolk
Ice cream   Nuts, peanut butter
Meat

Essential fatty acids are also found in fat and are indispensable for your baby's growth and healthy skin. Linoleic acid is one of the most important. Breast milk contains more than cow's milk, but both are good sources. The commercial formulas that use coconut oil may be low. If your baby is drinking skim milk, you should be sure to include foods in his diet that are high in essential fatty acids, such as:

Vegetable oil (safflower, corn, soy, peanut, wheat germ)
Chicken
Soybeans
Wheat germ
Nuts, peanut butter

The recommended daily intake of linoleic acid is 5-6 grams, which can be supplied by 1 tablespoon of vegetable oil.

Vitamins

Vitamins are small substances found in food and are necessary for growth and all the bodily functions. All the vitamins needed for good health can be found in food, or are synthesized in the body.

Water-soluble vitamins cannot be stored in the body

and foods containing these vitamins should be eaten every day. They are very perishable and can be lost in water, heat, and exposure to air. They are: vitamin C and vitamin-B complex (thiamine or B_1, riboflavin or B_2, niacin, pyridoxine or B_6, pantothenic acid, folic acid, B_{12}, choline, and biotin).

Fat-soluble vitamins can be stored in the body. The amounts that occur naturally in food cannot cause a harmful surplus in the body. However, supplemental forms of the vitamins can be taken in harmful amounts and should only be given under a doctor's supervision. They can be destroyed by high heat, drying, exposure to air, and rancidity. These vitamins are A, D, E, and K.

VITAMIN A

Vitamin A is essential for growth, good vision, and healthy skin, and for keeping the lining of the mouth, nose, throat, and digestive tract healthy and resistant to infection. Babies are unable to store this vitamin before birth, so it is necessary in their diet. The following animal foods supply large amounts of vitamin A:

Liver	Fish-liver oil
Kidneys	Fish
Egg yolk	Butter
Cheese	Whole milk, breast milk

Plant foods contain large amounts of carotene, which is converted by the body into vitamin A. The highest sources are *dark-green* and leafy vegetables, and the *deep-yellow* fruits and vegetables:

Broccoli	Carrots
Chard	Winter squash
Leafy greens	Sweet potatoes
Asparagus	Apricots
Green beans	Cantaloupe
Tomatoes	Mangoes

The vitamin, while found in many foods, can be destroyed by exposure to air (wilting), high heat, and rancidity. Skim milk and skim-milk products are very low in the vitamin since it is removed with the fat, and so they are often fortified with vitamin A.

Because the vitamin can be stored in the body, a continual overdose can be harmful to your baby. Dr. Fomon states that for normal infants living in countries with good living standards, "the hazards of vitamin-A overdosage exceed the dangers of deficiency." The amount of the vitamin that naturally occurs in food cannot result in overdose; however, the amounts consumed in supplements can reach high levels. Many foods have been fortified with vitamin A, especially nonfat dry milk, skim and whole milk, margarine, and cereals. Many brands of milk are fortified with up to 2000 I.U. (international units) per quart. A supplement may be prescribed, and you should never give your baby more than the prescribed amount of the supplement. If a little is good, more is *not* better. Try to keep track of the total vitamin A that your baby is consuming in natural foods, supplements, and fortified foods.

The suggested daily intake of vitamin A for a normal infant is 600 I.U. A daily dosage of 20,000 I.U. for as long as a month may be harmful.

VITAMIN-B COMPLEX

There are at least fifteen different B vitamins, which occur in many of the same foods. The best-known ones are thiamine (B_1), riboflavin (B_2), niacin, B_6, and B_{12}. These B vitamins are essential to the growing infant in many ways. They enable body cells to obtain energy from carbohydrates, they promote growth, good appetite, digestion, and healthy skin, and they keep the nervous system in balance. A deficiency in these vitamins can result in loss of appetite, irritability, fatigue, eye and skin problems, and poor growth. The B vitamins are found in high amounts in a variety of foods:

Pork	Dried peas, beans, lentils
Liver and organ meats	Soybeans
Fish	Peanut butter

Poultry
Milk (whole, skim)
Breast milk
Egg yolk
Cheese
Green leafy vegetables

Brown rice
Enriched cereals
Bananas
Sweet potatoes
Wheat germ
Brewer's yeast

All the B vitamins are water soluble, so they are easily lost in cooking water. They cannot be stored in the body and should be eaten daily. The vitamins are quite stable to heat, with the exception of B_6. Riboflavin is particularly sensitive to light, and foods that are served as main sources, such as milk, should not be stored in clear containers or left out in the light. The B vitamins are also lost when soda is used in the cooking water.

A deficiency in some of the B vitamins is more prevalent today because of the practice of refining flours, cereals, and rice, which results in a large loss of all the B vitamins. The Food and Drug Administration has approved levels of enrichment for refined flours and cereals; however, only thiamine, riboflavin, and niacin are added. Even a large intake of enriched foods can leave a baby deficient in the other B vitamins. One answer is to serve whole-grain cereals, unbleached or whole-grain flour, converted or brown rice, and other foods that are high in the B vitamins. Wheat germ and brewer's yeast can also be used as added fortifiers in your baby's food.

In general, if your baby drinks an adequate amount of breast or cow's milk, he will be receiving a good amount of the B vitamins, with the exception of niacin, which can be supplied by meats, poultry, and enriched cereals. The commercial formulas should be fortified with B_6 and will state so on the label. Advisable daily intakes of some of the B vitamins are:

	1 month	12 months
Thiamine	.12 mg.	.21 mg.
Riboflavin	.27 mg.	.44 mg.
Niacin	3.7 mg.	6.2 mg.

VITAMIN C

Vitamin C, or ascorbic acid, is needed by all body cells. It is crucial to growth, strong bones, and teeth. Current research indicates that it plays an important role in the body's resistance to infection, which is especially important for infants. Vitamin C cannot be stored in the body and must be supplied daily. A deficiency can result in scurvy, gum problems, and frequent infections. There are many high sources of this vitamin among foods:

Oranges	Orange juice
Grapefruit	Grapefruit juice
Lemon juice	Strawberries
Breast milk	Broccoli
Cantaloupe	Green pepper
Guava	Parsley
Papaya	

There are also many fair sources of vitamin C:

Watercress	Spinach
Asparagus	Collard greens
Tomatoes	Potatoes
Tomato juice	Kohlrabi
Kale	

In spite of the abundance of vitamin C in foods, the vitamin is highly unstable and can be lost in cooking or soaking water, or by exposure to heat, light, and air. Vitamin C deficiency, or scurvy, still occurs even in countries with high standards of living. Dr. Fomon states, "Failure of infants to receive adequate amounts of ascorbic acid can be traced primarily to faulty nutritional education of parents or to failure of physicians to realize that certain milks and formulas are deficient in content of ascorbic acid."

While the vitamin is usually adequately supplied through breast milk, cow's milk is a poor source, and a bottle-fed baby should receive some supplement from birth. Many commercial formulas are fortified and the labels should be checked as to the amounts. Some doctors recommend orange juice, others prefer to delay orange juice until the fourth or fifth month because of the possibility of an allergic reaction. Other supplements are ascorbic acid tablets and water-soluble vitamin concentrates.

The recommended daily intake is 30 mg. (milligrams) of vitamin C.

VITAMIN D

Vitamin D is one of the most important vitamins for babies. The first formation of bone is cartilage, and this vitamin is necessary for the absorption of calcium and phosphorus, which cause the cartilage to harden into bone. When a baby is deficient in vitamin D, he may have rickets, which is characterized by soft, curved bones, bowed legs, or knock-knees.

The vitamin can be produced in the body by the action of the sun on the skin, but this is not a reliable or adequate source. The main food sources are:

Cod-liver oil   Halibut-liver oil

It is also present in fair amounts in *liver, salmon, tunafish,* and *egg yolk*. The vitamin is added to many kinds of milk—whole, skim, evaporated, and nonfat dry milk powder. You must read the labels to be sure the milk is fortified with 400 I.U. per quart.

Vitamin D is given to babies from the first or second week, in the form of cod-liver oil, a water-soluble concentrate, fortified milk, or formula. You should give it during or just after a feeding to make certain that it is absorbed. Breast-fed babies also require vitamin D since it is not adequately supplied in human milk.

The advisable daily intake of vitamin D is 400 I.U. Some research has indicated that excess amounts may be harmful to infants. As with vitamin A, this vitamin should be prescribed as a supplement by your doctor, and you should be aware of the amounts in fortified foods.

VITAMIN E

Vitamin E is essential for your baby's development. It plays an important part in cell structure and contributes to growth, good muscles, nerves, and skin. The vitamin can be extracted and is available as alpha-tocopherol. It is also found in some foods:

> Breast milk
> Wheat germ, wheat-germ oil
> Peanut, soy, and safflower oil
> Whole-grain cereals
> Nuts

The vitamin can be destroyed by high heat and exposure to air. The practice of refining flours and cereals has removed much natural vitamin E from our diets, and the enrichment of flour and cereal does not include vitamin E. Since heating and chemical extraction of oils can destroy the vitamin, nutritionists recommend using unrefined oils.

Breast milk contains more vitamin E than cow's milk. The American Academy of Pediatricians in 1969 recommended that vitamin E be used in all infant formulas. The advisable daily intake of vitamin E (alpha-tocopherol) is 1.8 mg.

VITAMIN K

Vitamin K is a fat-soluble vitamin that is essential in blood clotting and liver function. It is found in several foods:

Spinach	Cow's milk
Tomatoes	Carrot tops
Cabbage	Cauliflower
Breast milk	Turnip greens

Yogurt is also a source since the yogurt bacteria will produce vitamin K in the body. The vitamin is adequately supplied for normal babies in breast milk, cow's milk, and formulas.

Minerals

Minerals are present in the body fluids as soluble salts and affect many bodily functions. *Calcium* and *phosphorus* are the basic elements of bones and teeth. *Iron* and *copper* are elements in the red blood cells. *Iodine* is essential for proper functioning of the thyroid gland. *Sodium, potassium,* and *magnesium* are other important minerals.

Most minerals are adequately supplied by a balanced selection of food. However, minerals are water soluble and can easily be lost if you soak food or cook with a large amount of water. Refining of flours, cereals, and rice also destroys minerals, so the whole-grain cereals and brown rice are better sources. Both breast milk and cow's milk can supply your baby with adequate amounts of most minerals, with the exception of iron.

IRON

Iron is a mineral that is essential to your baby's health. It combines with protein in the body to form hemoglobin, the substance which carries oxygen from the lungs to all the parts of the body. The body cells must be supplied with oxygen to sustain life. Iron also forms part of several enzymes that break food down so that it can be digested in the body. It is supplied by several foods:

Liver	Enriched bread and cereals
Kidneys	Green leafy vegetables
Egg yolk	Dried fruits
Dried peas, beans, lentils	Molasses
Meat	

Unless a mother is iron-deficient during pregnancy, the baby will be born with enough stored iron for at least the next four to five months. Both human and cow's milk are low in iron, but most commercial formulas are iron fortified. Your doctor may also prescribe a vitamin supplement that contains iron.

After your baby is eating solid food, you can add iron-fortified cereals, egg yolks, and the above foods to his daily diet as a source of iron. Molasses can be added to food or a bottle, but since it is a laxative, it must be used in very small amounts.

Although a baby's daily requirement for iron can vary with individual needs, an average daily intake of 6 to 8 mg. of iron is advised, from the time your baby is four to six weeks old, until at least eighteen months. If iron supplementation is begun at four months or later, then a larger daily amount of 10–15 mg. is advised. The average daily intake should not exceed 15 mg. According to Dr. Fomon, babies who are most likely to develop iron deficiency are those with low birth weight, those of multiple births (twins, etc.), and those who are born to mothers who have had several closely spaced pregnancies, or possibly who are low in iron during pregnancy.

CALCIUM

Calcium is the most important mineral in the building of strong bones and teeth. Infants have a particularly high need for calcium in the conversion of cartilage to bone and for their rapid growth. It also plays a large part in the prevention and relief of nervous tension and irritability. A calcium deficiency can result in rickets.

The highest source of calcium is *milk*, both whole and skim, breast and cow's milk. Other foods contain calcium in good amounts:

Ice cream	Collard greens
Cheese	Green beans
Nonfat dry milk powder	Broccoli
Kale	

Although spinach, chard, and beet greens also contain calcium, it is not in a form that is usable by the body and should not be considered a source of calcium. Fat is also important in the absorption of calcium by the body.

By the time your baby is a few months old, he should be drinking 1 quart of milk a day and continue to do so through childhood. This will adequately supply his need for calcium. The following foods contain the same amount of calcium as 1 cup of milk and can be used as supplements:

1 ounce semifirm cheese—Swiss, Cheddar, Muenster, etc.
3 tablespoons nonfat dry milk powder
1 cup custard
The advisable daily intake of calcium is 500 mg.

SODIUM

Your baby will receive an adequate amount of sodium, or salt, from milk, meat, and vegetables. It is unnecessary to salt your baby's food to your own taste, since babies do not show any preference for salted foods—this is an acquired habit. Research has indicated that a high intake of sodium by infant animals results in high blood pressure and hypertension in adult life. So the safest course is to avoid adding salt to your baby's food, and avoid those prepared foods that are highly salted. Be aware that sodium compounds are also used as preservatives in many foods..

IODINE

Iodine is an essential mineral for the maintenance of the body processes by its role in the functioning of the thyroid gland. If the activity of the thyroid is too slow, the body will store up energy as fat. If the thyroid is overactive, the body will burn up food and energy reserves too quickly.
Iodine is present in:

Shellfish	Salt-water fish
Cod-liver oil	Meats
Iodized salt	Vegetables

If you live in an inland area, a small amount of iodized salt can be added to your baby's food as a source of iodine. Be sure to check the label on table salt to make certain that iodine has been added.

PHOSPHORUS

Phosphorus is essential for the growth of strong bones and teeth and also many bodily processes. It is especially important to the rapidly growing infant.

This mineral is present in large amounts in these foods:

Liver	Whole-grain cereals
Fish	Peanut butter
Egg yolk	Brown rice
Dried peas, beans, lentils	Corn
Soybeans	Cow's milk
Cheese	

The advisable intake is 220 mg. daily.

How to Save Money

"Nutritional Cost"

Now that you know your baby's nutritional needs, let's look at how to buy foods in terms of their **"nutritional cost."** That is, how you can get the most food value for your money and also avoid foods which may be harmful for your baby.

Throughout this book I stress the *least expensive* ways to feed your baby. This economy is not the same thing as skimping. We all want our babies to have the best food possible, and we are ready to pay a high price for quality. However, the expensive foods are not necessarily the most nutritious and may even be harmful for your baby. For example, prime meats contain more fat and less protein than lower grades, and expensive processed foods contain additives and fillers and have often lost nutrients.

But you must also keep in mind that some less expensive foods may be poor nutritional buys. For example, unenriched white rice is less expensive than brown rice but also has lost many of the nutrients. Fruit "punches" may be less expensive than a juice, but they contain a much higher amount of water and sugar.

Instead, you should select your baby's food by considering its "nutritional cost"; that is, where can you find the most food value for the least amount of money. Look for the "$" on foods and recipes in this book. They are your best nutritional "buys."

If you look back over the lists of foods that are high in specific nutrients, you will see that the same inexpensive foods appear on many of the lists:

Soybeans*   Leafy greens—turnip, kale,
Liver* (beef, lamb)   spinach, collard, etc.
Kidneys*   Carrots
Egg yolk*   Dried peas, beans, lentils
Poultry*   Oranges
Nonfat dry milk*   Peanut butter
Milk*

Fruits and vegetables are always less expensive in season and in areas where they are easily grown. Near the end of the season you can prepare and freeze ahead. Fresh fruits and vegetables are usually less expensive than frozen or canned.

Meat protein will probably be the most expensive item on your list, but if you check the papers you can find sales on at least one type each week. Again, you can prepare a few weeks' supply and freeze.

Inexpensive Protein

Fortunately, there are other ways that you can serve complete protein and still economize. Remember the list of "incomplete" protein foods in the last chapter—cereals, rice, nuts, legumes (dried peas and beans), pastas, and wheat germ? They are all very cheap sources of protein. If you combine these foods with small amounts of the more

---

*These foods are all excellent sources of complete protein. Some of them may not appeal to you, but your baby was not born with specific likes and dislikes. Just remember to smile!

expensive protein foods in dishes such as beef and rice, or even serve them at the *same meal*, you will have adequate amounts of high-quality protein at a lower cost.

Even more economical is the use of "complementary" incomplete protein foods. Each of these foods has some amino acids that are lacking in the others. The trick is to put together the right combination of grains, seeds (nuts), and legumes to end up with complete protein. My rice-and-bean casseroles aren't family favorites, but babies love them! They purée and freeze very well.

In chapter 10, "Protein Foods," you will find more ways to combine these foods and specific recipes that your family might also enjoy. For a more detailed description of "complementary" protein foods and enough recipes to satisfy everyone, look up the books DIET FOR A SMALL PLANET by Frances Moore Lappé and RECIPES FOR A SMALL PLANET by Ellen B. Ewald.

How to Read Labels

When you consider the immense variety of foods that are available in a supermarket, shopping becomes a challenging game between you and the food industry. The secret of winning is very easy. Just read and take advantage of all the information that is printed on the labels for the protection of you, the consumer.

The U.S. Department of Agriculture and the Food and Drug Administration enforce several laws that cover all food that is sold in interstate commerce or is imported, and many states and localities also have their own laws. These acts require that the food be pure, wholesome, and honestly labeled. The label must include, when applicable, the grade; inspection shield; brand name; weight, measure, or count; description; dates; and a list of ingredients.

In this section I will help you to understand how you can easily use this information in buying the food that you will prepare for your baby. Of course, you will also be able to use your marketing know-how in shopping for the rest of your family. In the Bibliography I have listed additional sources of marketing information.

U. S. Grades

These grades are used to classify foods according to their appearance, such as size, shape, color, or by their tenderness. All the grades are equally wholesome, and the lower grades contain the same amount of nutritional value as the highest grade. In the case of meats, the lower grades contain even more protein. These grades are particularly useful in buying food to prepare as purées, since appearance and tenderness are irrelevant once you have puréed the food for your baby. The higher the grade, the more expensive the item usually is, and it is an unnecessary expense to use the top grade. Because the names of the grade vary according to the food, I have indicated the appropriate grade for the various foods in the recipe chapters. Here are some examples of grade marks:

You should always look for the initials "U.S." before the grade, since they indicate that it is a U.S. Department of Agriculture grade.

Inspection Shields

The shields appear on all meat, on poultry products, and also on many other foods. Their presence means that the food was prepared under federal supervision and inspected for wholesomeness. You should always try to buy foods for your baby that carry these seals. Here are some federal seals:

Products that do not come under federal control may still carry state or local inspection seals, and you should become familiar with them.

Brand Names

The label must contain the brand name or the manufacturer's name. You can easily recognize the well-advertised name; however, many supermarkets and other distributors have goods packaged under their own or a private label. Very often, the food is packaged by the same well-known manufacturer, who simply puts on a different label. Usually the private labels are less expensive than the well-known ones, since you do not have to pay for the cost of advertising. Because most of the food that you will buy for your baby comes under government inspection and grading, you can get the same food value and quality from the private-label brands and save money.

For many products, such as mayonnaise, canned fruits, juices, and vegetables, the government has established *standards of identity* which define minimum and maximum amounts of major ingredients. So you are assured of getting "at least" a certain amount of fruit and "not more than" a set amount of water in a can of fruit, regardless of the brand.

Weights, Measures, or Counts

This information on content must be printed clearly on the label. Always compare different brands according to their weight in order to get the most for your money. Do not be deceived by larger packages. You can also use these weights to compare different sizes of the same brand in order to see if you really are saving money by buying the larger size.

In many areas, *unit pricing* is required by law and it makes economical shopping easy and fast. Under each item is listed the price per weight or count. Take advantage of it, and if it is not required in your area, support your local consumer organization in passing such a law.

Description of Food

The name on the label must clearly and accurately describe the food, such as "sliced green beans," "orange juice," "whole carrots." If there are two main ingredients, the food that is present in the *largest amount* must be listed *first* in the name; such as "beans with pork" instead of the way we usually refer to it, as "pork and beans." Also, if a food resembles a food for which a standard of identity has been set, but does not contain the required ingredients, it must be labeled "imitation." The word "flavored" is also used to identify an imitation food.

Often, descriptions are added to the name of a food, and these are usually a good warning that the basic food has been modified. Cheese is a good example of this type of labeling. The word "food" in the label "pasteurized process cheese food" shows that the product contains less cheese, but added nonfat dry milk and water. The term "spread" in "pasteurized process cheese spread" indicates an even higher moisture content than the cheese "food." Instead of "orange juice," you can find cans labeled "orange drink," "punch," or " . . . ade." These beverages all contain more water than those labeled "juice." *In general you will get the most food value for your money and the least additives and fillers if you avoid those products whose names show modification of the basic food.*

There are two words that may be added to the name of a food to indicate added food value. The word "enriched" is added to the name of many cereals, flours, and baked goods. This means that the vitamins *riboflavin, niacin,* and *thiamine* and the mineral *iron* have been added at least in minimum amounts to replace the loss due to processing. Some brands contain amounts that are higher than the minimum, so it is worth your time to look at the amounts or percentages that are listed on the label. The amount of *iron* and *niacin* in cereals is particularly important since they will be one of your baby's main sources during early infancy.

The word "fortified" means that vitamins and minerals not normally in the food have been added to the product. It may also mean that the amounts of some nutrients have been increased above the normal amount.

Since these "fortified" and "enriched" foods are usually *more expensive*, read the label to see what has been added and consider if it is necessary for your baby. If not, you are spending money needlessly for nutrients that are naturally present in other foods that your baby eats. In the case of vitamins A and D, which may be added to many foods, excess amounts may even be harmful to your baby.

"Natural" Foods

In the last few years, the most popular words in food advertising and labels are *"natural," "organic,"* and *"whole."* The manufacturers are aware of the consumer's interest in unrefined, unprocessed, additive-free foods and they seize every opportunity to claim in large letters that their food is *"natural," "organic,"* or *"whole."* A survey showed that the majority of consumers believed that these foods were indeed better for them. **Don't be misled!**

These words have not been under government control and can mean anything the manufacturer wants them to mean. For example, one "natural" fruit drink contains some natural orange flavor, but is made almost entirely from chemicals and is artificially colored. Some foods contain large amounts of sugars and starches which, although "natural," are not good for you and are a waste of money.

The Federal Trade Commission has recently announced a definition for the term "natural" which is expected to become law and will be the standard for natural food advertising. The proposed standard requires that **in order** to be advertised as "natural," products may not contain synthetic or artificial ingredients and may not be more than minimally processed.

The agency determined that "minimally processed" foods could also be considered "natural" if the process was not far different from what a consumer could do in his own kitchen. Under this definition, minimal processing includes such things as washing or peeling fruits or vegetables; homogenizing milk or fruit juices; canning, bottling, and freezing foods; baking bread; aging and roasting meats and grinding nuts. Highly processed, high technology procedures such as puffing, extruding, and processes that changed the shape of things are not considered "natural." Anything that contains added sugar and salt, highly refined products or oils, other than cold-pressed oils, would not qualify as a natural product.

Read the small print in the list of ingredients to find out what you are buying. Avoid those brands that do not give a complete listing of contents. Many companies are even giving a list of ingredients on foods that have a "standard of identity" such as ice cream and mayonnaise. Do not be willing to pay extra just because a food is labeled "natural"!

Dating Codes

Most foods are marked with a code to indicate the packing date. Perishable foods always contain the last date on which the food may be sold. This date is used to help the owner of the store in removing spoiled foods and is often in coded form. However, in many areas, laws have been passed which require open and clear dating of perishable foods such as milk, eggs, and baked goods. Take advantage of these dates to buy the freshest food possible. Even where the date is coded, you can usually interpret it, since it is a combination of month, date, and, possibly, year. For example, 9039 usually means September 3, 1979; or 1023 on milk means October 23. Some baked goods use letters to indicate the day of the week. If your area does not have open dating, try asking your local grocer for information on interpreting dates of perishable items that you frequently buy. Where possible, buy brands that are clearly dated and labeled—they have nothing to hide!

"RDA" Nutritional Information

You may have seen the abbreviation "RDA" on a label and wondered what it meant.

"RDA" stands for Recommended Dietary Allowance and applies to the daily amount of a nutrient that is necessary to *maintain good nutrition* in the average healthy person. The amounts are established by the Food and Nutrition Board of the National Research Council. They currently apply to 16 nutrients.

This information on a label can be very helpful in selecting the product with the lowest "nutritional cost" and to help you plan a balanced, healthy diet. But keep in mind the specific needs of your baby and look for actual amounts of nutrients that may also be listed on a label. You can compare these amounts with the advisable daily intakes that are described in chapter 1.

List of Ingredients

This list must be clearly printed on the package and it is your most valuable aid in safe and economical food buying. If you read the list, you will know what is in the product and at least the relative amounts. The ingredients are listed in *descending* order of amount. **Thus, the ingredient that is listed first is present in the largest quantity.** If the label on a can of fruit drink reads "water, sugar, and juice," you will be buying more water and sugar than actual fruit juice. Although the drink may be priced lower than a fruit juice, this product may actually be more expensive in terms of its nutritional cost. Whenever you are in doubt about a product, or the name seems confusing, just read the list of ingredients!

ADDITIVES

It is even more important for you to read this list of ingredients so that you know what additives are in the food that you will be feeding your baby. There are almost 10,000 officially approved additives and most must be included on the label. However, there is a growing criticism of the adequacy of the testing methods which are used in determining whether or not a particular additive is safe. Some additives, such as MSG, which have been used for years have been found to be harmful when they are tested on infant animals. Your baby's relatively low weight and immature digestive system are two important considerations. The United Nations' FAO/WHO Expert Committee on Food Additives recommended in a 1961 report:

Foods that are specifically prepared for babies require separate considerations from all other foods as regards the use of food additives and toxicological risks. The reason for this is that the detoxicating mechanisms that are effective in the more mature individual may be ineffective in the baby. The committee strongly urges that baby foods should be prepared without food additives, if possible. If the use of a food additive is necessary in a baby food, great caution should be exercised both in the choice of the additive and in the level of use.

In addition, there is potential risk in the combination of two or more harmless additives, and also in the accumulation of some additives which are present in so many foods. The frightening part is that the effects of some additives may not show up until later in life and there is no way of taking back what your baby has eaten.

Obviously, the safest course is to avoid all foods which contain additives and one way is to make at home, from basic foods, everything your baby eats. However, if you'll excuse the old expression, you should not "throw out the baby with the bath-water." You will be very busy with a baby in the house, and this may not be the time to start baking bread or growing vegetables. It would be nice if you could take advantage of the convenience of some prepared foods in feeding your baby. Also, some additives are actual nutrients which are used to improve the value of the food and I have called these **"fortifiers."**

The most difficult job for the layman is to interpret or recognize the long technical names of the various additives which are printed in the list of ingredients. I have identified some of the most common ones and indicate why they are used. Some are highly controversial and are the subject of current research; others seem unnecessary and are used to improve appearance or texture or cover lack of quality. You will find them listed on a label either by their specific name or by their type, such as "preservatives."

Preservatives are used to delay deterioration or spoilage, which is an advantage with some perishable foods. However, they are often added to prolong shelf life of a product for unnecessarily long periods to increase its chances of sale. You can use a rule of thumb that if a product is inexpensive or is one that you will buy and use immediately, such as bread, select a brand without preservatives. Some common preservatives are *sodium chloride, sodium nitrates, sodium benzoate, calcium propionate, sodium propionate, sulfur dioxide, sodium sulphites,* and *sodium carbonate. Sodium nitrite* was strongly criticized in 1970 by Dr. Samuel Epstein, of the Children's Cancer Research Foundation, who has shown in research that it can produce harmful effects. Subsequent research has supported his results.

Some organic preservatives, which are generally accepted as harmless, are *acetic acid, tartaric acid, lactic acid, sorbic acid, citric acid,* and *benzoic acid,* and *tocopherols.*

Antioxidants are a type of preservative and some commonly used ones are *propyl gallate, BHT* (butylated hydroxytoluene), and *BHA* (butylated hydroxyanisole). The British Food Standards Committee has banned *BHT* from use in baby food and restricted its use in other foods because it has produced allergic reactions and is possibly related to cancer. Many other countries have also banned its use; however, it is one of the most widely used additives in America.

Emulsifiers are added to improve the texture or consistency of foods and include *monoglycerides, diglycerides,* and *disodium phosphate*. *Lecithin* is an organic compound found in egg yolks, soybeans, and corn and is generally accepted as harmless.

Stabilizers, or thickeners, are also used to add texture and consistency to food. They make food nutritionally expensive, since you are paying for and filling your baby up with a large percentage of nonnutritious fillers instead of the actual food. Some commonly used fillers are the vegetable gums *agar-agar, gum arabic, gum tragacanth,* and *pectin*. *Gelatin* is a thickener that does contain protein. Some cellulose compounds used are *methyl cellulose* and *carboxymethyl cellulose,* and these are currently under controversy. *Food starches*, such as tapioca, cornstarch, and rice starch, are nonnutritious and are difficult for babies to digest. Flour, when enriched or unbleached, can thicken while adding some nutrients; however, the terms "white," "bleached," and "wheat" flour indicate that the flour is merely a filler.

Hydrogenated, or partially hardened, is often used to describe oils that have been treated to a hydrogenation process to change them to a more solid state. Research now indicates that this process modifies the fatty acids in a way that might be dangerous to bodily functions, and most doctors and nutritionists advise against using them.

Artificial colors are coal-tar dyes and have long been controversial. These are completely unnecessary in food you will be serving your baby. Some *natural* food colors are annato, betain, caramel, carotene, chlorophyll, and saffron. These are just as unnecessary, but are less controversial.

Artificial flavors, or enhancers, are widely used and are also unnecessary in your baby's food. *Monosodium glutamate* (MSG) is an example of an organic-based additive that has been identified as potentially harmful to infants. *Hydrolyzed plant protein* is also used, and this is an early step in the production of MSG. [Salt is a natural flavoring that can be dangerous when it is overused.] [Some artificial flavorings are *amyl acetate* (banana), *benzaldehyde* (cherry, almond), and *citral* (lemon).] One wonders about the basic quality of the food when such enhancers, or added flavors, are considered necessary.

Sweeteners. The artificial ones, such as cyclamates and saccharin, have recently been banned or are under investigation.

There are also many forms of sugar, which may be called cane sugar, sucrose, corn syrup, sugar syrup, and dextrose. These are empty-nutrition additives which can depress the appetite and contribute to dental decay. It is not considered harmful to occasionally use prepared foods that contain these sugars, but you must be careful not to serve these foods as a steady diet or select foods which contain them as major ingredients.

FORTIFIERS

Vitamins and minerals are added to many foods, and in a sense, they are additives. However, their purpose is to replace those vitamins and minerals which have been removed through processing or to add nutrients that are not readily available in food. They are an attempt to improve the quality of our diet. Some common fortifiers are iron, thiamine, riboflavin, niacin, iodine, potassium iodide, and vitamins A, C (ascorbic acid), and D.

A recent development in food processing has been the use of low-cost *protein fortifiers* in various foods, especially those with incomplete proteins such as cereals, baked goods, noodles, spaghetti, soups, etc. This is an inexpensive means of improving the protein quality of foods with vegetable and grain proteins. They are either composed of nutrients found in foods or are essential amino acids. They will be listed in the list of ingredients on the label and include:

From animal protein sources: nonfat milk solids, cheese whey, egg-white solids, sodium caseinate, fish-protein concentrate, whey solids, and hydrolyzed-milk protein.
From vegetable sources: soybean flour, soybean protein, brewer's yeast.
Essential amino acids are lysine, methionine, threonine, and tryptophan.

When you prepare your own baby food, you also have the opportunity to add your own fortifiers. Molasses, rich in iron, can be used as a mild sweetener. Wheat germ, high in vitamin E and B vitamins, can be used as a thickener. Nonfat dry milk powder can be added to almost any food. Lemon and orange juice supply vitamin C and can be used instead of water.

So, if you read the list of ingredients, you will be able to select foods without *unnecessary* or *potentially harmful additives*. You can keep track of those which are under current controversy through the newspapers, consumer magazines, and the Federation of Homemakers. (See Bibliography.) You don't have to memorize these difficult names; instead copy the ones down that you want to avoid, and take the list shopping. You can even practice at home with labels on foods that you have already bought.

Remember that foods containing any additives should be served only occasionally for the sake of necessary convenience. If you are in doubt about any additive or see a long list of long names, just don't buy the food.

In general, the whole process of label reading is less time-consuming than you might think. Since you tend to use the same foods, once you have identified the best ones in terms of safety and nutritional cost, you can simply keep buying them. This is the best way to convey your preferences and objections to the food industry. It really can be a fun game and a rewarding one!

A Shopping Checklist

- Buy fresh fruits and vegetables in season.
- Buy other foods on sale or specials.
- Buy store or "no-name" brands.
- Buy lower grades when appearance or tenderness is unimportant.
- Read dating codes to buy fresh foods.
- Use unit pricing to buy the lowest-priced brand or size. Larger amounts are usually, but not always, a better buy.
- Read the list of ingredients to insure that you are not paying for unnecessary or harmful ingredients. Remem-

ber: "fortified," "natural," "enriched," or "organic" foods may not be your best nutritional buy!
- Do not buy highly refined and processed foods.
- Use "fresh" leftovers that might have been thrown away; the baby won't know the difference!
- Combine inexpensive incomplete protein foods in the same dish or meal.

Throughout the book I have indicated with the sign "$" those foods or recipes that are inexpensive in terms of their "nutritional cost." Under each food you will also find specific "best buy" information.

There is simply no reason for any baby to grow up nutritionally deficient, regardless of family income. It is also unnecessary to deprive the rest of your family by buying expensive foods for your baby. You will be able to save money while giving your baby the best possible start in life. This, I believe, is the best reason for you to prepare your own baby food!

3

Feeding Your Baby

As you read books, consult doctors, and talk with other mothers, you will find that everyone seems to have their own specific ideas on breast feeding versus bottle feeding, the age to start solids, which solids, schedules, sterilization, and so on. If you have other children you will already have your own way of feeding your baby. In spite of wide differences of opinion on the various aspects of feeding, babies seem to thrive. They are really very adaptable!

Most experts do agree that the important factor in successful feeding is a relaxed and confident mother. You will be able to maintain this attitude if you try to follow whatever methods are most convenient and comfortable for you. In this chapter, I have tried to show the various choices that you have among the methods that are generally recommended. Of course, if you regularly consult a doctor, he will give you specific advice. Just don't be afraid to ask questions!

Breast Feeding or Bottle Feeding

The first choice that you will make is whether to nurse your baby or use a formula. You should decide *before* you

33

go to the hospital, since soon after your baby is born, you will receive medication to prevent the milk from coming if you will not be nursing. This is not the time that you will feel like making the decision.

Breast feeding has become very common and most doctors recommend and encourage it for both physical and psychological reasons. Nutritionally, breast milk is nearly perfect and if you are eating a balanced diet, your baby will be well fed during his first six to eight months. Compared to cow's milk, it is higher in vitamins C, E, niacin, and in linoleic acid. Breast milk does not contain adequate amounts of vitamin D and iron; however, these can be given as supplements. It contains carbohydrates in the form of lactose, which is less sweet and more easily digested than the sucrose or dextrose usually added to formulas. There is less chance that your baby will have digestive trouble with breast milk, and it also supplies him with antibodies that will make him more resistant to infections.

There are also several advantages for you, personally, in nursing. This is really the most convenient, economical, and easy way to feed your baby. The milk is always available and sterile. You don't have to buy or mix formulas, sterilize bottles, or store them. Some women object that nursing may tie them down, but a daily relief bottle can be given and that gives you up to eight hours between feedings. If you feel that you may be too busy to nurse, remember that it also gives you a good excuse to retreat by yourself for a while and relax.

Then there is the all-important job of regaining your figure. You will do so faster since nursing naturally causes the uterus to contract. You will be supplying extra calories in the milk you produce, so you can eat great amounts without gaining weight and can even lose any extra pounds easily. Really a pleasure if you have been calorie-watching for the past nine months!

The only reason not to nurse is if you have strong feelings against it. If you are unsure, remember that you can wean your baby, or stop nursing, at any time. So it seems a good idea to try it, at least for two or three weeks. Before your baby is born, try to get some advice from other mothers who have nursed their babies. You should contact La Leche League, which distributes information on nursing and often has women on call to talk with about specific problems. There are now branches in most areas, or you can write to their main office. (See Bibliography.) Often, the local YWCA or a hospital will have information or courses on breast feeding. The government booklet "Infant Care" also contains a good section on breast feeding.

Here are some general suggestions on successful nursing:

- Get as much rest as possible.
- Eat a balanced diet, especially including as much milk as you can.
- Drink a good amount of fruit juices.
- Watch out for allergic reactions in your baby to foods that *you* are eating, and avoid them. These are also foods that may cause a reaction when he eats them as solids.
- Be careful of drugs you might take that can affect your baby. If you can, avoid using any drug.
- What *you* eat or drink will show up in your milk.
- Find a comfortable place to nurse—a rocking chair is excellent. Place a pillow under your arm.
- Don't worry about how much milk your baby is drinking. If he is gaining weight and seems satisfied, the actual ounces aren't important.
- If you have an older child who is suffering from acute jealousy, this is a good time to read him a story, or sing.
- If you do run into problems, call your doctor, or a friend who has nursed.
- If you begin to have pain in one breast, stop nursing on that side and contact your doctor at once.
- Get as much rest as possible.
- Relax!

Bottle feeding. If you decide not to nurse, a bottle is also a very satisfactory way to feed your baby. The hospital will put your baby on a specific formula and you will receive instructions when you go home. A recent development has been the use of commercial formulas, either in concentrated form or already mixed. Although these are more expensive than preparing your own, they are very convenient. Their composition does vary, but they should be fortified with vitamins D, E, and C, and iron. Dr. Fomon has questioned the use of vegetable oil in these formulas, since the lack of butterfat results in a very low intake of the cholesterol in saturated fat. In any case, their use should always be discussed with a doctor.

The Food and Drug Administration also warns that canned formula can become curdled and, if so, should not be used. Formula should not be stored at temperatures above 72° Fahrenheit.

HOW TO PREPARE A FORMULA

The classic way of preparing a formula is to dilute evaporated milk with boiled water and add sugar. This results in a composition that is similar to breast milk. Whole homogenized milk can also be mixed with sugar and water. The formula depends upon the individual needs of your baby, so follow the one prescribed by your doctor. Remember that cow's milk is lacking or low in vitamins D and E, iron, niacin, and also vitamin C.

If you do not have a doctor to help plan the formula, you can use these sample formulas. You would gradually shift from the first formula to the later formulas over the first two to three months, increasing the amount as your baby's appetite grows. By the time he is three months, if he is gaining weight and eating solids, you would give 24–32 ounces of undiluted whole milk, or evaporated milk that is diluted with equal parts water, and omit the sugar.

	FIRST FORMULA	LATER FORMULAS	
Evaporated milk	6 ounces	10 ounces	13 ounces
Water (boiled)	10 ounces	15 ounces	19 ounces
Sugar or corn syrup	1½ tablespoons	2½ tablespoons	3 tablespoons

OR

Whole milk (boiled)	12 ounces	20 ounces	26 ounces
Water (boiled)	4 ounces	6 ounces	6 ounces
Sugar or corn syrup	1½ tablespoons	2½ tablespoons	3 tablespoons

You will first divide the formula into six 3-ounce bottles, then six 4-ounce bottles. As your baby starts to drop the extra feedings, you will have five 6-ounce bottles, then four 8-ounce bottles.

Goat's milk and soybean-based formulas are also sold. These are given to babies who are allergic to cow's milk. Since they require nutritional supplements, *you should never use them without a doctor's instruction*.

As with nursing, before your baby is born, find a good source of information on sterilization and bottle feeding. Your doctor can recommend one, or send for one of the government booklets. (See Bibliography.) Remember that even if you are nursing you will occasionally give a bottle.

Sterilization of bottles and formulas is important when you are preparing a day's supply of formula that you will be storing in the bottles. The sterilization will slow down the growth of bacteria and spoilage. If you are making each bottle just before a feeding, or using an occasional bottle to supplement nursing, you can prepare the formula in a well-washed bottle. You should, however, use boiled water. Sterilization is usually stopped at around three months, the same time that you switch from formula to regular container milk. The age at which you can make this switch depends upon your baby's individual growth, and you should consult a doctor. The "Beverages" chapter covers the various types of milk you can use.

Since bacteria and germs will not grow on clean, dry surfaces, you do not have to sterilize feeding spoons, dishes, or the baby's toys.

Bottles. You have a wide choice in the type of bottle that you can use. The clear-glass bottles seem to me to be the most inconvenient to use because of the possibility of breaking. The clear glass will also allow light to destroy the riboflavin in the milk. There are plastic bottles in various colors which are opaque and so screen out any light. These can be sterilized as well as the glass bottles.

The most convenient bottles are the disposable, sterilized liners that fit inside an opaque plastic holder. The only part that you boil, and even that isn't always necessary, is the nipple that snaps on top of the holder. The nipple turns inside out and is very easy to clean. Besides their convenience, these disposable bottles have some advantages for your baby. The plastic bag will collapse as he drinks, so there is less chance of swallowing air. Also, the nipple is shaped so that it does not collapse and prevent milk from flowing—very frustrating to a baby. The only disadvantage in using these bottles is their expense. They cost from one cent to two cents apiece and you can use 8 to 10 bottles a day. One way of reducing this expense is to wash the bottles that are used for water and juice and reuse them. Of course, if you are nursing, these bottles are ideal for the occasional relief bottle of water or juice.

The **temperature** of the milk is often a major concern. The standard test is to drop some on the inside of your wrist, and it should feel warm. This test is used to prevent feeding a baby milk that is too hot; it does not mean that the milk must be warmed to this temperature. *Some hospitals do not warm milk for newborn infants.*

There are some clear advantages in feeding your baby milk directly from the refrigerator. The cold milk allows less chance of spoilage and you can save unused portions in the refrigerator for the next feeding. You also save those few minutes of listening to a screaming baby while waiting for the bottle to warm. If you are traveling, it is very convenient to be able to give a cold bottle. The important thing is to accustom your baby gradually to cold milk, then be consistent with this temperature.

So whether you decide to nurse your baby or use a formula in a bottle depends upon your own feelings. Most important is for you to have a confident and relaxed attitude toward the whole process. Your baby will respond to this more than to where his milk is coming from. You also may find that feeding was going well in the hospital but becomes unsettled when you first come home. Or the reverse may happen. Your baby may have difficulty feeding in the hospital and then settle down at home. Most feeding problems are usually resolved within the first two weeks, so just try to be patient and relax.

SUPPLEMENTS

Your doctor may also prescribe vitamins A, C, and D and iron supplements that you will give your baby from about three weeks through his first year. *Never give more than the amount prescribed.* They will usually be in the form of water-soluble drops that you can put in a bottle or directly in the mouth. If it is an oil-base vitamin, or fish-liver oil, you should give it immediately *after* a feeding by dropping it in the corner of his mouth, to make sure it is fully absorbed. If you are not nursing, do ask your doctor about supplements of vitamin E and linoleic acid, since cow's milk is lower in these nutrients.

If you cannot regularly consult a doctor, or purchase the concentrated drops of vitamins C and D, you should still give these supplements. Vitamin C can be supplied daily with a 3-ounce serving of orange juice or larger servings of other juices. (See chapter 12, "Beverages.") You can also dissolve a 50-mg. vitamin C tablet in a little water. This would be useful if your baby is allergic to orange juice. You can supply vitamin D with 1 teaspoon of cod-liver oil each day. (See chapter 1, "Nutrition," for amounts and sources of other vitamins and minerals.)

Schedules

A feeding schedule is more for your convenience than for your baby's needs. You will be able to plan your day if you know when your baby is going to eat. This is especially important if you are nursing. When you are feeding solids, you will want to choose mealtimes that best fit in with your family's schedule. The most relaxed time may be after you and your family have eaten.

In the first few weeks you will probably work out some compromise between your baby's demands and the schedule you prefer. If you are nursing, you should feed your baby at 3-hour intervals for the first few weeks to establish your milk supply.

The interval between feedings that you should aim for is

4 hours, and most babies naturally settle into this; however, a very young or small baby may become hungry in 2½ or 3 hours. You may allow him to cry a few minutes to encourage him to wait a little longer, but it will be painful for both of you to wait out the full 4 hours. Fortunately, the days of strict schedules are over. Even after your baby is on a schedule, don't be surprised if he wakes for a feeding at a strange time!

You will be able to gradually shift your baby to the 4-hour interval that is most convenient for you. The hospital usually starts the day at 7 A.M., which means feedings at 7 A.M., 11 A.M., 3 P.M., 7 P.M, and 3 A.M. If you like to stay up late and sleep late, you will give the first feeding at 9 A.M. Hopefully, your baby will soon drop the middle-of-the-night feeding. When he does drop a feeding and when you start adding solids, the whole schedule may shift around. So try to stay flexible, and you won't become a frantic clock watcher. If you are a person who dislikes keeping to any schedule, you do not have to follow one. Your baby will then be on "demand" feeding.

When you begin feeding your baby solids you will space them out so that they roughly fall into breakfast, lunch, and dinner. Again, this is for your convenience. We happen to live in a 3-meal-a-day society, but some research has shown that it may be healthier to eat more frequent, smaller meals. So you should not hesitate to give midmorning and midafternoon snacks, such as juice, fruit, or crackers if your baby is hungry. If he is eating healthy foods, you really can't spoil his appetite.

One thing to avoid is the "strung-out" meals which last a half hour or more as you try to get down one more bite. You can end up spending much of your day with a spoon in your hand, and your baby will never get the idea of specific meals. He may even come to resent spending so much time eating! Try to remember that if your baby does not eat much at one meal, he will be hungrier for the next one.

Why, When, and How to Introduce Solid Food

You will begin to feed your baby solid food in the form of purées to supply him with vitamins and minerals that are lacking in milk, and to satisfy his increasing appetite. He will gradually become accustomed to new tastes and textures, so that he will easily make the switch to regular family food.

There has been a significant change over the last ten years as to when solids are introduced into a baby's diet. In the past, cereals were begun around four weeks and by six months a baby was eating a wide range of fruits, vegetables, eggs, and meats. Now, pediatricians feel that early feeding of solids can result in food allergies and digestive problems.

There is still a variation among doctors, but most recommend that solid food should not be started until a baby is at least four months old. If a baby is gaining well, especially if he is breast fed, solids are often delayed until six months. By delaying until after eight months, you might chance weaning and feeding difficulties when you first introduce solids. In any case, you will be preparing baby foods for a much shorter time than I did!

The **When to Introduce a Food** table was created from the recommendations of several pediatricians and from personal experience, as a practical *order* for introducing the different foods. The *earliest* advisable ages are given but you can begin at any later time. After your baby is seven to eight months old, you have leeway of a month or so for any specific food, so don't consider this list as the last word. If a food shows up whole in a bowel movement, the baby's system is not mature enough to digest that food—just delay it for a month.

Many foods are included that you may not have considered "baby food"; however they are nutritious and often economical. Also, don't feel that you have to feed your baby every food that is listed here, and don't be afraid to try foods that may have been left out.

WHEN TO INTRODUCE A FOOD

AGE	CEREALS	FRUIT	VEGETABLES	PROTEINS
4 Months	Rice (dry infant cereal)	Orange juice		Yogurt (plain)
4½ Months	Other infant cereals— Oatmeal Barley High-protein	Banana (raw) Applesauce or Apple juice		
5 Months	Enriched— Farina, cream of wheat Cream of rice Pearl barley Wheat germ	Cooked— Pears Apricots Peaches Prunes Plums Nectarines		Yogurt (with any introduced fruit)
6 Months		Cooked— Pineapple Guavas Mangoes Papayas	Cooked— Carrots Green beans Winter squash Peas Tomatoes	
7 Months	Whole Grains— Oatmeal Whole Wheat Brown Rice Wheatena Ralston	Cooked— Cherries Grapes Raw—Pears	Cooked— Asparagus Broccoli Summer squash Celery Corn Potatoes	Egg yolk Egg-yolk custard Cottage cheese Grated cheese Chicken Turkey Soybeans
8 Months	Enriched— Noodles Spaghetti Macaroni	Raw— Apple Plums Apricot Citrus Grapes	Raw— Carrots Cooked— Beets Spinach Green leafy Rutabaga Turnip Parsnips Okra Legumes Peanut butter	Veal Liver Kidneys Beef Lamb Lean fish Whole egg

AGE	CEREALS	FRUIT	VEGETABLES	PROTEINS
9 Months		Any cooked Fruit Raw— Pineapple Tropical Cantaloupe Avocado	Any cooked vegetable Raw— Greens Tomatoes	Ham Pork Duck
10 Months	All table foods			

HOW TO INTRODUCE NEW FOODS

The way that you introduce a food is really more important than the taste or texture. Always offer a new food with a smile and some encouraging words. Your baby soon becomes an expert at interpreting your expression and can acquire your own likes and dislikes of specific foods. Here are some other suggestions:

- Give a new food in the morning or at lunch. If you give it at dinner and he has a reaction, you may be in for a sleepless night.
- Always start with a small amount—about one teaspoon for the first time—then increase daily.
- Introduce one food at a time and wait four days before giving another new food. Then, if he has an allergic reaction, you will know which food caused it.
- A reaction to a food may show up as a rash, hives, gas pains, vomiting, or diarrhea. Allergies are not very common, but they often occur in the same family, and with similar types of food.
- Some foods that may cause a reaction are orange juice, egg white, chocolate, nuts, berries, seafood, green beans, and green leafy vegetables; so watch out for these.
- If your baby does show an allergy to a specific food, wait one to two months, then try again. If allergic reactions occur frequently, you should consult your doctor.

- Your baby is most likely to accept a new food if you offer it at the beginning of a meal when he is most hungry. You can also mix it slightly with a favorite food such as a fruit. This is especially good for introducing meats and foods with coarser textures.
- When your baby first begins to taste solid food, his natural sucking response will cause most of the food to spill out. Do not feel that he is spitting out the food because he dislikes it; he will soon learn how to swallow. Some babies find it easier to manage a fairly thick purée, so you can try different consistencies of food.
- There is always the question of whether you offer solid food before or after the bottle. Obviously, if he has just finished a full bottle, he will not be interested in solid food. But if he is starving, he will not be in the mood to experiment. The best time to offer solids, at least in the early months, is after he has finished about half a bottle.
- If your baby shows an obvious dislike of a specific food after you have offered it at several meals, forget it for a month or find a substitute. Other than milk, no one food is really essential.
- If you will be using a reclining infant seat, get your baby accustomed to sitting in the seat before you offer food for the first time.
- If your baby starts coughing or decides to sneeze just as you have given him a mouthful of food, hold your hand an inch or so away from his mouth. A wet hand is easier to clean than a shower of puréed food all over you!

HOW TO INTRODUCE COARSER FOODS

It is to your own advantage and your baby's that he begin eating regular family foods as soon as he can. You will save preparation time and your baby will be getting the most nourishment from foods that have not been thinned. Also, when he is eating food that he can pick up and feed himself, he will have a feeling of independence and you will have the freedom from feeding him every bite. Since you can control the consistency of baby food that you prepare yourself, your baby will make the switch easily at an early age. An extra bonus from making your own baby food!

When your baby is six to seven months old, or easily eating fine purées, you can begin to gradually accustom him to coarser purées, then finely chopped food, then finger foods. Don't worry about how many teeth he has or doesn't have; he will be able to manage most foods very nicely with his gums.

Here are some general suggestions that I have found practical.

- Introduce your baby to each new consistency or texture very gradually—one food a day. Do not force them.
- Start with foods that are particular favorites—fruits and vegetables are good ones.
- If you have a blender or food processor, you can make a coarser texture by using a slower speed or a shorter blending time. It is very easy to make gradual changes.
- You can also begin mashing many foods with a fork.
- If you are thinning a food, start using less liquid.
- When you are giving a coarser food such as ground meat, mix it with a little smooth fruit or vegetable purée.
- Most important—do not look anxious; SERVE WITH A SMILE!

Planning a Balanced Menu

The most important part of feeding your baby is to make sure that you offer him a balanced menu of the foods that he requires. Experiments have even shown that, from a variety of foods, a baby will choose those that contain the necessary nutrients. Since your baby's basic needs are similar to those of the rest of your family, this menu planning will require very little additional time. It really is very simple—just become familiar with the four basic food groups and the number of servings from each group.

This book is designed to help you, with the recipe

chapters divided into the three main food groups—**Cereal Grains, Fruits/Vegetables,** and **Protein Foods.** The other important group, **Dairy,** will be satisfied by your baby's daily intake of formula or milk.

You can then select any food from within the basic group. This allows you considerable room for substitution in order to take advantage of foods that are available and convenient at a particular time, especially those that fit in best with family meals. For example, a serving of cereal grains does not always have to be cereal, you can also use rice or spaghetti. Or, if you don't have meat prepared, you can occasionally give an extra egg. Fruits and vegetables can be interchanged, and you don't have to serve a different one at each meal, or even each day. If your baby becomes tired of one food, he will let you know!

A balance among the food groups will give you the best nutrition, and it is unnecessary and time-consuming to try to offer a wide variety each day. Of course, too much of any one food should also be avoided, no matter how nutritious that food is. For example, one egg serving a day is recommended, but you should limit eggs to 7 to 9 in a week. Organ meats, such as liver, should not be served more than three times a week. Even milk should be limited to one quart a day. *Just remember that there is no "wonder food"!*

The following **Menu Planning Guide** indicates the daily servings of each food group and the sequence in which they are usually added to make up a complete menu. Although protein and calories are essential each day, many other nutrients can be stored so that you can also balance your baby's menu over a few days. The day is divided into breakfast, lunch, and dinner mainly for convenience, but you can serve these foods at any time during the day.

A "serving" is really whatever your baby will eat. In order to plan, you can count an average serving, for a six- to twelve-month baby, as *1–2 food cubes or 3–6 tablespoons*. A *"food cube"* is the amount that can be frozen in the form of an average ice cube, or *about 3 tablespoons*. (See **Food Cube** section in chapter 5.) Do try to give equal amounts of the various foods. If you are serving an "all-in-one" meal such as a stew, increase the amount to 3–6 food cubes.

MENU PLANNING GUIDE

	BREAKFAST	LUNCH	DINNER
4 Months	Cereal		Cereal
5 Months	Cereal	Fruit	Cereal
	Fruit		Fruit
6 Months	Cereal	Fruit	Cereal
	Fruit	Vegetable	Fruit
7 Months	Cereal	Fruit	Cereal
	Fruit	Vegetable	Fruit
	Egg Yolk	Cheese	
8 Months	Cereal	Fruit	Cereal
	Fruit	Vegetable	Fruit
	Egg	Protein	Vegetable
9 Months	Cereal	Fruit	Cereal/protein
	Fruit	Vegetable	Fruit
	Egg	Protein	Vegetable

Also snack of extra juice, crackers, etc.

So, from nine months on, your baby's daily menu will include:
3 protein foods (including 1 egg)
2 cereal grains (including 1 cereal/protein)
5 fruit/vegetable (including 1 serving of juice, 1 dark green or yellow)
3–4 cups milk (24–32 ounces)
This is the balanced diet that your baby should continue eating for several years!

Feeding Equipment

You will not need any special or expensive equipment to feed your baby. The important thing is to use whatever is most practical for you.

Feeding dishes can range from any small dish to an electric three-compartment feeding dish. The latter is the most expensive and is designed to keep the food at a constantly warm temperature. This can be a disadvantage if you leave the food in the dish for any period, since it is an ideal temperature for bacteria to grow. It will also accustom your baby to eating food that is always the same temperature and this can be a problem if you find yourself without this dish. There is no medical reason for your baby to eat food at a constant warm temperature.

The big advantage in using any warming dish is that you can quickly heat your baby's food without creating an extra pot to wash. You can use the inexpensive plastic dishes that can be filled with hot water; or a small heatproof dish that can be put in the oven or in a pan of hot water (a custard cup, heavy dish, or the Mini-Blend jar can be used). You can also wrap any food in aluminum foil and heat it in the oven. This is a fast way to heat a frozen "food cube." Of course, there is no reason why the food has to be warmed at all. Your baby will adapt to any temperature and you just have to learn to ignore the cries of outrage from other mothers and grandmothers!

A **spoon** should be small, narrow, and shallow—it does not have to be silver! A demitasse spoon is perfect if you have one and the small plastic picnic spoons are also a good size. When you first offer solid foods, try using a wooden tongue depressor, a dull butter knife, or a well-washed popsicle stick. These flat sticks are also good for your baby's early attempts at feeding himself.

A **bib** is a feeding necessity. Use a big plastic bib, with a catch-all pocket (see chapter 14 for instructions on making one), and a slide or snap fastener. Since a baby does not have much of a neck, it can be a real problem to tie a bib on. The plastic bibs can be easily wiped off, dry quickly, and are more practical than the terry-cloth or cotton bibs.

A **feeding chair** is not a necessity, but it is a great convenience. You won't have to juggle a wriggling baby and a spoon. The first chair to use is a plastic recliner that sits on a table and sells for as low as $5. It sits on the table and you can put your baby in it as young as three to four weeks.

When your baby is five to six months old, he may become very restless in a recliner, and it will be time to switch him to a high chair. Select one that is easy to clean, has a removable tray with a raised edge to catch spills, and a wide base so it won't tip over when your baby starts leaning over. I would have preferred a decorative antique cane high chair, which would have tipped easily and been impossible to clean. Luckily, I was talked out of it! If you do not have the room for a high chair, there are several seats available that either fasten to a chair or on to the edge of the table. Your baby then sits right at the table. These seats are less expensive than a high chair and are very practical for traveling.

When Your Baby Won't Eat

After you have planned balanced menus, carefully bought the food, and prepared nutritious dishes, you still have to get the food into your baby. This is probably the subject of greatest concern among mothers, yet you will have the most success if you can just relax and not worry about it. Again, serve with a smile!

Feeding is your baby's earliest contact with another person and just as food is essential for his physical growth, happy mealtimes will help him get the idea that people are really very nice. At one time, the thought was that a baby should consider eating as serious work, so playing was discouraged. The result was often a problem eater. There is no reason why you can't sing, make faces, or give your baby a toy to play with while you are feeding him. Most important is for your baby to look forward to mealtimes with pleasure.

You must not allow feedings to become a battleground over the choice of foods or the amount. If your baby dislikes one food, there is always another from the same food group that you can substitute. Your baby's appetite will also vary with each meal or each day. Since the baby food that you prepare will be inexpensive, you should not mind throwing out any uneaten portions.

It will also be easier for you to maintain this casual attitude if you can forget the idea that a baby must be fat to be healthy, and that it is a sign of success as a mother to have a fat baby, or stuff in as much food as you can.

Your baby is not a turkey and there is even a limit to how many nutrients he can use. Also, since your own baby food will not be laden with sugar and starches, you are less likely to have a fat baby. So be ready to resist advice from grandmothers and even total strangers on how to "fatten up" your baby.

There are some subtle ways that you can encourage your baby if he starts to show a lack of interest in eating.

- You can offer him some different foods or prepare foods with a coarser texture.
- Or he may be ready for finger foods as an attempt at feeding himself.
- If he seems restless in a reclining seat, change the position so he has something else to look at; or move him to a high chair if he can sit up.
- You can even try feeding him at the same time the rest of the family is eating, although this may take some organization on your part.

You may encounter real stubbornness, and your baby may decide to give up eating completely for a day or so. Remember that a baby has very few ways that he can assert himself and not eating is one of them. If you show that it bothers you and you make a feeding a major battle, you can have a problem eater. Your baby will probably still continue to drink milk and this will supply him with enough nutrients for a while. You can fortify his bottle (see Homemade Fortified Milk), but be careful not to give him more than one quart of milk a day or he may not become hungry enough to begin eating again. You may also not even attempt to feed him for a meal or two, and the chances are that he will forget why he stopped eating in the first place. This may be hard to do, but remember that babies do not want to be hungry and there has never been a case of a baby choosing starvation. Sooner or later he will begin eating again.

Self-Feeding

There will come the day when your baby begins to grab for the spoon, try to hit it out of your hand, or put his hands in the food. This means that he has the idea of feeding himself. If you discourage him and don't allow him to try, you may be feeding him for the next year. So, try to cheerfully accept the mess that is about to begin and consider that it is a step toward the day when he will be neatly feeding himself. There are some ways that you can at least control the mess.

- At first, you can give your baby a spoon to hold and play with while you are feeding him. This may satisfy him for a week or so.
- At the end of a meal give him a spoon or popsicle stick and let him practice with a thick purée such as bananas. If he tries to feed himself when he is hungry, he may become very frustrated and discouraged.
- If he begins fingerpainting on the tray with food, allow it for a few meals so that the novelty will wear off, then gently discourage it by removing the tray and ending the meal.
- If your baby feeds himself with his fingers, it is a step in learning, but keep offering a spoon.
- Put newspaper under the high chair.
- If he refuses to allow you to feed him altogether, but cannot manage a spoon well enough to eat an adequate amount, start serving finger foods. (See chapter 14, "Finger Foods.")
- When he seems ready to try a cup, buy a training cup with a cover, and give only a small amount at a time. Juices are most readily accepted from a cup.
- Unless you have a real aversion to a bottle, there is no reason to push him to drink from a cup. It is really more trouble for you.
- In general, do not discourage self-feeding, but do not force your baby into it.

Digestive Difficulties

Since your baby's digestive system might take a while to start working properly, he is likely to react to feeding with digestive problems. Here are some common ones to look out for, and some suggestions. Of course, you should always contact your doctor when one occurs.

Colic, or gas pain, may be very common during your baby's first three months. It is a result of food not being completely digested by the baby's immature digestive system, and your baby will show his pain by loud, constant crying and sharply drawing his legs up. It is very similar to hunger crying, but although the baby is calmed by eating, he soon begins crying again. Often the crying will follow a schedule, an hour or two at specific times during the day or night.

Your doctor may feel that it is an allergic reaction to a kind of milk and prescribe a special milk or formula. If it only occurs after eating certain foods, you can avoid them for a month or so. Most likely, the colic will be a painful stage for both you and the baby and you will just have to wait it out—with earplugs if necessary!

Rashes or hives are usually an allergic reaction to a specific food, and you can eliminate that food for a month or so. A light dusting with cornstarch will relieve the itching, but be careful not to get it in the baby's eyes or nose.

Often a baby of one to two months will develop a pimply rash that looks like adolescent acne. This is usually not related to a food allergy, but is caused by clogged pores. You should keep the baby's face well washed, and powder with cornstarch to dry up the excess oil.

Diarrhea, or very loose, watery bowel movements, can be a sign of teething, an oncoming illness, or a reaction to a specific food or to a spoiled food. If it continues for more than a day, your baby may become dehydrated, so you should definitely contact your doctor. The recommendation for mild cases is to increase the amount of liquid that the baby drinks. Diluted skim milk (or formula) may be given. Do not give boiled skim milk or add dry milk powder. Other foods that may help are carrot/rice soup, rice cereal, eggs, and bananas.

Celiac disease is a form of diarrhea in which the bowel movements are frothy and foul-smelling and contain undigested food. It is usually a result of an inability to digest and absorb food properly. You should contact your doctor, who will plan a special diet for your baby.

Constipation is usually not a serious problem. It is not necessary for your baby to have a bowel movement every day. You should watch out for hard dry movements that are painful. They may be softened by feeding him barley cereal, prune juice, or stewed dried fruits, or by adding dark-brown sugar or molasses to his bottle. *Do not give your baby an enema or laxative* (unless prescribed by a doctor), *or mineral oil*.

Vomiting is a forceful throwing up of a large amount of food. It may be caused by oncoming illness, a reaction to a specific food, or eating spoiled food. If it occurs frequently, it may be a sign of a more serious problem. In any case, contact your doctor.

A less serious but very annoying problem is when your baby "cheeses" or spits up a small amount of food as he burps. It may be caused by a difficulty in digesting fat or by just overeating. A switch to skim or half-skim milk may help, but ask your doctor first. Most babies outgrow it in several months, so be patient and always have a towel handy.

Feeding Your Baby Away From Home

We all travel around with our babies, and we are likely to be away from home at a mealtime. Here are some suggestions that may be helpful.

- If your baby is on formula, you can carry the individual bottles of commercial formulas that do not require refrigeration until they are opened. You just screw on a clean nipple. These formulas are also available in small cans, which are less expensive.
- If you are using bottles with the canned formula, or for water and juice, use the plastic disposable bottles that fit inside a holder. You won't have to worry about washing or sterilizing bottles.

- If you are using your own formula and you will need several bottles, you can save room in your thermos bag in the following way. Mix as much water and sugar as you need in a jar. Carry a can of evaporated milk, or place it in a thermos. Then you can mix each disposable bottle as you need it. Only the concentrated milk needs to be kept cold after opening.

- If your baby is off formula and drinking fresh milk, just carry the nonfat dry milk powder. It does not need to be refrigerated and you can mix each disposable bottle as you need it, right in the bottle. Use 2 ounces of dry milk for an 8-ounce bottle. Even if your baby is regularly drinking whole milk, the nonfat milk will not disagree with him. (See chapter 12, "Beverages," for specific information.)

- Solid food is not really necessary in the early months, and your baby probably won't mind missing a meal. If you do want to feed him solid food when you are away from home, you can look for an "instant" food. (See chapter 13.) *Do not introduce new foods when you are away from home.*

- You can also carry the frozen "food cubes" with you. Place enough cubes for a meal in a plastic bag, and they will defrost in time without any need for special storage. Some cooked fruits will keep for several hours. You can then feed your baby out of the plastic bag and throw it away. If you are carrying milk, the cubes will also help keep the milk cold.

- Be sure to accustom your baby to eating cold food and milk when necessary. This will be most convenient when you are traveling.

4

Equipment for Easy
Cooking and Puréeing

I have been saying, throughout this book, that it is easy as well as nutritious to prepare your own baby food. Your mother and grandmother might doubt this, but they did not live in our gadget-conscious modern world. You have a wide choice of equipment for easy cooking and puréeing of baby food. Some of these things you may already own. If not, they may be acquired at modest cost, and remember, this equipment is not limited to baby food. Your entire family will benefit from the many uses of your new equipment long after you have stopped preparing baby food.

Cooking With Steam

You probably have your own favorite cooking methods and utensils, but keep in mind that many of the vitamins and minerals are water-soluble and thus are lost in the cooking liquid. Many nutrients are also destroyed by high heat, long cooking time, and the cutting of food into small pieces before cooking.

There is unanimous agreement among nutritionists that the *steam method* of cooking best preserves the vitamins and minerals in food. One study showed that, in steam cooking, only 6 per cent of the vitamins were lost, while pressure cooking resulted in a 12 per cent loss. Boiling in water caused a loss of 29–39 per cent. Vegetables are most often the victims of the water-boiling method and yet they are eaten as a major source of nutrients.

In the *steam method*, the food is held above rapidly boiling water and cooks in the rising steam. While it is especially important that the food your baby eats is as nutritious as possible, this method also produces food that retains its natural flavor and color. Your entire family will appreciate these steamed fruits and vegetables that are both nutritious and flavorful. This method is also the easiest and simplest way of cooking. You can choose from a variety of low-cost utensils or improvise one of your own.

A **steamer/blancher** is a good utensil for the steam method. It consists of a deep pot with a tight-fitting cover and another pot that is completely perforated and fits inside the first pot to within one inch of the bottom. It is similar in appearance to a double boiler. The water in the bottom will boil and the food will cook in the rising steam without being immersed in the water. This utensil is sometimes called a blancher because it is used to quickly immerse fruits and vegetables in boiling water before freezing. It sells for as low as $6 and is available in many stores, especially those that carry home canning and freezing equipment, such as a hardware store. An imported, more expensive heavyweight steamer is sold in some stores that carry gourmet and professional cooking equipment. Since you may use the steamer daily, the extra cost may be justified; however, the inexpensive steamer is quite adequate.

Steam baskets are also sold for use in steam cooking. There are several types available for $3–$8. Most are adjustable to fit inside any pot you already own to convert it into a steamer by raising the food out of the cooking water. You must be sure that the steam basket fits well inside the pot so that the cover will fit tightly. One disadvantage of the steam basket is in removing it from the pot.

Since all parts are inside the pot, it is not difficult to burn yourself. Also, if you have a full pot, the basket may tip while removing it.

Chinese cooking has become very popular and you can easily find an inexpensive **Chinese bamboo steam basket.** This flat round basket with a cover can be set in a wok or over a pot. It holds a good amount of food and can be handled easily.

Since the main principle in the steam method is to keep the food supported about one inch above the bottom of the pot, just out of the water, you can improvise in creating your own steam basket. A small colander might fit inside a large pot or you may have a round wire rack of the kind used in baking. If you are in the country, you may use well-washed stones in the bottom of the pot, probably the oldest means of steam cooking. Remember, whatever you use as a platform, it must have holes in it to allow the steam to come through.

A **double boiler** is a common utensil that will give almost the same results as a steamer for some foods, and is also useful for making custards and cooked cereals. Since the food cooks at a temperature below boiling, some of the bacteria that cause spoilage may not be destroyed. You should be especially careful in storing foods cooked this way. A double boiler can be purchased for as low as $5.

If you already own and are familiar with the use of a **pressure cooker,** you may wish to use it to prepare your baby's food. This method of cooking with steam under high pressure has the advantage of reducing the cooking time; however, you must be careful not to overcook the food. The cost of a nonelectric pressure cooker is around $15 and an electric one can be bought for $25–$30. If you buy one, look for the Underwriters Laboratory Seal as a check on quality and follow the manufacturer's instructions. An improperly used or malfunctioning pressure cooker can be dangerous.

An **electric crockpot** is also useful. This is a heavy-weight, tightly sealed utensil which maintains a low heat. The food simmers slowly, steaming in its own juices for 10–12 hours. This slow cooking retains the vitamins and minerals and tenderizes the food. Thus, it is especially good for meats and poultry. Several foods may be combined and it is suitable for making large quantities. The main drawback to this utensil is its price—$20–$30. A heavy stone or earthenware casserole used in a very slow oven would produce the same result; however, you might find it impractical to have the oven in use for the necessary length of time.

Aluminum foil and the clear roasting wraps offer simple means of nutritious cooking of almost any food. The food is tightly sealed in a double layer of foil and bakes in a slow (325° F.) oven. The cooking time for most food is slightly longer than with the steamer. This is a very good way to cook meats, since the slow moist heat will soften the tough fibers for easier puréeing. The cooking time for meat is about the same as with potting or braising. There is no need to add any water since the food will steam in its own juices. The tight seal will prevent the loss of those vitamins that are destroyed by air.

The cleanup is effortless—just throw the foil away. But this can also be a disadvantage if you are concerned with cost. The roasting bags are convenient for cooking large amounts, for combining different foods, or for foods which contain a large amount of juice. If your oven is already in use in preparing the family meal, it is very convenient to use foil to cook baby food at the same time.

Instead of foil, you can also use a heavy baking dish with a tight-fitting cover. Unless the food is very juicy, it will be necessary to add a little water when you begin cooking.

In general, here are the points that you should remember when selecting and using any steaming equipment.

- Buy a large utensil so that you can cook a large amount of food, or combine different foods, at the same time. This will save you cleanup and preparation time.
- Make certain that the lid is tight-fitting and heavy enough so that the steam cannot lift it. You can add curtain weights if necessary.
- Steam food whole and in the skin whenever possible. It is most nutritious and saves you cutting and peeling time. It is even easier to remove skin or pits of fruits and vegetables after cooking.

- Be careful not to let the water in the bottom of a steamer boil away during a long cooking time.
- Rinse the pot immediately after use for easy cleaning.

Microwave Ovens

A microwave oven is expensive and definitely not something you would buy just to prepare baby foods. It will save preparation time and can be a big help in quick defrosting of food cubes. Most of the nutrients are retained since the foods will cook in their own juices. In shopping for a microwave oven, you have a wide choice of styles and features. There are the least expensive countertop portable models, double ovens with the microwave oven on top and the conventional oven on the bottom, and combination ovens where both microwave and conventional cooking can be done in the same oven. Options include automatic defrosting (or low power settings), a variable power setting, a browning element, and a turntable that rotates the food while cooking. All manufacturers have to meet federal standards of safety.

Specific instructions are not included for microwave cooking of baby foods, but the recipes for baking and steaming (without additional liquid) can be used. Ovens vary, so follow the cooking times that are given in the instruction manual for your oven.

The Electric Blender

In the past, food had to be scraped and strained in small quantities. No wonder we heard that making our own baby food would be difficult and time-consuming! Fortunately, **electric blenders** and **food processors** have revolutionized the preparation of baby food.

The modern high-speed blenders can quickly and easily purée almost any food, even meats and poultry, into the finest consistency for the youngest infant. The blenders range in type from 4 speed to 16 speed, and some have specialty features or solid-state controls. The prices will vary accordingly, from $13 for a basic blender to $70. You can find many blenders in the $13–$30 range that have the necessary speed for processing baby food.

SELECTING A BLENDER

Here are some features that should be considered:

- Solid-state controls, which assure even processing at the lower speeds regardless of the load factor, are not a necessity in processing baby food where you will usually use the higher speeds. This feature does cost more.
- A blender with a *wide base* and larger blades is convenient because you do not have to cut the food into small pieces before blending. This blender is also excellent for processing *large* loads quickly and evenly. However, the wide base is a disadvantage in puréeing a small amount, since the food will disperse along the sides away from the blades.
- Blenders with *narrow* bases are more suitable for making *small* amounts.
- Do not use the small drink blenders or coffee mills to process baby food.
- It will be necessary with most blenders, when puréeing a heavy consistency, or a small amount, to carefully move the food from the sides of the container into the blade area with a rubber spatula. It is safer to stop the blender.
- The *Mini-Blend jar,* an Oster blender attachment, is an innovation that offers the ideal solution for processing a small amount (1 cup or less) of food. The Mini-Blend jar is a heavy 8-ounce jar that screws onto the blade assembly, replacing the large container. After the food is puréed, a cap can be screwed on the jar and the jar can be used for storage. You will save your time and effort by blending, feeding, and storing in the same jar. You will find it most practical for puréeing leftovers, or food from the current family meal, into baby food. It is also very convenient to reblend food,

in the container, to add more food, or to change the consistency.

- The Oster blender is sold with one jar, but additional jars are inexpensive. Other jars, such as home canning jars, with a 2½-inch neck and the proper screw thread, can be used, but may be less efficient in blending. Be careful not to use a light jar since the action of the food and the blades may cause it to break. In using any jar, do not fill it more than ¾ full to allow for expansion of the food during processing.
- Some other blenders can also accommodate the Mini-Blend and similar jars, although they are not advertised with this feature. You may check for this on your own blender by unscrewing the container from the base (if possible), and attempting to screw on a Mini-Blend or canning jar.
- The *cycle* or *pulse* feature on some blenders is useful in chopping foods evenly. The blender will stop at intervals during processing. This is an advantage in controlling the coarseness of purées that you are preparing for an older baby. However, it is not a necessity and may add to the cost of the blender.
- Another advantageous feature of a blender is the ability to add ingredients through the top while it is operating, without removing the entire lid.

USING YOUR BLENDER

Your blender will easily process baby food if you use it properly and care for it. If you are not satisfied with the blender you already own, you may not be following the manufacturer's instructions. In general, these are the important things to remember in using any blender:

- Read the instruction book carefully. If you do not have one, you can write to the manufacturer, giving the model number.
- Set the blender on a clean, dry, solid surface.
- Be sure the cover is firmly in place before starting, and add ingredients through the top if possible.

- Do not remove the container from the base while the motor is running. Never leave the blender while processing.
- When using an older or less powerful blender, start the motor on a slower speed before adding ingredients, then switch to a faster speed.
- If liquids are used, pour them in before adding the dry ingredients.
- If the blender has a small base, cut the food, especially meats, poultry, and cheese, into one-inch cubes.
- Allow boiling or steaming foods to cool slightly before blending.
- If you are puréeing a small quantity and it disperses along the sides, stop the motor, push the food down with a rubber spatula, and restart. It may be necessary to repeat this several times.
- Do not allow the motor to labor when processing a heavy or thick load. Either stir to introduce air, add liquid, or switch to a higher speed. If the mixture is very thick, make only a small amount at a time.
- If there is any burning smell, shut the motor off immediately, clean the blades, and check the repair directions.
- Clean your blender immediately after use by adding some detergent and water and running the blender on a medium speed for a few seconds. Finely puréed foods can stick like glue if they are allowed to harden. Eventually the turning ability of the blades will be slowed.
- Do not put the blade assembly in the dishwasher because the lubricating oils will wash away and the blades will not turn easily, thereby putting strain on the motor.
- Remember that most blenders will not mash potatoes, grind raw meat or poultry, or extract juices from fruits and vegetables.

The way that you use your blender for preparing your baby's food depends upon the speed selectors and the general condition of your particular blender. In general, you will be using the highest speeds (*blend, frappé, purée*) to process food for the youngest infant. These speeds will produce the finest consistency. As you prepare various types of food, you will soon find the proper speeds.

As your baby becomes accustomed to solids, and after a food has been introduced, you can begin reducing the blender speed or processing time or using the cycle feature for a coarser consistency. If the baby has difficulty swallowing or digesting a particular consistency, it is easy to thin or reblend the food. However, your aim should be to accustom your baby to eating increasingly coarse food until he can chew and swallow small bits of ordinary table food at family meals. An electric blender will give you the most control and ease in regulating the consistency of your baby's food.

REPAIRING YOUR BLENDER

When you are regularly using your blender to process your baby food, any breakdown is a major inconvenience. There are several faults that you can test for and repair yourself before you surrender your blender to the repair shop.

1. If the blender will not start and makes no sound: Plug another appliance into the outlet. If that does not start, then the outlet is at fault, not the blender.

    If the other appliance does start, then check the electric cord and the plug on the blender. If these are disconnected, you can buy a replacement plug at any hardware or five-and-ten store.

2. If the blender hums and tries to start: *Stop the blender*. Remove the blender container from the motor base, start the blender to see if the mechanism that turns the blade assembly now turns. If it does not, then the fault is in the motor itself, and you will probably require professional repair. If you have access into the blender base, you can try to clean any encrusted food, then oil.

    If the motor is turning, then your problem may be the common one of a frozen blade assembly. Food has probably become lodged around the blades or under the turning axle. Soak the blade assembly in detergent or a penetrating oil, then clean with a brush and thin thread or dental floss, then lubricate. If the problem persists, you may be trying to process too heavy a load.

3. If the motor overheats or smokes: *Stop the blender*. Clean out any dust and food to allow for better cooling. Lubricate any parts of the motor you can reach. Clean the blade assembly as in the preceding section.

4. If the blender is very noisy or vibrates: *Stop the blender*. Check the blades for accidental bending and straighten them. Lubricate the blade assembly and gearbox. If the problem persists, you will need professional repair.

Used carefully, the electric blender is a valuable aid in processing your baby food. It is fast, effortless, allows you to make large or small quantities, and gives you control over the consistency of the food. A blender or a food processor is also the only way you will be able to prepare many raw foods, such as citrus purées, that are highly nutritious. If you do not already own one, try to purchase even a low-cost or used blender. It's a good investment. Aside from substantial savings in making your own baby food, the blender offers many uses and savings for the entire family.

The Food Processor

A food processor has all the advantages of a blender—plus some! The only things it doesn't handle as well are very small amounts of some foods and large amounts of liquid (it will leak out through the center shaft). A processor is more effective in handling large amounts and thick purées; it will purée just about anything you would use as baby food.

The price range is higher than for blenders—from around $40 to $250. This is an expensive item just to prepare baby foods, but it will have a long and useful life in your kitchen. For example, you can whip up two loaves of bread in five minutes and easily save money on a staple food!

SELECTING A FOOD PROCESSOR

The original food processor is the Cuisinart®, available in improved and larger models. There are now many other manufacturers that sell less expensive ($40–$140) food processors and there is a running argument among users as to which is better. Some people report that the slicing, chopping, and ability to handle heavy loads suffers on the less expensive processors. Before you make a purchase you should talk to some owners and check a consumer comparison survey. I have never heard any complaints about the Cuisinart other than its price ($140–$250). The lowest-priced model is adequate for preparing baby foods and for most kitchens. Some features that should be included are:

- A warranty (the Cuisinart has a 15-year warranty on the motor).
- A pulse switch to give you more control over processing.
- The ability to knead bread.
- An automatic circuit breaker to protect against overload and motor burnout.
- A safety feature that prevents use when cover or bowl is not secured properly.

USING YOUR PROCESSOR

Before you use a food processor, carefully read the manufacturer's instruction book. The following suggestions are applicable to most processors:

- Insert metal blade before adding food.
- Handle the blades very carefully and keep out of children's reach.
- Before processing, cut most food into cubes 1½ inches square; hard vegetables and tough meats should be cut into smaller cubes. Soft fruits and vegetables can be added in large pieces.

- Do not overfill the processor.
- If the motor labors, stop and remove some of the food.
- If the blade jams on a hard lump of food, unplug machine and remove lump. In fact, it is safest to unplug the processor when not in use or when changing parts.
- For purées, begin with little or no added liquid, then add a tablespoon at a time as necessary.
- For coarser purées, cut food into same-size cubes so it all ends up the same coarseness. Watch your time!
- Remove pits and seeds before processing.
- Rinse processor immediately after using.
- To soak the processor bowl, leave the blade in place and the bowl will fill to the top.

REPAIRING A FOOD PROCESSOR

The only check I would advise on a nonoperative processor is whether the wall outlet is working; just plug in another appliance. If the outlet is all right, follow the manufacturer's instructions on obtaining repair service.

Other Ways to Purée

As handy as a blender and food processor are, there are alternative methods of processing food, which are still adequate, although slower. Some of these utensils are even more practical for processing small amounts. Also, they are easy to carry or are readily available if you go away from home.

Food mills can be purchased in small or large sizes for $4–$8. The food is placed in the basket, and as you turn the rotary handle the blade presses food through holes in the bottom of the basket. It is actually a more automatic version of the spoon-and-strainer method. It is, however, considerably faster and requires less effort. The food mill strains *most cooked foods*, with the exception of meat, to a smooth consistency acceptable to even the youngest infant. It also works well with *soft, raw fruits* such as bananas, pears, and plums. Meat and poultry will require more effort and will be processed more coarsely. The mill will purée liver or organ meats to a strained consistency that is fine enough to serve as a first meat food. *You may also prefer to use a mill to remove seeds, skin, and fibers from fruits or vegetables.* If you cannot use an electric blender or processor, you will find the food mill is a very adequate utensil for processing your baby food, either in large or small batches.

One indication of the increasing popularity of home-prepared baby foods is the appearance of inexpensive ($4–$10) food mills that are sold specifically for puréeing baby foods. They are compact and a very convenient way to purée small amounts of food from family meals or when away from home. Some mills prepare a finer purée than others, but all can prepare at least the consistency of junior foods.

Also available are electric food mills with different blades for puréeing baby foods of various textures. They are very effective; however, they process small amounts at a time and are expensive in terms of their limited usage.

Graters come in a wide range of types, sizes, and prices. Most will process food suitable for an *older baby*, with similar consistency to the junior foods. If you own one, experiment with various foods to see if you can achieve the right consistency for your baby. You may even use it for grating some raw fruits and vegetables. A grater is particularly useful in processing small amounts, so if you have an electric blender which does not work well with small loads, you may also want to use a grater.

A rotary grater, such as a Mouli, is especially efficient for making small amounts. The food is placed in the small magazine and is grated as you rotate the handle of the drum. By varying the pressure on the cover of the magazine, you can grate a fine or coarser consistency. It is safe, easy to clean, and small enough to carry when traveling.

Strainers are probably the oldest means of processing baby food, but they require time and effort for most foods. The food is strained by pushing it through holes in the strainer with the back of a spoon. This is impractical for making large quantities. Strainers vary in size and in the fineness of the holes. A fine strainer will purée fruits and vegetables comparable to the strained foods for the youngest infant. They are not usable for any meat or poultry.

The one strainer that you should keep handy, even if you are using a blender for other foods, is a *small, very fine strainer* to strain juices for your baby's bottle. You can carry it when traveling to prepare small servings of soft fruit and vegetables.

Forks and spoons are the most available and least expensive means of preparing baby food. You will find them adequate for mashing some soft foods to a coarse texture. Some foods, such as bananas, egg yolks, or canned pears, can be mashed finely enough for the youngest infant. If a fork or spoon is the only means available at a particular mealtime, don't be afraid to experiment. A hungry baby can become very adept at swallowing!

Miscellaneous Utensils

There are also several ordinary household utensils that you should use in preparing baby food. You probably already own them.

- A stiff brush for cleaning fruits and vegetables. The most nutritious method of cooking produce is in the skin, but it must be free of dirt and chemicals.
- A good sharp paring knife with the slot in the middle of the blade. If it is necessary to remove the skin on produce, this knife will take the thinnest layer.
- A juicer for preparing fresh citrus juices. A manual juicer can be bought for around $3, while an electric juicer costs $20 and up. A juice extractor, sold through health-food stores, can be used for any fruit or vegetable juice. They are very expensive, starting at $60, and not necessary.
- An egg beater, if you do not have a blender, for preparing fruit or egg beverages.

As you can see, the type of equipment that you will use in preparing your baby's food depends upon the amount of money, time, and effort you want to spend. You may already own many of these utensils or suitable substitutes. If you can coordinate preparation of your baby's food with that of the rest of the family, using the same equipment, you will save both money and effort. Just look at any piece of equipment and ask how you can use it. Discovering new uses for common utensils can be fun!

Recommended Equipment List

Paring knife
Vegetable brush
Rubber spatula
Hand juicer
Six-quart steamer/blancher
Aluminum foil
Electric blender—varying speeds, good quality, with Mini-Blend jars; or food processor
Food mill
Small, fine strainer

5

The Safe and Healthy Way
to Store Foods

Nutritious, well-balanced meals may be planned for your baby, and the freshest and best-quality foods purchased. However, you may still end up with food that is lower in vitamins. Storage is very important in the preservation of vitamins that can be destroyed by exposure to air and light. Improper handling and storage can also be dangerous to your baby's health, since bacteria, which are present in all food, can grow to harmful levels in just hours.

How Spoiled Food Can
Affect Your Baby

Babies are particularly susceptible to digestive upsets and when you notice "something" did not agree with your baby, what may really have happened is that bacteria in poorly kept foods were causing the upset. The discomfort usually takes the form of gas or diarrhea. Other forms of bacteria can produce toxins which can be more harmful and even fatal. You should be aware of the dangers of improper handling and storage. The U.S. Department of Agriculture has published the following information on these bacterial illnesses:

Salmonellosis is caused by bacteria which are widespread in nature and live and grow in the intestinal tracts of human beings and animals. The bacteria grow and multiply at temperatures between 44° and 115° F. The symptoms are severe headache, following by vomiting, diarrhea, abdominal cramps, and fever. Infants are particularly susceptible and, of course, cannot tell you some of their symptoms. These bacteria in food can be destroyed by heating the food to a temperature of 140° and holding for 10 minutes, or to a temperature even higher for less time. Refrigeration at 45° or below inhibits the increase of these bacteria, but they remain alive in the refrigerator, in the freezer, and even in dried foods.

Perfringens poisoning is caused by bacteria that grow in cooked meats, gravies, and meat dishes that are held without the proper refrigeration. The symptoms are nausea without vomiting and acute inflammation of the stomach and the intestines. To control the growth of surviving bacteria on cooked meats that are to be eaten later, you must cool the meats rapidly and refrigerate them immediately at 40° F. or below.

Staph poisoning produces mild symptoms of vomiting, diarrhea, and abdominal cramps that are often attributed to other causes. The growth of bacteria that produce the toxin is inhibited by keeping hot foods above 140° F. and cold foods at or below 40° F.

Botulism is caused by a toxin that is produced in cans or sealed containers where there is an absence of oxygen. The toxin produces severe symptoms of double vision, inability to swallow, speech difficulty, and progressive respiratory paralysis, with possible fatality. The bacteria can be destroyed by the high temperatures obtained only in a pressure canner. This form of poisoning can occur through improper home canning methods, especially with meats and vegetables. If you suspect a food, throw it away without tasting.

You should always contact a doctor if anyone in your family shows signs of the above-listed symptoms.

SIGNS OF SPOILAGE

While it is not always possible to detect—by taste, smell, or appearance—when food has become spoiled, some common signs are:

- Off odors
- Mold (green or white fuzzy spots)
- Fermented odor of fruit juices
- Rancid odor or flavor
- Slime on meats or poultry
- Sour tastes in bland foods
- Cans which are bulging, leaking, or spurting liquid when opened. *These conditions may be caused by botulism and the contents should be thrown away without tasting.*

General Rules of Handling and Storing Foods

If this introduction to the various types of food poisoning frightens you a little, that's good! If you are familiar with the possibilities of food poisoning, it need never occur with your baby or the rest of your family so long as you follow the basic rules of proper preparation and handling. Time and temperature are the important factors and the danger lies in holding foods for any length of time at temperatures above refrigerator temperature and below serving temperature of hot food. Remember:

- Work with clean hands when preparing food.
- Work with clean utensils, especially grinders, blenders, can openers, cutting boards. The bacteria in these surfaces can be destroyed by rinsing the utensil with chlorine laundry bleach in the proportion recommended on the package or bottle.
- Cook or prepare a food immediately after removing it from refrigeration. If you use an automatic oven, re-

member not to hold the food in the oven more than three hours before cooking.
- Cooked food, if not served immediately, should be cooled as quickly as possible. Put the dish in cold water if it cannot be put immediately in the refrigerator. Keeping the food cold will inhibit the growth of food-poisoning bacteria.
- The temperature range of 60°–120° is the most dangerous zone; one in which bacteria multiply quickly.
- When you are using leftovers as baby food, purée and use the recommended storage time from when they were first prepared.

PURÉES NEED SPECIAL CARE

Prepared baby food is particularly susceptible to spoilage, since the food is usually creamed, puréed, or ground. More important, you probably serve your baby food that is warm, instead of hot or cold, and this is the temperature at which bacteria grow rapidly. The electric warming dishes are designed to hold food at this dangerous temperature. How often have you warmed food in preparation for a feeding, and then spent half an hour or more preparing your baby? Many babies are also notoriously slow eaters and a feeding may last another half hour. If he does not eat, you may feel the baby is not hungry just now, and put the food aside for a while. **Remember that from the time the food is taken from the refrigerator, or out of the fresh jar, bacteria can be growing.** If there is leftover food, you can put it back to use at the next feeding, but the new refrigeration will only slow the bacterial growth, which has occurred while the food has been out. Instead, follow these basic habits:

- If you prefer to warm your baby's food, do it immediately before his feeding.
- Only warm as much food as he usually eats, then throw away the leftovers if it has been out for more than a half hour. (Since your homemade food was not as expensive as the commercial, you won't feel so guilty if you waste some.)

- Serve cold foods that adults usually eat cold, such as fruits, custards, and puddings. Even the youngest infant will eat cold food if he is accustomed to it from birth. In addition to the lessened danger of food poisoning, you will find it very convenient when traveling or in a hurry.

Now, let's go into some detail on the various ways you can store your baby's food, both before and after you prepare it.

Pantry Storage

While most of the foods that you will use in preparing your baby food will require at least refrigeration, some foods can be stored in the pantry. The pantry or area used for storage should be in the coldest part of the kitchen, and away from the oven and refrigerator exhaust. A basement, where the temperature is 60°–68° F., is a good place for storage of certain vegetables and for long-term storage of canned goods. While most of the pantry foods will not spoil to a harmful degree, they will lose quality and texture. In general, keep most pantry foods, other than vegetables, covered, preferably in airtight containers, and dry. The following list gives suggested storage times for those foods you are most likely to use in preparing your baby's food.

FOOD	TIME
Cereals, ready-to-eat	4 months
dry	6 months
Evaporated milk	1 year
Nonfat dry milk	6 months
Flour	1 year
Honey, molasses	1 year
Rice	2 years
Pastas	2 years
Bread	1 week
Crackers	3 months

FOOD	TIME
Sugar—brown	4 months
granulated	2 years
Fruits, dried	6 months
Vegetables, dried	1 year
Soups, dried	1 year
Bananas	Until yellow with brown spots
Oranges, grapefruit, other citrus fruits	1 week
Melons	1 week
White potatoes, sweet potatoes onions, hard squash, eggplant, rutabagas	1 week at room temperature 5 months at 60° F.
Peanut butter, unopened	9 months

Note: Storage for canned foods is covered in the section on Canned Foods.

Refrigerator Storage

Most fresh and perishable foods and all cooked foods require proper refrigeration. The low temperatures will retard spoilage by slowing the growth of bacteria and will also prevent the loss of essential nutrients. When storing food in your refrigerator, you should be aware that different areas can vary in their temperatures.

- The temperature range in the middle of the refrigerator should be 38°–42° F.
- The chill tray, or meat keeper, which is usually located next to the freezer compartment, should be the coldest area, about 32°–35° F.
- Milk, cheese, and other dairy products should also be kept in the coldest area.
- The temperatures at the bottom of the refrigerator and in the door are the highest.
- Heavy frost on the freezer unit and warm weather can cause temperatures to rise several degrees. At those times it may be necessary to use a colder temperature setting.

- The newer frost-free refrigerators and freezer combinations usually have more uniform temperatures, but different makes can vary.

The only way that you can be sure of setting your refrigerator controls to the proper setting is to check the temperature with a refrigerator thermometer or a common outdoor thermometer. At night, place the thermometer in the area of the refrigerator that you want to test so that it does not touch any metal surface or grill. In the morning, read the thermometer when you open the door for the first time. If the temperature in the center of the refrigerator is 42° or above, change your control to a lower setting, and check again in a day or so.

Your refrigerator should be kept clean and any spoiled food should be removed immediately, since bacterial decay can be passed to other foods. The movement of air in the refrigerator will cause drying and loss of vitamin C, so tightly wrap, or cover, all foods, using plastic wrap, plastic bags, airtight containers, or foil. Beware of the practice of using aluminum foil to wrap small amounts of leftovers. Since you can't see the contents, it's easy to forget about these little packages until they have spoiled. Raw meat, poultry, and fish should be loosely covered to retard the growth of bacteria. (The only exceptions to covering are fruits and tomatoes, which keep longer uncovered.)

Since you often do not know how fresh the food is when you purchase it, use it as soon as possible and look for signs of spoilage before using. These storage times are based on the proper degree of refrigeration.

FOOD	TIME
DAIRY	
Butter, margarine	1–2 weeks
Yogurt	5 days to 2 weeks
Cheese—cottage, ricotta,	5 days
cream, Neufchatel,	2 weeks
American, Cheddar, Swiss, etc.	2 weeks, if sliced, 3–4 weeks, whole
Milk—liquid, reconstituted	4–5 days
Evaporated, in open can	4–5 days

FOOD	TIME
Eggs—in shell, raw, cooked	2 weeks
yolks and/or whites	2 days
Custards, puddings, etc.	4 days
FRUIT	
Apples	2 weeks
Apricots, avocados, grapes, nectarines, pears, peaches, plums, rhubarb	1 week
Berries, cherries	1 week
Pineapples, ripe	4 days
Raw purées	1 day
Cooked purées	1 week
VEGETABLES	
Asparagus, broccoli, Brussels sprouts	3 days
Cabbage	1–2 weeks
Cauliflower	3–5 days
Carrots, beets, radishes	1–2 weeks
Green peas, limas, corn	1–2 days
Lettuce and green, leafy	1–2 days
Other vegetables	3–5 days
Cooked purées	4 days
MEATS, FISH, POULTRY	
Uncooked meat	
chops, roasts, steak,	3–5 days
stew, ground	1–2 days
liver, kidneys, etc.	1–2 days
Cooked meats and meat dishes	2–3 days
Gravy, broth, or stuffing	1–2 days
Fish—fresh or cooked	1–2 days
Poultry—uncooked	1–2 days
Frankfurters	4–5 days
Ham—whole, halves, steaks,	5–7 days
canned, unopened	6 months
Cold cuts, cured meats	
sealed	3–5 days
vacuum packages	2 weeks
OTHER FOODS (opened)	
Wheat germ	2 months
Cooking and salad oils	3 months
Honey, molasses	1 year
Peanut butter	6 months

Freezer Storage

The freezer gives you the best opportunity to conveniently feed your baby with home-prepared foods. One of the most common reasons that women give for using commercial foods is that it is too much trouble and time to make and purée food for each meal. Now, the freezer enables you to prepare and store several months' supply of food at one time—baby food that is fresh and ready to feed to your baby at a minute's notice.

Freezing preserves the nutritive value of food better than canning, and the value is nearly equal to that of fresh foods. The protein, fat, and carbohydrate content of food is not affected by freezing. There is little loss of vitamin C in frozen fruits and other vitamins and minerals are well retained.

Freezing foods will also prevent the growth of bacteria when the food is stored around 0° F. and used within the recommended time. The organism that produces the botulism toxin in canned nonacid and protein foods does not grow in frozen foods.

HOW TO CHECK YOUR
FREEZER TEMPERATURE

While we usually think of freezing temperatures as anywhere below 32° F., the long-term storage of high-quality foods requires a temperature of 0° F. or below. Storage temperatures above 10° F. will result in a rapid loss of nutritional value and quality. You can check your freezer temperature with an outdoor thermometer in the same way that you check the temperature of your refrigerator. Do not rest the thermometer on the freezer coils; instead place it on a frozen package in the middle of the freezer. Leave it in overnight and take a reading in the morning. If your freezer temperature is above 5° F., and you cannot set it lower, plan to store the frozen baby food for less than the recommended times. In the side-by-side refrigerator/freezers, there are often areas in the freezer that are above 10°F. These shelves should not be used for long-term storage.

WHAT AND HOW TO FREEZE

You can freeze almost any raw or cooked food that you have prepared as baby food. You can save time and money by buying seasonal or sale foods and preparing large quantities of baby food. Or, you can also save time and money by puréeing and freezing small quantities of food that are left over from family meals. Here are some basic principles of proper freezing which will give you a ready supply of safe and nutritious foods for your baby.

- Cook or prepare food as soon after buying as possible, to prevent loss of nutrients and spoilage.
- After cooking, chill the food quickly in the refrigerator and freeze immediately.
- If you are using leftovers, don't allow them to sit at room temperature for too long. If possible, *purée* and freeze the leftover food immediately after the meal.
- It is important not to stir air into the puréed mixtures before freezing, so purée the food, then allow it to settle. Watch out for this if you are using a blender.
- It is safe to freeze *cooked* baby food that has been prepared from frozen *raw* meats, fish, poultry, fruits, or vegetables.
- *Do not freeze* any baby food that has been prepared from food *already cooked, frozen,* and *thawed.* (See the section in this chapter on refreezing.)
- Freeze the food as quickly as possible to preserve the quality. Place the food directly on the freezing coils for fast freezing. If possible, lower the freezer temperatures below 0°F. when freezing large amounts.
- Wrapping materials are very important in terms of preservation and time-saving. Since the dry air of the freezer can produce a loss of moisture and nutrients, you must use a wrap that is moisture-resistant and as airtight as possible. Rigid containers of aluminum or plastic and flexible freezer wraps, such as aluminum

or plastic freezer bags, can be used. The flexible wrapping requires that the ends be sealed with tape, and bags should be closed. A new type of storage bag even allows you to freeze food, then heat it by placing the entire bag in boiling water. Ordinary paper, waxed paper, and thin plastic wraps are not suitable.

These storage times are based on a freezer temperature of 0°F. The food may not spoil when kept longer or at higher temperatures, but it may lose nutritional value and quality. The following USDA times are given for fresh food that you may freeze before preparing and for raw and cooked baby food. Many people have reported that they have successfully frozen baby foods for 1–2 months longer than these recommended times.

FOOD	TIME
FRESH	
Ground pork	3 months
Ground beef, lamb, veal	4 months
Roasts, steaks	
beef	1 year
lamb, veal	9 months
pork	6 months
Fish, lean	6 months
Chicken	1 year
Turkey, duck	6 months
Liver, kidneys, etc.	3 months
Citrus-juice concentrates	1 year
Fruit	1 year
Vegetables	8 months
Butter, margarine	9 months
Cottage cheese	3 months
Cream cheese	1 month
Other cheese	3 months
Milk	3 months
Ice cream, ice milk, sherbet	1 month
Eggs, whites, and/or yolks	1 year

FOOD	TIME
COOKED OR PREPARED	
Baked goods	1–2 months
Ground beef, lamb, veal	4 months
Ground pork	2 months
Ground ham	1 month
Liver, kidneys, etc.	1 month
Frankfurters	1 month
Bacon	1 month
Luncheon meats, cold cuts	1 month
Fish	2 months
Poultry	3 months
Fruit purées	1 year
Vegetable purées	1 month
Combination dishes with gravy, sauces, etc.	1 month
Soup—bean, split pea, lentil	2 months
Steamed pudding	6 months
Frozen desserts	1 month

REFREEZING FOOD

You may want to refreeze food that has become accidentally thawed because of power failure. If the power fails, most freezers will maintain temperature below freezing for at least two days if the door is not opened. Or, you may begin to thaw food and then decide not to use it. It would be wasteful to have to throw the food away and you should be aware of when you can safely refreeze food.

- If there is any off odor to the food, throw it away.
- Any food that is partially thawed and still contains ice crystals may be refrozen.
- Uncooked foods that are completely thawed, but are held at refrigerator temperature for no longer than one day, may be refrozen. If the food has warmed above refrigerator temperature, do not refreeze.
- Cooked foods which are completely thawed cannot be refrozen. This applies to many baby foods.

• Commercially frozen fruits, vegetables, and red meats can legally be thawed and refrozen if they have been held at refrigerator temperature for a day. Try to avoid buying any frozen foods that have been refrozen since there may be a loss of nutrients, texture, and flavor. Signs to look for are frost inside the package, boxes which are solid on the bottom with space at the top, and sweating or battered packages.

FOOD CUBES

Since puréed and frozen baby food will spoil quickly after thawing, it is most efficient to freeze baby food in individual portions that can be taken out for a day's meals or, even better, before each feeding. I strongly recommend the following method of freezing your baby food as both convenient and safe.

1. Cool the puréed food quickly.
2. Pour it into ice-cube trays. The individual plastic cubes are ideal if you can find them. Cover with wrap.
3. Freeze the food cubes quickly.
4. For long-term storage, transfer the frozen food cubes to plastic *freezer* bags, cover and seal.
5. **Date and label the containers. Frozen baby-food purées all look the same.** In general, keep the protein foods, cereals, vegetables, and fruit in separate containers. It's easier to select a meal.
6. Before a meal, take out the food you want to serve. Allow half an hour to thaw at room temperature, or you can thaw and heat the cubes quickly in the oven or warming dish.

You will find this method is really the key to feeding your baby easily and conveniently with food you have prepared yourself. You can always keep an adequate supply on hand and you will never need to rush to prepare food for a hungry baby.

Canned Foods

Canning is a widely used form of preserving food. Commercially canned foods are usually safe from food poisoning and retain a large amount of vitamins and minerals, although less than frozen foods. Many of the foods that you will feed your baby can be prepared directly from cans, so it is important to know how to buy and store canned goods.

- Do not buy or use cans that are leaking, have bulging ends, or spurt liquid when opened. These may be signs of botulism and the food should be thrown out without tasting.
- When buying vacuum-packed jars, be sure the lid has not been opened.
- The ideal temperature for storing canned goods for more than one month is 65°F. At this temperature vitamins are well retained for as long as a year.
- In general, the longer the storage period and the higher the storage temperature, the greater the loss of nutrients.
- Read the labels carefully to select brands of canned goods which have the fewest additives and are without unnecessary sugar or salt.
- Remember that ingredients are listed in *descending* order of amount. Thus, the ingredient that is listed first is present in the largest amount.
- Where possible, buy food that is packed in its own juices. *About one third of the water-soluble vitamins and minerals in canned food and vegetables will be in the liquid*. To get the full nutritive value, use this liquid or juice as a thinner when preparing your baby's food. Or strain it and serve it as a beverage.
- Wash the top of a can before opening. If you are opening a vacuum-packed jar with a turn-off lid, rinse under the edge of the lid. The air rushing in when you open the jar will pull in any dirt under the lid. When you open a vacuum-packed jar, listen for the

"pop" sound. If you do not hear it, the jar may have been previously opened and the food spoiled.

- Opened canned food can be covered tightly and stored in the refrigerator in the original jar for the recommended time. I prefer not to store food in opened metal cans.

The maximum storage times for opened canned food that is stored in the refrigerator at 35°–40°F. are as follows:

Meats	3 days
Fish	2 days
Poultry	2 days
Fruit	1 week
Vegetables	3 days
Soups	3 days
Tomato-based sauces	5 days
Citrus juices	3 days
Evaporated milk	4–5 days

HOME CANNING

Canning your own baby food is an alternative to the frozen "food cube" method, especially if you do not have adequate freezer space. If you are already an experienced home canner and you own the necessary equipment, canning your prepared baby food is convenient and safe. You may do your baby-food purées at the same time you are canning food for the family. You can use the smallest size canning jars.

Unless you are already doing your own canning, it will not be worth the time and expense to start for the few months that you will be preparing baby food. Fruit is the one food that might be worth experimenting with, since it is inexpensive and nutritious in season. For tomatoes and fruits that contain acid, the safe method of canning is quite simple. The method used is called the "boiling-water-bath canner."

- Use a metal pot with a tight-fitting cover and a rack on the bottom on which to rest the jars. The steamer/

blancher described in the **Equipment** chapter can be used.

- Prepare the fruit or tomato purée as for baby food.
- Pour the hot purée in the clean jars. The jars and lids should be freshly washed, but do not need sterilization.
- Pack within ¼ inch of the top and close the lids.
- Immerse the jars in the boiling water. Make sure that the tops of the jars are covered with an inch of water.
- Cover and boil for 10–15 minutes.
- Store as for commercially canned fruits.

Other vegetables, meats, poultry, and fish can only be safely canned with a pressure canner, following specific times for each of the various foods. Improperly canned vegetables and protein foods can allow the growth of the toxin that causes botulism—the most harmful of food poisoning. If you are interested in learning how to can all types of food, send for the booklets published by the Department of Agriculture that are listed in the Bibliography or buy a good canning cookbook.

6

The Baby-Food System

Since you probably want to spend as little time as possible preparing your own baby food, in the following recipe chapters you will find everything you may want to know about any food you choose to prepare for your baby. You should not have to refer to any other cookbook. But first, here are the essentials of the easy baby-food system, and it really is easy if you know how.

How to Plan

The most important fact to remember in preparing your own baby food is that you must *plan ahead*. The last thing that you want to do is to cook and purée your baby's meal while he is shrieking with hunger. Just as you would buy a supply of the commercial baby foods, you should plan to keep on hand a supply of frozen food cubes (see **Food Cubes** in chapter 5); or fresh, canned, or frozen "instant foods." (See **Instant Baby Food,** chapter 13.) This supply is particularly important when your baby is young and eating only a limited variety of foods. Even when your baby is older and is eating more family foods, this planning is very convenient.

You can also save money by preparing large amounts of foods that are in season or are on sale. You don't have to worry about a large variety, just make a balanced selection of a few highly nutritious foods (see chapter 1, "Nutrition") and use the simplest recipes. Or prepare a large supply of all-in-one meals, such as stews.

Just remember not to make more food than your baby will eat in the recommended safe freezing or storage time. Also, do not make a large amount of a food until you have successfully introduced it to your baby. This is especially important with the foods that tend to cause allergies.

You can plan to feed your baby entirely from this store of home-prepared or *instant* foods as conveniently as if you were buying baby food. Of course, if a family dish is ready and suitable, you can always purée it and serve it to your baby.

How to Save Time

The easiest and most convenient time for you to prepare baby food is when you are already in the kitchen making your family's food. You will also save time and effort by making large amounts of various foods at the same time. To save preparation and cooking time:

- Prepare the *same kind of food* for your baby that you are making for your family. The recipe section is designed so you can easily look up any food. For example, if you are cooking fried chicken, put a few pieces in the steamer for Chicken Purée. This will also save you time marketing.
- Use the *cooking method* that fits in with the way you are already cooking. (But never fry foods for your baby.) If you are using your oven for roasting, then use a recipe for baking or aluminum-foil steaming.
- Whenever possible, use leftovers from family meals.

To save cleanup time:

- Cook your baby's food in the same pots or steamer that you have used for your family's vegetables.
- Cook several fruits, vegetables, meats, etc., in the same pot, baking dish, or steamer. You can then purée them separately or in any combination.
- Remember that you can cook almost any food by wrapping it in aluminum foil and steaming it in a 325°F. oven. There is no cleanup; just throw the foil away.
- Purée different foods, one after another. You will only need to quickly rinse between processing each food. It is always easier to use equipment when it is already out.

How to Use Leftovers

One of the easiest and most economical ways to prepare baby food is to combine leftovers from family meals. The cooking is already done. You can use any food that you have already introduced, as long as it is not highly seasoned or fried. Just be sure that the food, especially the meat, poultry, or fish, has not been kept for more than a day. Use "fresh" leftovers!

You can even *plan* to have leftovers from the family dishes that your baby can eat. If you make a large batch, you can freeze enough for a month or two and always have a nutritious meal on hand. Or you can purée just a small amount to serve your baby the next day. It's even easier if you have a blender with the Mini-Blend jar—you can blend, store, warm, and serve the meal and only wash one jar.

Meal-in-one Leftover Purée

Here is a well-balanced, all-in-one meal that you can prepare from any leftovers. The recipe will help you use the right amounts and types of food, but you can use your imagination and the **Food-Combination Guide** in combining other foods.

> 1 cup cubed cooked poultry, meat, organ meat, fish
> ⅔ cup vegetables or fruit (raw or cooked)
> ½ cup cooked rice, noodles, or cereal
> 1 cup (or less) liquid (cooking juice, vegetable, or fruit juice)

1. Place liquid in blender or processor. Add other ingredients.
2. Purée to desired consistency.
3. Freeze in food cubes at once. Can be kept frozen for 1–4 months depending on the type of food that is used. (See chapter 5.)

YIELD: 3 cups or 15 food cubes or 4–5 meals.

How to Purée

The type of equipment that you use to prepare purées depends upon what is available, as well as the consistency that your baby will swallow. In general, you should gradually increase the coarseness of the food so that your baby easily makes the transition to finger and family foods at an early age. This is one of the advantages in making your own baby food. If you make a food too coarse and your baby rejects it, you can just go back to a smoother texture.

Under the specific foods, I have suggested the best equipment to use in preparing purées of different textures. Here are some general guidelines.

- Use an **electric blender** for almost any food. You can vary the speed and blending time for a smooth or coarse purée. The only foods that should not be puréed in a blender are those with skins (if your baby is not eating skins), fibers, such as raw celery, and seeds.
- A **food processor** can be substituted for a blender in all recipes unless otherwise indicated. As with a blender, do not process skins (unless the baby is eating them), raw celery, or seeds. To purée small amounts

of food, you will have to stop the processor once or twice to push down the food from the sides of the bowl.

A food processor will more easily prepare thick, heavy purées—just start with a few short chopping pulses, then let it run, checking consistency at 5-second intervals. To prepare the smoothest purées, process the solid food first until it is thoroughly chopped, then add liquid as necessary. For most foods, you will require *less* liquid than specified in the recipes.

Fruits and very tender vegetables will need little or no additional liquid. Harder-textured vegetables (raw or slightly cooked) and some meats can be puréed into a texture smooth enough for most babies; however, they will not be as smooth as when puréed in a high-speed blender. This should not be a problem since your baby will be older when introduced to these foods and should not mind a coarser purée.

You can also experiment with some family foods in a processor that can't easily be prepared in a blender or food mill. I quickly turned pancakes, quiche, and even oatmeal bread into purées!

- Use a **food mill** for most foods except meats and poultry. Organ meats can be puréed, but it is a very slow process. The food mill is an excellent way to purée while removing skins, fibers, and seeds of either raw or cooked foods. (You will find it is easy to cook a food unpeeled or cored, such as apples, and then strain with the food mill after it has been cooked.) The mill also produces a very smooth purée.

- A **hand grater** can be used to grate small amounts of raw vegetables such as carrots or beets. These foods will not be as smooth as those made with a blender. Chilled meats and poultry can also be grated very fine. A rotary grater is the easiest to use.

- A **strainer** is a slow version of a food mill. It will make a very fine purée of most foods but is not suitable for meats and poultry.

- **A fork or spoon** is adequate for preparing coarser purées or for mashing smooth foods such as egg yolks or bananas. You can also use a spoon to scrape smooth purées from some raw fruits or cooked meats.

See **Equipment** chapter for more specific instructions on purées.

THINNING—THICKENING

Many of the purées that you will make will need some kind of thinning, a few will require thickening. I have found that the terms "a little" and "enough" liquid are not satisfactory. If you make a mistake in preparing a large amount of baby food, you will end up with either soup or glue. So, in all the recipes I have given specific amounts for thinning and thickening your purées. Depending on your own baby's preferences, you can change the amounts. *Remember that the thicker a purée is, the more original nutrients the specific food serving will contain.*

One of the advantages of making your own purées is that you can thin purées with more nutritious liquids than plain water, and thicken them without using refined flour or food starch. **This is where you can make every bite count!**

NUTRITIOUS THINNERS	NUTRITIOUS THICKENERS
Fruit juice	Egg yolk (hard-boiled)
Vegetable juice	Wheat germ (whole or ground)
Cooking or canning water (boiled down, without salt)	Soybean purée
Evaporated milk (undiluted)	Whole wheat or soy flour (in cooked purées)
Milk (whole or skim)	Cooked whole-grain cereal —oatmeal, rice
	Nonfat dry milk powder

A specific thinning liquid or thickener may be mentioned in a recipe. If you do not have it on hand, you can pick a substitute from the above list.

FOOD-COMBINATION GUIDE

Here is another way to change the consistency and flavor of your baby-food dishes without using liquid thinners or sweeteners. You can combine foods according to their tastes and juiciness, either when cooking or during a feeding. The following guide is useful as a quick reference, and you can have some fun in making up some unusual, but nutritious combinations. Your baby may love peanut butter and bananas, or peaches and lima beans, or fish and oranges.

	THIN	MEDIUM	THICK
	Apple, sweet, cooked	Beets, raw	Parsnips
	Apricots	Carrots	
	Beets, cooked	Banana	
	Cherries, sweet	Corn	
	Grapes, sweet	Peas	
	Guava	Apple, sweet, raw	
SWEET	Mango		
	Melon		
	Nectarine		
	Papaya		
	Peaches		
	Pears		
	Banana		
	Asparagus	Avocado	Cereal
	Cucumber	Beans, green	Cooked dried
	Mushrooms	Beans, wax	peas, beans,
	Squash, summer	Cauliflower	lentils
BLAND		Artichoke	Potatoes
			Rice
			Egg yolk
			Chicken
			Fish
			Meat

	THIN	MEDIUM	THICK
	Apple, sour, cooked	Apple, sour, raw	Peanut butter
	Berries	Brussels sprouts	Wheat germ
	Eggplant	Broccoli	Ham
	Grapefruit	Leafy greens	
SOUR	Lemon	Pineapple	
OR	Orange	Turnips	
STRONG	Onions	Rutabagas	
	Okra		
	Pepper		
	Rhubarb		
	Cherries, sour		
	Tomatoes		

How to Use and Modify the Recipes

The recipes in the following chapters contain specific detail and you can "go by the book." I have also shown how you can modify any recipe to *your* convenience. This is more important than using the exact ingredients or cooking methods and is really the key to the easy preparation of baby foods. Please feel free to substitute as shown in the previous section on **How to Purée.** Just keep in mind the general principles of healthy simple cooking.

Most of the recipes are also simplified in the use of seasonings and flavorings. The last thing you want to do is to accustom your baby to the controversial adult preferences for salted or sweetened foods. So resist the temptation to taste and season the baby foods that you are preparing. You do want to teach your baby to enjoy the natural flavors of foods that can be simply and easily prepared.

COOKING METHODS AND TIMES

One thing to avoid is *overcooking*. Just because you will purée a food does not mean that you have to cook it to a pulp. Many foods even become tough and stringy when they are overcooked. I have also found that the longer you cook a food, the more likely you are to forget and leave it on the heat. Burned liver has a powerful smell and it is almost impossible to clean the pot! In general, cook your baby food to a minimum, just until it can be easily puréed and digested.

Fortunately, **the most nutritious cooking is the simplest.** Many vitamins and minerals can be lost in water, air, or high heat. So try to steam your baby food in a tightly covered container, with little or no water, and over a low heat. The cooking times given in the recipes, especially for fruits and vegetables, are minimum times for whole food. You can decrease cooking time by cutting food into smaller pieces, but you will lose nutrients. You may have to increase the time if you are using equipment other than a blender or processor.

SALT

Dr. Lewis K. Dahl, head of the Research Medical Service of Brookhaven National Laboratory, has stated, "A baby's needs for salt are amply satisfied by the salt it gets from either mother's or cow's milk." Your baby will also obtain natural salt from many foods he eats, especially meats. So there is no need to add salt in food that you prepare especially for your baby, and research has shown that high intake of salt in infancy might be related to high blood pressure in later life. Very few of the recipes in this book contain salt. If you are preparing food for the rest of your family and want to use salt, try to add it after you have separated your baby's portion. But, for the sake of convenience, you may occasionally feed your baby a family dish that contains some salt. Remember, it is the use of *large* amounts of salt that may be harmful. If you live in an inland area, your baby may even benefit by the use of small amounts of iodized salt as a source of iodine.

FATS AND OILS

Whether or not you use saturated fats (butter) or unsaturated fats (vegetable oils) in cooking food or preparing purées depends upon your doctor's advice. Most recommend using *unsaturated* fats. (See section on **Fat** in chapter 1.) *Linoleic acid* is an essential fatty acid that is best supplied by corn, soy, peanut, and safflower oils and in mayonnaise. Butter contains almost no linoleic acid. The one type of fat that most doctors and nutritionists feel should be *avoided* is the hydrogenated or hardened vegetable oils, which are used in solid shortenings or margarine. If you use margarine, read the labels and select the ones that list *liquid (vegetable) oil* as the first and major ingredient. Remember that cottonseed oil should be avoided and also palm and coconut oils, which are high in saturated fat.

SWEETENERS

There are very few foods that will require sweetening for your baby to eat them. Although children and adults put a value on "sweets" and dislike very sour foods, it is unlikely that your baby has been born with these preferences. Research has shown that babies cannot tell the difference between sweet and sour tastes. You can test this out on your baby. Just give him a slice of lemon, and the chances are he will suck it with relish. So there is no need to load his food with sugar and train him in a habit that can contribute to tooth decay and overweight in later years. Your baby will get enough natural sugar from fruits, vegetables, and milk. You may also combine naturally sweet fruits and vegetables with sour ones. However, if you want to use sugar, as when you are preparing a dessert for the whole family, you may choose sweeteners other than refined white sugar; sweeteners that do have food value other than carbohydrates.

Molasses is the brown syrup that remains when most of the sugar has crystallized. It contains more vitamins and minerals (especially high in iron) than any other form of sweetening. The darkest molasses (blackstrap) contains the most nutrients and is often used as a fortifier. It can have a laxative effect.

Brown sugar is usually refined sugar that has molasses

added; however, this does add some vitamins and minerals, especially in the dark-brown type.

Raw sugar, often called turbinado sugar, is not refined. You can find it in health-food stores and some supermarkets, but it is fairly expensive in spite of the lower processing cost.

Honey contains the same amount of vitamins as brown sugar, but is lower in minerals. The type of sugar in honey is fructose, which is easily digested since it is already in a form that can be absorbed by the body. The lighter-colored honey usually has the mildest flavor. Some honey is graded by the government and the grade B or choice is adequate for use in cooking.

Do not feed honey to a baby younger than twelve months.

Store molasses, brown sugar, and honey in tightly covered containers in a dry place for several months. If honey crystallizes, you can place it in a pan of warm water until the crystals disappear.

If you do use sweeteners:

- In most recipes you can substitute brown sugar or honey in place of white sugar. Use ¾ cup honey for each cup sugar and decrease liquid by ¼ cup.
- Do not use honey in making teething cookies, since the honey will keep the baked goods moist. Use brown sugar.
- Molasses can be substituted for up to half of the amount of sugar that the recipe calls for. Decrease liquid by ¼ cup for each cup of molasses.
- You can add very small amounts of dark molasses (¼–½ teaspoon) to your baby's bottle once a day as a fortifier, but remember that blackstrap molasses can act as a laxative.

MEASUREMENTS

Since you may want to change any recipe to make either a single serving or a month's supply, these equivalent measures are useful.

3 teaspoons	=	1 tablespoon
⅛ cup	=	2 tablespoons
¼ cup	=	4 tablespoons
⅓ cup	=	5 tablespoons + 1 teaspoon
½ cup	=	8 tablespoons
⅔ cup	=	10 tablespoons + 2 teaspoons
¾ cup	=	12 tablespoons
1 cup*	=	16 tablespoons
2 cups	=	1 pint
4 cups	=	1 quart

SUBSTITUTIONS

Here is a handy list to use with any recipe, showing how to substitute a more nutritious ingredient or what to use if you do not have a certain food on hand.

1 whole egg = 2 egg yolks

1 cup buttermilk = 1 cup milk + 1 tablespoon vinegar or lemon juice

1 cup whole milk = ½ cup evaporated milk + ½ cup water = 1 cup skim milk + 2½ teaspoons vegetable oil

1 cup skim milk = ⅓ cup nonfat dry milk powder + 1 cup water

1 part corn starch = 2 parts flour = 4 parts dry infant cereal

1 cup white flour = ¾ cup whole-wheat flour + 1–2 tablespoons more liquid

1 cup white or whole-grain flour: replace 3 tablespoons with soy flour

1 cup dry cereal: add up to ½ cup wheat germ

The following recipes are divided into chapters according to their main nutritional food group—"Cereal Grains," "Fruits," "Vegetables," and "Protein Foods." I have arranged the recipes in this way so that you can easily select a balanced diet for your baby. (See **Planning a Balanced**

---

*1 cup makes about 5 food cubes. 1 food cube equals about 3 tablespoons or 1½ ounces. (See **Food Cubes,** chapter 5.)

Menu in chapter 3.) Some recipes, such as desserts, stews, leftovers, custards, etc., are combinations of different food groups.

You will see there is a very wide variety of foods, including some you may not have thought of as baby food. You can easily look up any food that you have on hand, or are preparing for your family, to see if and how you can serve it to your baby. Please do not feel that you have to try every food or recipe.

Most of the recipes give very basic and easy instructions on how to prepare a food in the most nutritious way, and, short of puréeing, *they can be used to prepare plain food that anyone can enjoy*. There are also some recipes that are often *family favorites* and that only require puréeing for your baby to enjoy them.

In selecting and using any of these recipes, remember to always keep in mind what is most convenient for *you*! Remember that those foods and recipes marked "**$**" are the best "nutritional buys."

7

Cereal Grains

The various cereal grains are highly economical sources of protein (incomplete), carbohydrates, minerals, the B vitamins, and vitamin E. They also contain trace elements that are essential in a balanced diet. You should include 2–3 servings in your baby's daily menu. The grains are processed into many products that your baby can eat— cereals, flour, pastas, baked goods, rice, etc. The different grains are:

Oats (highest in protein, iron, and fat)

Wheat (used mainly for flours and cereal, possible source of allergy)

Barley (slightly laxative)

Rice (lowest in protein, good for treatment of diarrhea)

Corn (corn meal and grits)

Rye and buckwheat

The amount of nutritional value in any cereal grain depends in large part on the way it was processed or refined. All cereal grains start out as *whole-grain*. If they are processed, the *bran*, which is the outer covering, is removed and a large amount of the B vitamins and minerals is lost. Often the *germ*, or heart of the grain, is removed. This is the most nutritious part of the grain and contains the highest amounts of protein, minerals, vitamin E, and the essential fatty acids. If the bran and germ are removed, the resulting grain is mostly starch, highly refined, and should *not* be counted as a *cereal* serving, since it lacks the iron, protein, and other nutrients that are essential to your baby.

The federal government, in order to prevent deficiencies, has set minimum levels of voluntary enrichment for four of the nutrients lost in the refining process—thiamine, riboflavin, niacin, and iron. The other B vitamins, vitamin E, and many minerals are still missing in refined, enriched cereal grains. Do read the label for the term "enriched" and read the list of ingredients to identify those products that may be enriched such as breakfast cereals, baked goods, pastas, and rice. You can also compare the levels of enrichment, since some brands use higher amounts than the minimum levels. In general, the "enriched" products are more expensive than the original whole-grain products, since you are paying for the cost of refining, and also enrichment.

In the wide variety of cereal products, it is confusing and difficult to identify those products that are *whole-grain*. Often the label will proudly state "whole-grain" or "stone ground." Some other products are whole-wheat flour, unbleached flour, rye flour, cracked wheat, barley, oatmeal, oat flour, brown rice, whole-wheat cereals, kasha, and whole-grain corn meal. It is worth your time and money to read labels in order to buy whole-grain products or at least enriched ones. Remember that these cereal grains are your baby's main sources of many of the essential nutrients.

If you understand and keep in mind the differences between the various grains and ways of processing, you will be able to select the most nutritious products, which include *cereals; rice; pastas, flours,* and *baked goods;* and *wheat germ.*

Cereals

Nutrition: Cereals are high in incomplete protein, iron, and B vitamins, and contain fair amounts of vitamin E and minerals. The cereals are particularly important in your baby's early months to supply the iron and niacin that are low in milk.

Introduce: In general, the dry infant cereals can be started as early as four months, enriched refined cereals at five months, and whole-grain cereals at seven months.

Buy: As you have seen, the amounts of the nutrients vary due to the type of processing and enrichment. So, it is important to look at the different types of cereals that you can feed your baby.

Precooked dry infant cereals are produced by the major commercial baby-food companies. They include oatmeal, barley, mixed cereals, rice, and high protein. They have been refined, then enriched with high levels of niacin, riboflavin, thiamine, and particularly iron. The amount of enrichment is the same for each cereal made by the same company; however, the amount of enrichment varies among the different companies. The *high-protein* cereals provide two to five times more protein at the same cost.

It is important to read the nutritional information on the packages since the manufacturers may change the levels of enrichment and you should select those with the highest amounts. Remember that the nutritional information or percentages are based on one ounce of dry cereal, which will make a serving of ⅓ cup. This may be more than most babies, especially in the early months, can eat at one meal. It may be more realistic to consider that one ounce as two cereal servings.

You should also remember that the other B vitamins and minerals that were lost in processing may not have been replaced. *But, most important, these cereals do offer the highest source of iron and are the most convenient to prepare and the smoothest in texture.* So you should serve them to your baby.

Do not use the sweetened variety of these cereals, since they often contain additives. The sweetening is unnecessary and only accustoms your baby to sugar at the earliest possible age. You should *avoid the wet-pack* jars of cereal, or cereal-fruit, cereal-egg combinations. As of this writing, their iron enrichment is far below that of the dry cereals. You are also paying a very high price for a jar that is more than 80 per cent liquid. Since you are feeding your baby cereals to give him specific nutrients, you should be sure that he is getting them by selecting and diluting the cereal yourself, always with milk or formula.

Whole-grain cereals are more difficult for very young babies to digest, but they can be introduced by seven months. *They should not be given to a baby who has diarrhea*. These cereals supply all the B vitamins, especially B_6, B_{12}, and folic acid, plus the other minerals that are in the original cereal grains. Their iron level is not as high as the dry infant cereals, but by this time your baby will be getting iron from meat, egg yolk, and other foods.

You can conveniently purée the same types of whole-grain cereals that you serve your family, such as oatmeal, Ralston, Wheatena, kasha, and barley. There is a Swiss cereal, Baby Familia, that is often available in supermarkets or can be ordered. This is a highly nutritious and convenient whole-grain cereal that is precooked and only requires thinning with milk. "Granolas" that contain a high percentage of sugars should not be used.

The refined enriched cereals include enriched farina (wheat), enriched cream of wheat, and enriched cream of rice. Again, read the labels and select the brand with the highest level of enrichment. Some may be fortified with vitamins A and D, and calcium; however they are usually more expensive and these vitamins are supplied in other foods that your baby is eating. The level of their iron enrichment varies and often is lower than that of the dry infant cereals. Read the label to make certain that ½ ounce of the uncooked cereal or 3½ ounces of the cooked cereal supplies at least 6 mg. of iron. These cereals can be used if no other cereal is available, but you may as well serve the dry infant cereals until your baby can eat the whole-grain cereals.

Store all cereals in tightly covered containers at cool room temperature and they may be kept for several months. Cooked cereals can be covered and stored in the refrigerator for 1–2 days. If your family does not regularly eat cooked whole-grain cereals, and you want to feed them to your baby, you will find it convenient to cook a quantity and freeze the cereal in food cubes for up to one month. *Two cups of cooked cereal will make about 10 cubes or servings.*

PREPARING CEREAL

In general, when preparing a specific cereal, you should follow the instructions that are printed on the box. To increase the nutritional value or save time, you can also:

- Dilute all instant cereals with milk or formula, usually 1 part cereal to 6 parts liquid. You should gradually decrease the amount of dilution so that the cereal is as thick as your baby will eat. *It is the cereal that is important here, not the milk.*
- You can fortify the dry infant cereals by mixing in grated or regular wheat germ. (See **Wheat Germ,** this chapter.) Use about ½ teaspoon wheat germ for each teaspoon of dry cereal.
- In a blender or processor you can grind regular oatmeal very finely so that it is more easily digested. One part of the ground oatmeal can be mixed with 3 parts hot milk. This ground oatmeal can also be used as a nutritious thickener.
- If you want to serve your baby cooked whole-grain cereals at any early age, you can also strain or purée them after cooking. However, the amount of iron will still be less than in the dry infant cereals.
- Pearl barley can be cooked, then mashed with a small amount of milk. It is one of the more digestible whole-grain cereals.
- You can always use milk instead of water when you are cooking any cereal. The milk is important in supplementing the incomplete cereal protein. Reconstituted nonfat dry milk is an inexpensive milk to use in cooking.
- Cooked cereals will be creamier and smoother if you put the cereal into the cold water, or milk, and then bring them to a boil together.
- You can use any instant cereal as a nutritious thickener for juicy fruits and vegetables. Add ¼–½ teaspoon dry cereal to each ¼ cup of purée (or 1–2 teaspoons per cup).

- You can also save any cooked cereal that is left over from the family breakfast, or even make some extra, to use as a thickener.
- Purée cooked cereal, adding milk 1 tablespoon at a time.

Flour, Pasta, Baked Goods

Nutrition: Flour and products made from flour—breads, noodles, spaghetti, crackers, etc.—have the same nutritional value as the grains that they are made from. They can be substituted for a cereal serving; for example, *1 slice whole-wheat bread = ½ cup oatmeal = 2 tablespoons whole-wheat flour*. As with any cereal grain, the nutritional value depends on the amount of processing and enrichment. Durum flour, often used in pastas, contains the most protein.

Introduce baked goods like hard crackers and toast around nine months as a teething food, but your baby will not eat enough at first for this to count as a cereal serving. Spaghetti and noodles can be added around eight months. Unbleached or whole-wheat flour can be used as a thickener at any time.

Buy: It is very important for you to read labels on flour and flour products in order to buy those that are whole-grain or enriched. *Do not buy* or use any refined flour or product that lists as the main ingredient: "flour," "wheat flour," "white flour," "rice flour," or "bleached flour." These cannot be counted as a *cereal* serving. Remember that if it is enriched, it will read "enriched flour."

Whole-grain flours are often listed as "whole-wheat flour," "unbleached flour," "rye flour." You should avoid the whole-grain breads which contain entire pieces of grains, since these will be difficult for a young baby to digest. They can be served from nine to ten months on. Soy flour contains the largest amounts of many nutrients and the protein is also complete. It can be substituted for one eighth of the flour in any recipe. Unbleached and whole-wheat flours can be substituted in most recipes calling for "flour," with the exception of cake flour. Other whole-grain flours are available in special stores, but these require the use of recipes that are designed for them.

Starches: You should not confuse starches with flours. Starches are extracted from cereal grains and they are almost completely carbohydrate. *They do not contain protein, vitamins, or minerals that are present in flours.* Starches are widely used as thickeners in prepared foods, especially in the commercial baby foods. They are also difficult for your baby to digest.

You can recognize these starches in the list of ingredients by the names "cornstarch," "rice starch," "tapioca," and "modified food starch." *Do not buy* any prepared food that contains these as major ingredients. *Do not use* these to thicken any of your home-prepared baby foods. If a recipe calls for starch, you can substitute twice that amount of flour.

Store flours in tightly covered containers in the refrigerator for long periods or in hot weather. Breads and pastas should be placed in plastic bags and stored at room temperature.

USING FLOUR

Besides the common use of flour in recipes for baked goods, there are other ways that you can use enriched, whole-wheat, and soy flour.

- You can use a small amount of flour to thicken cooked fruits and vegetables.
- You can substitute flour for cornstarch (nonnutritive) in most recipes if you use twice the amount.
- Supplement the protein in flour by adding nonfat dry milk powder to any recipe. You can add at least 2 tablespoons of nonfat dry milk powder for each cup of liquid that is used. Mix the powder in with the dry ingredients.
- Substitute 2 tablespoons of soy flour in each cup of flour called for in a recipe.
- You can use whole-wheat bread crumbs, finely ground in a blender, as a thickener for fruit and vegetable purées.

- You can soften graham crackers, arrowroot cookies, and other enriched baked goods that will absorb milk into a soft mush. These are a change from the regular cereals and are a good instant food. Do read the labels on these products to avoid those with additives, especially the controversial preservative BHT.
- Whole-grain or enriched breads and cakes can be sliced and baked in a very slow oven (250° F.) until they are very hard. The slices make excellent teething foods and snacks.
- Using your food processor, you can make any easy cereal purée from family foods such as pancakes and breads—especially good is oatmeal bread!

Pancake/Bread Cereal

**For 1 medium pancake or slice of bread,
add 1–2 tablespoons milk.**

1. Place baked goods in processor and allow to run until fine crumbs.
2. While processor is running, add milk until desired consistency is reached.
3. Serve within 2–3 days or freeze for up to 1 month.

USING PASTA

- When pastas are combined with small amounts of *protein foods*, such as in spaghetti and meat balls, they make economical *cereal/protein* dishes that are filling dinner dishes. (See *Noodle and Cheese Pudding*.)
- Do not wash noodles or spaghetti before cooking. After cooking, drain the noodles of most excess water but do not rinse them. You can use a small amount of the cooking water as a thinner and add some nonfat dry milk powder as a protein supplement.
- You can also easily purée any pasta dish that you have cooked for your family as long as it is not highly seasoned and does not contain foods that you have not already introduced.

- You can even plan to cook an extra amount and take out your baby's food before adding seasonings or foods that he is not accustomed to.
- Pasta dishes can easily be mashed and puréed, using a strainer, food mill, processor, or blender. You may have to add a little more milk or juice to thin, about ¼–½ cup for each cup of pasta.
- These puréed foods may be frozen in food cubes for up to 1 month.
- You can use any of the canned pasta dishes and you will save preparation time. They are almost instant foods since they require only a blender or food mill for smooth puréeing. Read the label carefully to avoid those with additives and fillers.

$ Noodle and Cheese Pudding

This is a good family dessert that you can serve your baby as a *cereal/protein* dish at any meal, especially for a light, nourishing supper.

    1 box broad noodles
    2 eggs, beaten (egg yolks alone may also be used)
    2 cups cottage cheese
    ¼ cup raisins
    ½ cup brown sugar or honey
    ½ pint sour cream or yogurt
    2 tablespoons melted butter
    2 tablespoons lemon juice (optional)
    1 teaspoon cinnamon (optional)

1. Preheat oven to 350°F. Lightly butter casserole.
2. Cook noodles in boiling salted water.
3. Drain and cool slightly.
4. Mix noodles and other ingredients together in casserole.
5. Bake for 50 minutes.
6. Purée with any equipment, adding a small amount of milk to thin, if necessary.
7. You may freeze the casserole, or purée, for up to 1 month.
YIELD: 6–8 servings (adult).

$ Macaroni and Cheese

This is a good family dish that you can serve your baby as a purée or a finger food.

    1 8-ounce package macaroni (shells, twists, etc.)
    ¼ pound mild American cheese, thinly sliced or grated
    2 tablespoons butter
    ¼ cup nonfat dry milk powder (optional)
    2 cups milk (whole or skim)

1. Preheat oven to 350°F.
2. Lightly grease a casserole. Or use several small individual baking dishes or cups.
3. Cook macaroni according to package instructions for use in baking.
4. Drain the macaroni, do not rinse.
5. Arrange macaroni in casserole in layers with the cheese and bits of butter.
6. Mix the nonfat dry milk powder with the milk. Pour over the casserole.
7. Bake for 45 minutes.
8. Prepare as a purée in strainer, blender, or food mill. You can also mash a small amount with a fork for a coarser purée. You should not need any additional thinning. Or serve whole pieces as a finger food.
9. Store in refrigerator for 3–4 days. Or, freeze for one month.
YIELD: 3 cups or 15 food cubes.

$ Wheat Germ

Nutrition: Wheat germ is the most valuable part of the wheat cereal grain, yet it is often removed during the refining of wheat in cereal and flour. It contains the greatest amount of protein, minerals, all the B vitamins, and linoleic acid (an essential fatty acid). Wheat germ is also one of the few good sources of vitamin E, which many doctors feel is very valuable in an infant's diet and is found in lower quantities in cow's milk than breast milk.

Introduce wheat germ around five months after you have introduced wheat as a cereal. Since wheat is a possible source of allergies, you should begin with a very small amount. If your baby has no reaction, it can be an important addition to his diet.

Buy: You may think of wheat germ as a "health" food and difficult to find. However, it is available in most supermarkets either plain or sweetened with honey. You should avoid using the latter.

Store wheat germ in a tightly covered container in the refrigerator for 2–3 months. Since it contains oils, it is likely to become rancid if left at room temperature.

USING WHEAT GERM

The texture is fairly hard and mixed with milk it may be a difficult consistency for a young baby to swallow. You will get the smoothest texture by grinding it in a blender and cooking it with milk for 5 minutes, or allowing it to soak until soft. Raw wheat germ, if you can find it, is more tender.

- The best way to introduce and use wheat germ is to grind it, then mix it with a food that has a smooth consistency, such as bananas.
- When you mix wheat germ with another food, always add extra liquid, about twice the amount of wheat germ. Allow the purée to stand a few minutes to soften the wheat germ.
- You can add wheat germ, either ground or whole, to juicy fruits and vegetables as a thickener. Use about 1 tablespoon for each cup of purée.
- You can also mix 1 part wheat germ to 2 parts dry infant cereal and you will have almost the nutritional value of a whole-grain cereal.

As you can see, you will be able to use your imagination in finding ways to use wheat germ in your baby's food. You may find nutritious and tasty combinations that your entire family will also enjoy.

$ Rice

Nutrition: Rice is a cereal grain that can be used as a cereal or in many main dishes and desserts. It can also be used as a nutritious thickener. It contains less protein than the other cereal grains, but it is a good source of the B vitamins, especially niacin. The amount of nutrition depends upon the type of processing.

Brown or natural rice contains all of the nutrients in the rice—it is a whole grain. You can find this in most supermarkets and should use it whenever possible.

Converted or parboiled has been processed so that some of the B vitamins are carried into the grain before the bran or outer part is removed. It is a white rice, easily digestible, and is the next best rice nutritionally. If the converted rice is also enriched, it may be even higher than brown rice in iron and thiamine.

Enriched polished rice has had many of the vitamins and minerals removed during processing. Thiamine, riboflavin, niacin, and iron have been added according to government standards. It is lower in protein than converted or brown rice. I can see no reason to use this instead of the converted rice. The instant or quick-cooking rice may also be enriched.

Polished white rice that has not been enriched should not be used since it has a very low nutritional value. Rice flour is made from this highly processed rice and is usually unenriched.

Introduce converted or enriched rice as a cereal as early as five months. Because of the bran, you should not introduce brown rice until your baby is around seven to eight months hold.

Store rice in a tightly covered container at cool room temperature for up to two years. Cooked rice may be covered and kept in the refrigerator for 2–3 days. You may also freeze it as a purée for one month. This is convenient for rice that requires longer cooking times.

COOKING RICE

- To retain the nutrients, especially thiamine, do not wash the rice before cooking and do not drain or rinse the rice after it is cooked.
- Use only as much liquid in cooking as can be absorbed by the time the rice is soft, usually 2–3 times the amount of rice.
- You may use milk as the cooking liquid to supplement the quality of the rice protein. When you use milk, do not cover the pot or else the milk will boil over.
- If you cook rice in a double boiler, you can cover the pot and it will require very little watching or stirring.
- The cooking times given here are for brown or converted rice. If you are using precooked or instant enriched rice, use the cooking times on the package.
- A nutritious time-saving way to cook rice is to use the same pot and cooking water in which you have just prepared a vegetable, or stewed chicken, etc. Just measure the desired amount of liquid, bring to boil, and add the rice.

$ Basic Rice Purée

This makes a good substitute for a serving of cereal.

    1 cup brown or converted rice
    3 cups water, vegetable juice, or milk
    ¼ cup nonfat dry milk powder (optional)
    ¼ cup milk

1. Place rice and liquid in pot and bring to a boil.
2. Reduce heat and simmer uncovered for 30–45 minutes or until the rice is soft. Add more liquid if necessary.
3. Cool and purée with any equipment, adding ¼ cup milk, and optional nonfat dry milk.

YIELD: 2 cups purée or 10 food cubes.

VARIATION

$ **Rice and Wheat-Germ Purée.** Add ¼ cup of wheat germ during the last 10 minutes of cooking.

$ **Leftover Rice Purée.** Use any rice that is left from a family meal and thin with 2 tablespoons of milk for each cup of rice.

$ **Rice Cheese.** Purée with ¼ cup grated cheese or ½ cup cottage cheese.

$ Soybean/Rice Purée

This dish is high in protein and can be used as an economical substitute for a serving of meat. Double the amount for a cereal/protein serving.

> ½ **cup soybeans**
> 1½ **cups water**
> ½ **cup brown or converted rice**
> 1 **cup skim milk (or water)**
> ½ **cup skim milk**

1. Soak beans overnight in water; or bring to a boil, cover, and allow to sit for 2 hours.
2. Boil rapidly for 1 hour, uncovered. Reduce heat to simmer.
3. Add 1 cup of skim milk, and rice.
4. Simmer uncovered for 45 minutes. Stir occasionally and add more water or milk if necessary.
5. Cool and purée, adding about ½ cup of milk to thin.
YIELD: 2½ cups or 12 food cubes.

$ Rice Pudding

This is a nutritious dessert that counts as a cereal and is also high in protein. The rest of your family can enjoy it as a dessert or an unusual breakfast food.

1 cup rice, brown or converted
4 cups milk (whole or skim)
2 eggs beaten (you may also use only the yolks)
2 tablespoons nonfat dry milk powder (optional)
½ cup sweetener (brown sugar or honey) (optional)
1 teaspoon vanilla (optional)

OVEN METHOD

1. Butter casserole. Preheat oven to 325°F.
2. Mix rice and milk in casserole and bake uncovered for 1 hour or until rice is soft. Stir every 15 minutes.
3. Mix a little of the rice mixture with the beaten eggs, then mix the eggs and any optional ingredients into the casserole.
4. Bake for 15 minutes.

DOUBLE-BOILER METHOD

This will require less watching.
1. Bring the milk and rice to a boil in the top of a double boiler. Place on the bottom part, cover, and steam for 45 minutes.
2. Remove from heat. Stir some rice or milk into the beaten eggs, then mix the eggs into the rice and milk. Add any optional ingredients.
3. Return to heat and stir until the spoon becomes coated. Cool pudding and purée with any equipment. No additional thinning should be necessary.

Variation

Rice/Fruit Pudding. Add ½ cup of fruit purée (apricot, peach, plum, berry, or banana are good) after the rice is cooked and before mixing in the eggs.

$ Rice and Meat Dishes

If you prepare main dishes with rice for your family, you can easily use them as baby food as long as they are not highly seasoned and your baby has already been introduced to all the main ingredients. The protein of the meat will improve the quality of the rice protein and you will have an economical and nutritious dish for your baby.

- For each cup of the rice and meat dish, purée with about ⅓ cup of milk or tomato juice as a thinner.
- These are good dishes for introducing your baby to a coarser texture in preparation for eating ordinary family meals.
- If you purée these dishes the same day they are made, you can freeze the purée in food cubes for up to one month.

$ Sautéed Rice

This is a nutritious, easy, and economical all-in-one dish that can be made from leftovers. You can use it as a main dish for your family and purée some for your baby's dinner.

½ cup chopped onions (optional)
½ cup chopped leafy greens (optional)
2 tablespoons butter
1 egg, beaten
2 cups cooked brown or converted rice
½ cup cooked diced chicken, liver, beef, or pork
2 tablespoons soy sauce

1. Sauté onions and leafy greens in butter.
2. Add egg and scramble lightly.
3. Stir in rice, meat, and soy sauce.
4. Cook over low heat for 5 minutes.
5. Purée with a blender, processor, or food mill, adding about ¼ cup milk to thin.
6. You may freeze the purée for up to one month.
YIELD: 4 cups.

8

Fruits

Fruits are among the first solid foods that you will feed your baby. They are high in natural sugar, an easily digested source of carbohydrates, and they contain good amounts of minerals, especially phosphorus and iron. Some fruits are major sources of vitamins A and C. By the time your baby is several months old, he should be eating daily one serving of citrus fruit and at least two servings of other fruits.

Fruits are also the easiest and most economical baby foods that you can make yourself. Many fruits can even be served raw and mashed only with a spoon. Most do not require any thinning or added sweetening, so every bite will contain the most nourishment. You can choose from among the wide variety of fresh frozen, canned, and dried fruits.

Fresh Fruit is inexpensive, flavorful, and highly nutritious when it is selected and stored properly. Many fruits are given grades based on appearance and size, such as U.S. Extra Fancy, U.S. Fancy, and U.S. Extra #1. You can save money by buying the lower, but equally nutritious, grades for use as baby food. You should select those fruits that are in season, since they are inexpensive and the best quality. You should also take advantage of specials on very ripe fruit that you will use immediately or freeze.

Ripe Fruit contains the most sugar and vitamins and is easiest for your baby to digest. You can buy unripe fruit and ripen it at home if it was mature when picked. Fruit is *mature* when it was fully grown when picked. If fruit is *immature* when picked, it will not ripen properly and will be lacking in flavor and nutrients. (The signs for recognizing mature fruit are given under the specific fruit.) Fruit will ripen at room temperature and should not be placed in the refrigerator or in the sun.

Before storing fruit, sort out any bruised or decayed pieces, since they will cause the other fruit to spoil more quickly. Whether or not you should wash a fruit before storing depends on the specific fruit. You should always wash fruit before using to remove any pesticides.

Raw Fruit has the highest nutritional value and will require the least preparation—it is one of your best "instant foods." Most babies can eat raw fruit at quite an early age and really enjoy the taste.

- The skin of raw fruit is more difficult to digest and should not be included in the purée until your baby is at least eight months old and the fruit has been introduced.
- You can remove the skin with a sharp knife, by blanching, or by using a food mill or strainer to purée. For an individual serving of some fruits, such as peaches, you need only to cut the fruit in half and scrape out the pulp.
- Always try to cut or peel the fruit just before using to prevent the loss of vitamins.
- Most raw fruit can be frozen either whole or puréed in food cubes for as long as one year and this is very practical for seasonal fruits.
- Raw-fruit purées spoil quickly so you should plan to use them within two days.

Cooked Fruit. The main purposes of cooking fresh or frozen fruit are to soften the texture or improve the digestibility of less than ripe fruit. Most fruit only needs to be cooked for the young baby or when first introducing a fruit. The main cooking methods are BAKE (in the skin, or aluminum foil); STEW in a little water or in a double boiler (good for very juicy fruits); or STEAM in a steamer (ideal for any fruit with a fairly thick skin which will retain the juice).

You should choose the cooking method which fits in best with your daily family cooking. For example, if you are roasting, wrap some fruit in foil and bake it at the same time. In general, fruit should be cooked over low heat for as short a time as possible. If only a fork or spoon is available for mashing, it may be necessary to cook the fruit until it is very tender. If water must be used in cooking, or juice is produced from cooking, use it in the purée or save it as a thinner or beverage. In these recipes, little or no liquid is used in cooking.

Fruit should always be cooked in the skin in order to save the most vitamins and minerals. Cooked skins can usually be puréed with the fruit unless the skin is very thick or sour or there is a large amount of skin, such as with grapes. The skin should be removed when you are introducing purées to a very young baby.

Cooked purées can be frozen in food cubes for as long as 1 year and some are also easily canned at home. They can be stored in the refrigerator up to one week. (See **Storage** chapter.)

Frozen Fruit has the same nutritional value as fresh fruit if it has been frozen and stored properly. Select packages that are solidly frozen and not stained. In the case of fruits that are out of season, the frozen fruit may be better quality and less expensive. You will prepare frozen fruit in the same ways as fresh fruit and it can be substituted in any of the recipes. Since it is usually cleaned, you will even save some preparation time. The cooked purées can be frozen in food cubes.

Canned Fruit retains a very high amount of vitamins and minerals, although less than fresh or frozen fruit. It should be stored at cool room temperature and used within a year. This is a very convenient form of fruit, since it is already prepared, cooked, and often mashed. They are some of your best "instant foods," with some soft enough to purée with a fork or spoon.

The "U.S. Grade B" canned fruits are economical for use as baby food. Be careful not to buy cans that are leaking, bulging, or badly dented. If the fruit is packed in a vacuum glass jar, listen for the "popping" sound when you open it to make sure that the jar was not already opened and the fruit spoiled. **Before opening, always wash the top of a can or the underneath edge of the lid of a glass jar in order to remove any dirt.**

Try to buy fruits that are packed in their *own juice*, or in water, instead of syrup. The juice or water should be used in thinning the fruit or other purées, or served as a beverage, since this liquid can contain as much as *one-third of the vitamins and minerals*. If you can only buy fruit that is packed in syrup, the light syrup will contain less sugar than the heavy syrup. Always drain this fruit and *do not give the syrup to your baby*. This fruit should not be served too often because of its extra sweetness. Read labels carefully to avoid canned fruits that contain additives, such as artificial color or flavor.

Opened canned fruit, whole or puréed, may be stored in the refrigerator for up to one week. It may also be frozen in food cubes for future use.

Dried Fruits are a good source of minerals, especially iron. They are high in sugar, but lower in vitamin C than other forms of fruit. Dried fruit can be introduced around five months or at the same time as the cooked fruit. Dried fruits include apples, apricots, dates, peaches, pears, prunes, and raisins. They also make excellent "finger foods."

Buy well-sealed, clean containers and try to feel if the fruit is pliable. Many dried fruits have sulfur dioxide added as a preservative and may have a laxative effect, so use these sparingly. Try to buy dried fruits that are packed without preservatives and added sugar. Store dried fruits in tightly covered containers at cool room temperature or in the refrigerator for up to six months.

Apples

Nutrition: A well-balanced, good source of vitamins and minerals.

Introduce cooked at four to five months. Raw at eight months. A peeled whole apple, given as a finger food, is useful in cleaning your baby's teeth and massaging sore gums.

Buy firm apples of any variety for cooking, ranging from tart to sweet. They are most plentiful in fall and winter months. Avoid apples which have a shriveled appearance from too-long storage, soft apples, and those with large bruised areas.

Store apples in a cool pantry for several weeks; or wash, dry, and store uncovered in the refrigerator.

Instant Use: Applesauce.

Finger Food: Peeled, whole apple.

Raw Applesauce

Jonathan, Grimes Golden, Delicious, McIntosh, Cortland, and Northern Spy are good varieties to use raw. Always prepare just before using or sprinkle with lemon juice to prevent browning.

1 medium apple
1 teaspoon lemon juice

1. Peel if necessary, core, blend on high speed. (Add 1 tablespoon fruit juice if apple is very dry.) Or grate with a rotary grater.
2. Add lemon juice.
3. Store in refrigerator for 1 day or freeze larger amounts.
YIELD: ½ cup purée or 3 food cubes.

Raw Apple/Carrot Purée

½ medium apple (cored, peeled if necessary)
½ carrot (wash, do not peel)
2 tablespoons fruit juice
1 teaspoon lemon juice

1. Purée all ingredients in processor or blender, or grate apples and carrot. Mix with juice.
2. Store in refrigerator for 1 day or freeze in food cubes.
YIELD: ½ cup purée or 3 food cubes.

Applesauce

8 medium apples (2 pounds)

1. Preheat oven to 350°F.
2. Wash and core apples.
3. Wrap single apples in a square of aluminum foil, twisting the corners over the top of the apple so it is tightly sealed. Or, place apples in tightly covered baking dish with a little water.
4. Bake ½ hour for the softer varieties; 45 minutes for harder apples.
5. Purée with food mill or strainer to remove skin, or scrape out pulp for a single serving with a spoon. Use blender or processor to purée apple and skin.
6. Store up to one week or freeze in food cubes.
YIELD: 3 cups or 15 food cubes.

VARIATION

Steam apples in steamer for 12–15 minutes. You can leave the apples whole and then remove the skin and cores with a food mill.

Stewed Dried Apples

   1 **cup dried apples**
   2 **cups water**

1. Soak apples in water for 30 minutes.
2. Bring apples and water to a boil.
3. Cover and simmer 20–30 minutes.
4. Cool.
5. To purée, the stewed apples should be soft enough to mash with a fork. Use a food mill or blender for large quantities.
6. Store or freeze as for applesauce.
YIELD: 2 cups or 10 food cubes.

Apricots

Nutrition: A very good source of vitamin A.

Introduce cooked around five months; raw at eight months.

Buy apricots that are plump, with a uniform golden-orange color. Ripe apricots should yield to a gentle pressure on the skin. They are in season during June and July. *Do not buy* apricots that are dull, soft, or mushy (overripe); or very firm, pale yellow, or greenish-yellow (immature).

Store unripe apricots uncovered at room temperature, not in the sun, for several days until ripe. Store *ripe* apricots uncovered in the refrigerator for 3–5 days.

Finger Food: See Apricot Leather.

Raw Apricot Purée

   1 **pound ripe apricots** (1 apricot is usually adequate for a single feeding.)

1. Remove skins of apricots by plunging them in boiling water for 30 seconds, then run cold water over them while you rub off the skins. Or, remove skins by puréeing in food mill.

2. Remove the pits.

3. Very ripe apricots can be mashed with a fork. For large quantities or the smoothest purée, use food mill, processor, or blender.

4. Store purée in refrigerator for one day. Or, freeze in food cubes for up to one year.

YIELD: 2 cups or 10 food cubes.

Stewed Apricots

1 pound ripe apricots
2 tablespoons fruit juice

1. Wash. If it is necessary to remove skin, dip in boiling water, then rub off skin under cold water. Or, remove skins by puréeing in food mill.

2. Bring apricots and juice to a boil. Cover and simmer for 10 minutes or steam for 10 minutes; do not add more juice.

3. Cool, pick out pits.

4. Purée in processor, blender, or food mill for smoothest purée. You can mash with a fork for a coarser texture.

5. Store in refrigerator for 5–7 days or freeze.

YIELD: 2 cups or 10 cubes.

VARIATION: BAKED APRICOTS

1 pound ripe apricots

1. Preheat oven to 375°F.

2. Place washed apricots in covered baking dish, adding a small amount of water. Or, wrap tightly in aluminum foil (good for a single serving).

3. Bake for 20 minutes.

4. Proceed as for Stewed Apricots.

Stewed Dried Apricots

1 cup dried apricots
1½ cups water

1. Soak apricots in water for 1 hour.
2. Bring apricots and water to a boil.
3. Cover and simmer 15–25 minutes.
4. Cool. Mash with fork, or use a blender or processor for large quantities or a finer purée.
5. Store and freeze as for Stewed Apricots.
YIELD: 1½ cups or about 8 food cubes.

Avocados

Nutrition: A good source of unsaturated fat, some protein. High in linoleic acid, an essential fatty acid.

Introduce raw around nine months. They are not suitable for cooking.

Buy avocados that are either light green with smooth skins; or dark green or brown with rough, leathery skins. Both varieties are good eating and are in season from November through May.

Do not buy fruit with dark, sunken spots or cracked surfaces, both signs of decay.

Store unripe avocados at room temperature, out of sun, for 3–5 days until they have ripened, so that they yield to gentle pressure of the skin. *Ripe* avocados may be held in the refrigerator for 3–5 days.

Instant Use: Most babies will eat avocado purée without any thinning; so that the fruit can be mashed or scraped with the back of the spoon as it is removed from the skin. An avocado is a good food to use when traveling.

Finger Food: Remove skin and cut in pieces or strips.

Raw Avocado

¼ very ripe avocado
1 teaspoon milk or citrus juice

1. Wash avocado.
2. Cut through skin to pit and remove ¼ of the fruit.
3. Peel back skin and mash avocado with a spoon, thinning with liquid if necessary.

To store leftover purée in the refrigerator for up to one day, sprinkle with lemon juice to prevent browning and tightly cover. Store the rest of the avocado in the skin, tightly wrapped, in the refrigerator for up to three days.

YIELD: 1 serving.

Frozen Avocados

2 medium avocados
4 tablespoons lemon juice

1. Wash and peel avocados.
2. Mash fruit with the lemon juice. If a blender is used, push mix down with rubber spatula for smooth blending. A processor is best for this thick purée.
3. Pour immediately into ice cubes; cover and freeze.
4. Keep frozen for 4–6 weeks.

YIELD: 2 cups or 10 food cubes.

Bananas

Nutrition: High in carbohydrates, good source of vitamins A and C. High caloric value.

Introduce raw, very ripe, or baked bananas as one of your baby's earliest foods, at around four to five months.

Buy fruit with firm bright skins, either greenish, yellow, or brown, depending on the stage of ripeness. *Do not buy* fruit that is bruised or shows soft spots, since it will spoil quickly; or fruit with discolored skins, or a dull, grayish appearance which shows that the bananas have been exposed to cold and will not ripen properly.

Store unripe bananas (green to solid yellow skins) at cool room temperature (60°–70°F.), away from sun. They will not ripen in the refrigerator and the cold will cause a loss of quality. Bananas will ripen in 3–5 days and the best eating quality is reached when the skins are solid yellow with brown spots or streaks. The riper the banana, the more digestible it is for a baby; so you may use bananas with completely brown skins as long as the fruit itself is unbruised. *Ripe* bananas should be stored in the warmest part of the refrigerator for up to two days.

Instant Use: See following recipe.

Finger Food: Cut in small pieces.

Raw Bananas

This is one of the easiest fruits to prepare.

1. Use a very ripe banana.
2. Remove only the peel of the part of the banana that you will be using in one feeding. For a very young infant, start with ¼ of the fruit.
3. Mash the banana with a fork or the back of a spoon until it is smooth.
4. It is not necessary to add any liquid or sugar.
5. The banana purée should not be saved, since it browns quickly. The unused portion of the banana should be wrapped, in the skin, and can be stored in the refrigerator for up to two days. Ripe bananas can also be peeled, wrapped tightly in aluminum foil, in meal-sized portions, and frozen for several months. Thaw in the foil and use immediately.

Baked Bananas

If you must use greenish or yellow bananas that are not yet ripe, they should be baked to improve their digestibility.

1. Preheat oven to 450°F.
2. Peel banana.
3. Place in buttered baking dish, or wrap tightly in aluminum foil.
4. Bake about 10 minutes until tender.
5. Mash enough for one feeding with a fork or spoon.

Store whole baked banana in baking foil, tightly wrapped, in the refrigerator for one day.

VARIATION: BROILED OR SAUTÉED BANANAS

Unripe peeled bananas may also be sautéed in a small amount of butter, or broiled 3 inches from the heat until slightly browned. Prepare and store as for Baked Bananas.

Berries

Nutrition: Blueberries, raspberries, blackberries, cranberries, etc., contain fair amounts of many nutrients. Strawberries are very high in vitamin C, almost as high as the citrus fruits.

Introduce raw and cooked at about nine months. Since berries sometimes cause allergic reactions, give only small amounts at first.

Buy firm, dry fruit which is in season from May through August. *Do not buy* berries which are crushed or show a white fuzzy mold. Avoid boxes which are wet or stained with berry juice.

Store berries whole, uncovered in a flat pan, for 1–2 days in the refrigerator. Remove any spoiled berries, since decay spreads quickly. Do not wash or stem the berries before storing.

Finger Food: Whole berries for babies over one year.

Raw Berries

1 quart box of berries (Do not use cranberries.)
½ teaspoon honey

1. Wash berries just before using.
2. For a purée, press the berries through a strainer or food mill to remove the skin and seeds.
3. Mix with honey. (For a single serving, use only a few drops of honey to sweeten.)
4. Cover tightly and store in refrigerator for 1 day. Or, freeze in food cubes.

YIELD: 2 cups or 10 food cubes.

Stewed Berries

Cooking will destroy the vitamin C in strawberries.

1 quart box of berries

1. Wash berries.
2. Put berries in top of double boiler.
3. Cook 15 minutes.
4. Cool and mash. Strain out skin and seeds.
5. Store purée in refrigerator for up to one week or freeze in food cubes.

YIELD: 2 cups or 10 food cubes.

VARIATION

Since berries contain a high proportion of juice, they are good to combine with other fruit purées, either raw or cooked. The juice will serve as a natural thinner.

Cranberry Sauce

1 pound cranberries
¼ cup water (or fruit juice)
¾ cup honey

1. Wash and sort cranberries.
2. Bring water and honey to a boil.
3. Add fruit, cover, and simmer 5–10 minutes until berries pop.

4. Use food mill or strainer to purée and remove skin.

5. Store purée in refrigerator for up to one week. Freeze in food cubes, or can.

YIELD: 3 cups or 15 food cubes.

Cherries

Nutrition: Sweet cherries are quite high in natural sugar.

Introduce cooked at seven months, raw at nine months.

Buy firm, dark cherries with shiny skin. They are in season during June and July. *Do not buy* shriveled fruit with dry stems or brown discoloration which indicates decay.

Store *unripe* cherries at room temperature to ripen in 3–5 days. Put ripe cherries, uncovered, in refrigerator for 1–2 days. Do not stem or wash.

Finger Food: Sweet cherries are a messy fruit and the pits must be removed; but babies love them. Serve after baby is one year old.

Raw Cherries

1 quart or pound ripe eating cherries (Royal Anne, Napoleon, Bing, Black Tartarian, Republican, Lambert, Windsor)

1. Wash cherries and remove stems. If purée is to be prepared with a food mill or blender, remove the pits with the metal end (with eraser removed) of a pencil.

2. Mash cherries using strainer, food mill, processor, or blender. The skin is thin enough to be digestible for older babies, if a blender is used.

3. Store purée in refrigerator, tightly covered, for one day. Or, freeze in food cubes for up to one year.

YIELD: 2 cups or 10 food cubes.

VARIATION

Since cherries contain a large amount of juice, they are a good fruit to combine with more solid fruits such as apples or bananas.

Stewed Cherries

1 quart or pound sweet or cooking cherries (Montmorency or English Morello), **or 30-ounce can sour cherries** (Sour cherries are one of the few canned fruits that should be stewed to sweeten them.)

½ cup honey (use only with sour cooking cherries)

1. Wash, stem cherries.
2. Place honey and cherries in double boiler or heavy saucepan.
3. Simmer over low heat for 15 minutes.
4. Cool, and remove pits with a fork or slotted spoon (easier than pitting raw cherries).
5. Mashes well with fork. Use food mill or blender for quantities and when first introducing fruit.
6. Store cooked purée in refrigerator for up to one week. Or freeze for up to one year.
YIELD: 2 cups or 10 food cubes.

VARIATION

Since cherries contain a large amount of juice, they are a good fruit to stew in combination with a more solid fruit; just omit the liquid recommended for stewing the particular fruit.

$ Citrus Fruits

Nutrition: All the citrus fruits—oranges, grapefruits, lemons, tangerines, limes—are excellent sources of vitamin C. The pulp is also a source of certain vitamins and minerals.

Introduce as juice as early as 4 months. (See "Beverages," chapter 12.) Raw purées can be given by eight months. Since vitamin C is destroyed by heat, citrus fruits should not be cooked. To prevent a rash, wash your baby's face immediately after feeding him a citrus fruit or drink.

Buy citrus fruits that are firm and well shaped. Select

the heaviest fruits for the size, since the weight indicates the amount of juice in the fruit. Select those fruits with smooth skins, another indication of juice. If the skin is rough or wrinkled, the skin is likely to be thicker with less flesh to the fruit, with a large amount of pulp. Russeting, a tan or blackish mottling or specking on the skin, does not affect the quality of citrus fruit. These fruits are most plentiful and inexpensive during the winter months.

Do not buy citrus fruits that show signs of age (dull, dry, or hardened skin) or signs of decay (soft, discolored areas on the peel, water-soaked areas, or punctures).

Oranges: The *Parson Brown, navel (seedless),* and *pineapple* oranges are best for purées or as *finger food.* The *valencia* orange is better for juice. The seedless variety is more convenient for making purées. Oranges are required by state regulations to be well matured before picking, so skin color should not be used as a guide to quality. Oranges with a greenish cast, or spots, are as good as those which show a deep orange color (often more expensive). Some of those oranges with the brightest color have had artificial color added and must be so marked. There is some question as to the health hazards of this practice, but in any case it is unnecessary and may add to the cost of the orange.

Grapefruit: As with oranges, grapefruits are picked ripe and are ready for eating. There is little difference between the white or pink varieties. The seedless types will save you some time when preparing purées.

Lemons should have a rich yellow color. Those with a pale or greenish-yellow color will be more sour.

Limes must be mature when marketed and should be a dark green color. The small Key limes may have a yellowish color.

Tangerines should have a deep yellow or orange color. Very pale yellow or greenish fruit may be lacking in flavor. This is the one citrus fruit where the skin should feel loose and puffy. Since the skin peels easily and the fruit is usually quite sweet, tangerines make good finger food.

Store citrus fruits at cool room temperature (60°–70°F.) for about one week. They may be stored for a short while in the refrigerator.

Finger Food: Wash orange, slice into sections.

If you own a blender or processor, the following recipes will allow you to make full use of all the nutrition in a citrus fruit, both in the juice and the pulp.

Raw Apple/Grapefruit

1 medium apple
½ medium grapefruit

1. Wash, peel, and core apple.
2. Cut rind from grapefruit, remove seeds.
3. Purée apple and grapefruit in blender or processor (a slightly rougher purée).
4. Store in refrigerator for 3 days or freeze for 1 year.
YIELD: ¾ cup or 4 food cubes.

VARIATIONS

Apple/Orange. Use 1 apple, 1 orange.
Banana/Grapefruit. Use 1 banana, ½ grapefruit.
Banana/Orange. Use 1 banana, 1 orange.
Carrot/Orange. Use 1 carrot, 1 orange.

Grapes

Nutrition: Grapes are high in sugar and low in vitamin C.

Introduce cooked at seven months, raw at eight months.

Buy well-colored, firm grapes that are strongly attached to the stem. The green seedless variety are sweetest when they have a yellowish cast to them.

Do not buy soft or wrinkled grapes (indicative of freezing or drying), grapes with bleached areas around the stem end (indicative of poor quality), or leaking fruit which shows decay.

Grapes are most plentiful in late summer and fall. The Thompson variety is thin-skinned, sweet, and seedless, which makes it ideal as a finger food. You can also buy this variety canned.

Store grapes at room temperature, out of the sun, until ripe. Keep ripe grapes uncovered in the refrigerator for 3–5 days. Do not wash before storing.

Finger Food: Serve whole after child is 1 year old.

Raw Grapes

1 pound grapes
2 tablespoons wheat germ

1. Wash grapes.
2. Purée with food mill or strainer to remove skin. There is so much skin in proportion to the pulp that a blender will still leave pieces of skin in the purée. It would also be too difficult to digest.
3. Mix in wheat germ to thicken.
4. Store, tightly covered, in the refrigerator for 2 days or freeze in cubes.

YIELD: 2 cups or 10 cubes.

VARIATION

Grapes contain a large amount of juice and are very sweet, so they are a good fruit to combine with hard, sour fruits.

Stewed Grapes

1. Follow instructions for raw purée.
2. Stew in double boiler or simmer over low heat for 10 minutes.

Melon/Cantaloupe

Nutrition: Cantaloupes are the most common and generally the least expensive of the melons. They are an excellent source of vitamin A and a good source of vitamin C.

Introduce raw cantaloupe at nine months. It should never be cooked.

Buy cantaloupes that are mature, either unripe or ripe. Since proper selection is considered to be an art, it is worthwhile to go into some detail. A well-chosen cantaloupe is sweet, juicy, and highly nutritious. A *mature* cantaloupe shows three signs: 1) The stem should be gone, leaving a smooth, symmetrical stem scar. If the scar is jagged or torn, the melon was picked before it was mature. 2) The netting, or veining, should be thick, coarse, and corky, and should stand out in bold relief over some part of the surface. 3) The skin color (ground) between the netting should have changed from green to a yellowish-gray or pale yellow.

A *ripe* cantaloupe will have a yellowish cast to the rind, a pleasant odor when held to the nose, and will yield to light thumb pressure on the blossom end (opposite the scar or stem end).

An *overripe* cantaloupe should be avoided, since the flesh will be soft, watery, and tasteless. Signs of overripeness are a strong yellow rind color, softening of the entire melon, or mold growth in the stem scar.

Store mature, unripe melons at room temperature, out of the sun, for 2–4 days until ripe. Use immediately when ripe.

Finger Food: Sticks of cantaloupe are an excellent finger food, since they are sweet and juicy. It is a good substitute for carrots as a source of vitamin A.

Instant Use: Cantaloupe can also be used as an easy single serving of fruit. Just cut a slice and scrape the melon with a spoon as you feed your baby.

Cantaloupe Purée

½ very ripe cantaloupe
2 tablespoons wheat germ

1. Cut rind from melon, make sure that all the green is removed.
2. Cut melon into cubes and purée in processor or blender, adding wheat germ.

3. Serve at once or freeze immediately. The purée spoils very quickly.

YIELD: 1 cup or 5 cubes.

VARIATION

Cantaloupe purée is very sweet and thin because of the large amount of juice in a melon; so it is a good fruit to combine with a sour or hard fruit or vegetable.

Nectarines/Peaches

Nutrition: An excellent source of vitamin A.

Introduce cooked at two months, raw at five months.

Buy peaches or nectarines which are firm, but beginning to soften. The skin color should be yellow or creamy. The freestone variety is best for raw purées or for eating fresh. The clingstones are used mainly for cooking. Some good varieties are Elberta, Hale, Hiley, and Golden Jubilee.

Do not buy fruit that is very hard or has a green ground color. These are immature and will not ripen properly. Also avoid very soft fruit or those with large flattened bruises, since these are signs of decay.

Store unripe fruit at room temperature until ripe. Keep ripe fruit uncovered in the refrigerator for 3–5 days.

Finger Food: Peel and cut in pieces. Since nectarines have thinner skins, it is not necessary to peel for an older baby.

Instant Use: Cut in half and scrape with a spoon.

Raw Peaches/Nectarines

1 pound freestone peaches

1. Wash and remove skin by dipping in boiling water for 1–2 minutes, then rub off in cold water.
2. Remove pits.
3. Purée, using any equipment. A blender should be used when making purée for a young infant.

4. Store in refrigerator for 1–2 days, or freeze for 1 year.

YIELD: 2 cups or 10 food cubes.

Cooked Peaches/Nectarines

1 pound peaches (any variety)

1. Wash fruit. When mashing peaches with a fork or blender, remove skin. Otherwise, leave whole. The skin of nectarines is thin enough to purée in a blender.
2. Steam 15–20 minutes or bake—in covered dish with a little water or wrapped in aluminum foil—for 20 minutes at 375°F.
3. Cool.
4. Remove pits and purée. (For a single serving, cut in half and scrape with a spoon.)
5. Store cooked purée in refrigerator for 5–7 days, or freeze for 1 year.

YIELD: 2 cups or 10 cubes.

Stewed Dried Peaches

1 cup dried peaches
1½ cups water or juice

1. Soak peaches in water for 1 hour.
2. Simmer peaches, covered, in soaking water for 30–40 minutes.
3. Purée with any equipment.
4. Store as for cooked purée.

YIELD: 1½ cups or 8 food cubes.

Pears

Nutrition: Pears are high in natural sugar and fair in vitamins A and C.

Introduce cooked at five months and raw at seven months.

Buy firm pears that have begun to soften, so that you can be sure that the pear will ripen. The color of the pear depends on the variety, and the best pears for using raw are: Anjou or Comice (light to yellowish green); Bosc (greenish to brownish yellow with russeting); Bartlett (pale or rich yellow, red); or Winter Nelis (medium to light green). These varieties are in season from August until April.

Do not buy fruit that is wilted, shriveled, has dull skin, or weakening of the flesh near the ends (signs of immaturity). Soft spots on pears indicate that decay has begun and the fruit is overripe.

Store unripe fruits at room temperature until they begin to soften. Keep ripe washed pears in the refrigerator for 3–5 days.

Instant Use: Ripe pears can be halved and scraped with a spoon. Canned pears can be mashed with a fork.

Finger Food: Remove skin and cut in pieces.

Raw Pears

1 pound (3 or 4) pears (Bartlett, Bosc, Anjou)
1 tablespoon citrus juice

1. Wash fruit.
2. If using processor or blender, peel and remove core.
3. Purée, and add citrus juice to prevent browning.
4. Use in 1 day, or freeze immediately.
YIELD: 2½ cups or 12 cubes.

Cooked Pears

1 pound pears (any variety)

1. Prepare as for Raw Pears.
2. Bake whole in a covered dish, with a little water in the bottom (or wrap in aluminum foil), for 20 minutes in a 350°F. oven, or steam firm whole pears for 20 minutes, or broil halved pears, adding a little butter, for 7 minutes (good for single serving).

3. Purée in processor or blender (or mash with a fork).

4. Store in refrigerator for 5 days, or freeze for up to 1 year.

YIELD: 2½ cups or 12 food cubes.

Pineapple

Nutrition: Pineapple contains a good amount of natural sugar and balanced amounts of several vitamins and minerals.

Introduce cooked at six months, and raw at nine months.

Buy mature pineapples, either ripe or unripe. Mature fruit will have a pineapple odor, a very slight separation of the eyes, or pips, and the spikes or leaves at the top can be easily pulled out. The fruit should also be firm and shiny, with heavy weight for its size. The mature, unripe fruit will be dark green in color, which will change to orange or yellow as it ripens.

Do not buy fruit with sunken or slightly pointed pips, dull yellowish-green color, and a dried look. These are immature and will never ripen properly. Also avoid bruised fruit with discolored or soft spots, or traces of mold—all signs of decay, which will spread quickly.

Store unripe pineapples at cool room temperature (60°–65°F.) 3–5 days until ripe. Never ripen in the sun. Ripe pineapple should be tightly wrapped to contain the odor and stored in the refrigerator for up to 2 days. Ripe fruit will spoil quickly, so plan its use carefully.

Raw Pineapple

1 medium pineapple (2 pounds)

1. Wash, cut off crown end and stem end.
2. Stand upright and cut off skin from top to bottom.
3. Remove the eyes with a sharp knife.
4. A few sweet grapes or pieces of cantaloupe can be added as sweeteners.
5. Cut fruit in small chunks and purée in processor or

blender only. (If your blender is not powerful, cook fruit first.)

6. Store in refrigerator for 1 day, or freeze at once.

YIELD: 2 cups or 10 food cubes.

Cooked Pineapple

1 medium pineapple

1. Prepare pineapple as for raw purée.
2. Place cut fruit in steamer and cover. Steam for 10–15 minutes.
3. Cool and purée *in processor or blender only*.
4. Store in refrigerator for up to 5 days or freeze for up to 1 year.

YIELD: 2 cups or 10 food cubes.

VARIATION

Pineapple contains an enzyme which has some tenderizing action; so combine this fruit or use the juice in cooking any meat or poultry.

Canned pineapple that is packed in its own juice is available. Since it only requires blender puréeing, the canned fruit can save you time.

Plums/Prunes

Nutrition: Plums are a good source of natural sugar. The Italian prune plums can have a laxative effect.

Introduce cooked at five months, raw at eight months.

Buy any variety of plum for cooking. For eating, the Red Beaut, Burmose, Laroda, Duarte, President, or Queen Anne are the sweetest and juiciest. Prunes are purplish to bluish black. They are in season from June through October. Look for fruit with good color and shiny skins that are firm but beginning to soften. *Do not buy* fruits with skin breaks, or brownish discoloration. The immature fruit is hard, poorly colored, and often shriveled.

Store plums at room temperature until ripe, then refrigerate uncovered for 3–5 days.

Finger Food: Slices of plums are good finger food, but the baby should be old enough to digest the skin, since peeled plums can be very messy. Whole plums should not be given, since the pits are quite small and might be swallowed or choked on. Dried pitted prunes are also excellent as a finger or teething food.

Raw Plums

1 pound (about 15) ripe eating plums
1 tablespoon citrus juice

1. Wash fruit and remove pits.
2. Purée in food mill or strainer to remove skin. (The skin is usually too sour or tough to purée in blender.)
3. Add citrus juice to prevent browning.
4. Store in refrigerator for 1 day or freeze at once.

YIELD: 2 cups or 10 cubes.

Note: Some varieties may be very juicy and require some thickening—use wheat germ or cereal.

Cooked Plums

1 pound plums—any variety (good for hard fruit)

1. Wash fruit.
2. Steam whole for 15 minutes or bake in covered dish or aluminum foil for 20 minutes at 375°F.
3. Cool and remove pits.
4. Purée in blender unless skin is very sour. Any other equipment can also be used.
5. Store cooked purée in refrigerator for 5 days, or freeze for 1 year.

Note: Some varieties may require thickening, or cooking down the liquid.

YIELD: 2 cups or 10 cubes.

Stewed Dried Prunes

1 cup dried prunes
3 cups water

1. Simmer prunes, covered, in water for 30–40 minutes.
2. Cool and remove pits.
3. Purée with any equipment.
4. Store as for Cooked Plums.
YIELD: 3 cups or 15 cubes.

Rhubarb

Nutrition: Rhubarb has balanced amounts of vitamins and minerals. It is technically a vegetable, but is served as a fruit. Use only the stalks; the leaves are poisonous.

Introduce cooked at eight months. Never use raw.

Buy fresh, firm stems with a bright, shiny look and a large amount of pink or red color. It is most plentiful in May and June.

Do not buy stalks which are either very thin or very thick (likely to be tough or stringy). Also avoid stalks that are wilted or flabby, since they are not fresh.

Store rhubarb in refrigerator for 3–5 days.

Rhubarb

2 pounds rhubarb
¼ cup honey or brown sugar

1. Wash rhubarb, cut in 2-inch pieces.
2. Bake covered or in aluminum foil for 30 minutes at 375°F. or stew in top of double boiler, or over low heat, for 15 minutes.
3. Add sweetening.
4. Use either strainer or food mill to purée and remove fibers for the smoothest purée, or purée in blender or processor.

5. If purée is too thin, thicken with wheat germ or cereal.

6. Store in refrigerator for 1 week, or freeze for 1 year.

YIELD: 2½ cups or 12 cubes.

Tropical—Mango, Papaya, Guava

Nutrition: The tropical fruits are often ignored, yet are highly nutritious. Mangoes and papayas are an excellent source of vitamin A and good in vitamin C. Guavas are as high as orange juice in vitamin C and may be a substitute if your baby is allergic to orange juice.

Introduce raw at eight to nine months.

Buy: Unfortunately, these fruits are difficult to find and are expensive away from their growing area. Mangoes are in season from May to July, and the other fruits vary. Select fruit that is firm and free from bruises.

Store tropical fruit at room temperature until ripe. Mangoes and papayas should be very soft. The ripe fruit can be wrapped in waxed paper and refrigerated for 2 days.

Instant Use: These fruits can be halved and scooped out with a spoon. They are also available canned and can be easily mashed with a fork.

Finger Food: Halve; cut out small pieces or strips.

Raw Tropical Fruit

If you find a quantity at reduced prices, take advantage of it. As with melon, cut in half, scoop out, and purée. Freeze at once for up to 1 year.

9

Vegetables

Vegetables are an essential part of your baby's menu. They supply many vitamins, minerals, and carbohydrates. Fresh vegetables in season have the highest nutritional value, with frozen vegetables almost as high. As with fruits, canned vegetables are lower in some vitamins, but are more convenient and still supply adequate amounts of nutrients. Color is the most essential key to the amount of vitamins in vegetables, with the **deep yellow, orange, or dark green** vegetables containing the largest amounts. You should include at least one of these vegetables every day, along with a serving of some other vegetable. *Carrots, spinach,* and *beets* naturally contain nitrates, which, in *very* large amounts, may interfere with the oxygen-carrying capacity of blood. They can and should be a regular part of your baby's diet—in reasonable amounts. **Remember that there is no "wonder" food!**

One of the greatest advantages in preparing your own vegetables is the large variety that you can choose from. Many of the most nutritious vegetables, especially the green leafy ones, are unavailable in the commercial baby foods. If your baby dislikes one vegetable, you will have a wide range from which to select a substitute. The chances are that your baby will love the vegetables that you prepare yourself, with their natural flavors and textures. Since studies have shown that babies have no preference for the taste of salt, it seems logical that babies may even object to highly salted vegetables. These dislikes can continue through childhood and your child may never eat enough of the vegetables that are so important to his health. But if he acquires a taste for natural vegetable flavors as an infant, the battle is over before it has begun.

Another reason to prepare your own vegetables is their economy and ease of preparation. Buying in season and taking advantage of specials can amount to large savings. Very often you will be able to use vegetables that you have prepared for the rest of the family and might have thrown away as leftovers. Only simple cooking is required for most fresh or frozen vegetables and all of the purées can be frozen as food cubes. Most canned vegetables require no cooking, only puréeing. You should spend the most time and care in selecting and storing vegetables, so that you get the most nutritional value and flavor.

Fresh Vegetables. You should use these whenever possible for the most nutrition, flavor, and economy.

- Buy those that are in season and freshly picked for the maximum nutrition and flavor.
- Grades on vegetables are not required. Where you do find them, the U.S. Fancy grade is given on the basis of appearance, which is not essential in baby food. The lower and usually less expensive U.S. Grade No. 1 is adequate. Your best guide to quality will be your own judgment on the appearance and maturity of the vegetables.
- If the official USDA grade shield does appear on a package, it indicates that the product was inspected during the packing and that at the time of packing, it met the requirements of the grade shown on the package.
- Plan the use of what you buy, since most vegetables lose their freshness and quality within 2–5 days.

Most vegetables should be stored in plastic bags in the crisper section of your refrigerator. This will prevent drying and wilting, which causes a loss of vitamins, especially vitamin C. Root and tuber vegetables should be stored at cool room temperature for a short while, and in basements for a month or more. Before storing, cut out any decayed parts or sort out spoiled vegetables to prevent the spread of decay.

There are a few vegetables that a baby can eat raw. Do serve those frequently, since they will be highest in food value, and your baby will acquire a liking for the taste of raw vegetables. If a baby cannot digest raw vegetables, pieces will appear in the bowel movement and you should then postpone them for a while.

To preserve nutrients, always cut or peel raw vegetables just before serving, and do not soak any raw vegetable. You can use a blender to liquefy the raw vegetable with water or juice. You can also grate small amounts of raw vegetables and moisten them with vegetable oil or juice.

Cooked vegetables. There are several ways that you can cook vegetables; however, the ones that are easiest and retain the most nutrients are the **steam** and **bake** methods.

To **steam** almost any vegetable, use a steamer/blancher or an equivalent. (See chapter 4.) The main principle is to suspend the vegetables above a small amount of boiling water in a pot with a tightly fitting cover. Many vegetables can and should be steamed in the skin, and you can combine different vegetables in the same pot. If a vegetable requires lengthy steaming, add water as it boils away.

Bake any vegetable that has a thick skin, such as potatoes or winter squash, in the skin. This is a convenient method when you are already using the oven for a regular family meal. Most succulent or juicy vegetables can be baked at 325°F. by wrapping them tightly in foil or by placing them in a tightly covered dish with a tablespoon or two of water. Then the vegetables will steam in their own juices.

To **boil** some root and tuber vegetables that require lengthy cooking, place them in boiling water that just covers, in a tightly covered pot. If at all possible, bake instead of boil these vegetables. Do boil down the cooking water and save it as a thinner, since it will contain vitamins and minerals.

To preserve nutrients, with any cooking methods, do not cut the vegetables. Most of these recipes give cooking times for whole vegetables. If you really are in a hurry, you can usually reduce the cooking time in half by slicing the vegetables. Never add salt or soda to the cooking water. If you must salt your family's vegetables, do it after cooking.

The cooking times given in the recipes are only guides. Remember that you want to *cook to the minimum* for easy puréeing. If you are using a blender, the vegetables may require less time. If you are mashing by hand or with a food mill, you will have to cook them longer so they become more tender. Young or small vegetables will be more tender using less cooking time.

Remember that vegetables that are cooked, saved, and reheated will lose some vitamins, especially vitamin C. They may be stored for up to 3 days in the refrigerator; however, the best way to store cooked purées is to freeze them in food cubes.

To can vegetables, you will need a pressure canner. You must follow detailed canning instructions to prevent botulism, a serious food poisoning, in canned vegetables. (See chapter 5.)

Frozen vegetables can be substituted for fresh in any of the recipes. You can save considerable time by using them, since the washing and cutting are already done. These are almost as nutritious as fresh vegetables, and offer a wide range from which to choose, especially during the winter months when many vegetables are not in season.

They will be more expensive than fresh vegetables in season, but there are several ways that you can save money. Buy cut vegetables instead of whole ones, and avoid fancy cuts or mixtures. Buy Grade B or Extra Standard vegetables, which are as nutritious, but more mature and less uniform than the highest Grade A. Grade C or Standard is the lowest grade, which usually indicates vegetables with the strongest flavor and firmer texture. Your baby may object to this taste, especially when the vegetable is first introduced. If not, using Grade C will result in considerable savings.

Do not buy packages that are damp or sweating (signs of defrosting) or stained (defrosted and refrozen). Frozen vegetables will maintain their quality for as long as eight months if the freezer temperature is kept at 0°F.

In general, you may follow the cooking times on the package, but use your steamer instead of boiling them in water as is usually suggested. Do not defrost the vegetables before cooking.

Most vegetables are sold in 10-ounce packages, which will yield 1–1½ cups of purée, or 5–8 food cubes. The large bags of vegetables are very economical, and you can either make a large amount or pour out only as much as you need. You can cook *raw* frozen vegetables, then purée and freeze the purée.

Canned vegetables are not as nutritious as fresh or frozen, but you do have a wide selection, and they are very convenient to use as an instant food. You can save money by buying the cut or diced styles and also the Grade B or Extra Standard for use in purées.

Do not buy cans that are leaking, badly dented, or bulging. If you buy the vacuum-pack jars, make sure that there is a popping sound when you open one. If not, the jar may have been opened and the food spoiled. Thoroughly wash cans or lids before opening.

These canned vegetables will require very little preparation. They are already cooked and only need puréeing. Most will require a food mill or blender for the smoothest consistency, but you can mash them with a fork to the texture of "junior" foods. The important thing to remember in using any canned vegetable is that the *liquid that it is packed in contains ⅓ the nutrients* in the vegetable. To use this liquid, drain the vegetables, then boil down the liquid. It can then be used to thin the vegetables, or in other purées. You can also strain it and serve it as a beverage. The *exception is the salt brine* that some vegetables may be packed in. Try to avoid buying this style, but if you do use it, discard the liquid. Never boil canned vegetables before puréeing, since you will lose additional vitamins and minerals. You should only warm them slightly, even serve them cold.

For most vegetables, a 15- or 16-ounce can will yield about 1½ cups purée, or 8 food cubes. This can be refrigerated for up to 3 days or frozen for 1 month.

Consistency. Most vegetables, when first introduced, will require a little thinning; however, the least amount is the most desirable in terms of nutrition. *You can start with 1–2 tablespoons of liquid for each cup of vegetable.* The liquid should be either cooking water or canning liquid (reduced), juice, or undiluted evaporated milk. If your doctor approves, a small amount of butter, 1 teaspoon for each cup of purée, can be added to any vegetable to improve the consistency, and this is a good way to add fat to your baby's diet if he is drinking skim milk. Wherever possible, combine a thin vegetable, such as tomatoes or summer squash, with a thick one, such as potatoes or cooked dried beans. Here is where you can be most creative in selecting vegetable combinations for your baby. You can also combine vegetables with fruits. (See **Food-Combination Guide** in chapter 6.)

Very few vegetables will require thickening, but when it is necessary, use about 1 tablespoon of wheat germ or cereal to each cup of vegetable.

You will soon find the consistency that your baby prefers. It is important not to thin with water or thicken with starch.

A food processor will not prepare as fine a purée as will a high-speed blender for hard raw or lightly cooked vegetables such as carrots, but it should be smooth enough for most babies.

Since the storage times are the same for most vegetables, I have listed them here for easy reference. Any variations will be given under the specific vegetable.

REFRIGERATOR		FREEZER
Fresh	**Canned or Cooked**	**Fresh:** 8 months
Whole: 3–5 days	Whole or	Raw purée: 1 month
Purée: 1 day	purée: 4 days	Cooked purée: 1–2 months

Artichokes

Nutrition: They have fair amounts of vitamins and good amounts of minerals, especially potassium.

Introduce around seven months. They are a good finger food when they are cooked until very soft.

Buy compact, tightly closed heads that are heavy, with green, fresh leaves. Do not buy artichokes with spreading brownish leaves. Their peak season is March through May and they are easily grown in warm areas.

Store in refrigerator for 3–5 days.

Artichokes

This is a vegetable the entire family should share. The leaves are pulled off, ends dipped in lemon and butter, and eaten. When the leaves are all eaten, lift out the light-colored cone of leaves and the fuzzy center. Now it's the baby's turn. Just mash the remaining heart with milk or the lemon-butter sauce.

1 artichoke per person

1. Wash under running water, trim ends flat.
2. Steam, tightly covered in 2 inches water, with 1 tablespoon oil and 1 tablespoon lemon juice, for 45 minutes or until tender.

Asparagus

Nutrition: Asparagus is a fair source of vitamins A and C. Babies love its mild taste and smooth texture.

Introduce cooked at seven months.

Buy: Asparagus is very expensive unless it is in season— April and June. Buy rich green spears with closed, compact tips.

Do not buy spears that are ribbed with up-and-down

ridges or tips that are open, spread out, or decayed. These
are all signs of aging, which means toughness and poor
flavor. Very thin or thick stalks also indicate toughness.
Avoid very sandy asparagus, since the sand can lodge in the
tips and is very difficult to remove. Frozen and canned
asparagus are available; the latter may have stannous chloride
added as a color preservative.

Store asparagus in a plastic bag, in the coldest part of
the refrigerator, for up to 2 days.

Finger Food: A steamed stalk of asparagus is tender and
easy to handle.

Asparagus

1 pound asparagus

1. Prepare asparagus by breaking off each stalk as far
down as the green. Remove scales with a knife and scrub
in water to remove the sand.

2. Steam for 12–18 minutes or bake for 20 minutes in
dish or foil, at 325°F.

3. You will make the smoothest purée by removing the
fibers with a strainer or food mill. A blender or processor
gives a slightly coarser consistency.

4. The purée should not require thinning or thickening.

YIELD: 1½ cups purée or 8 food cubes.

Beans, Green and Wax

Nutrition: Both varieties are equally high in vitamin A
and calcium.

Introduce cooked at six months.

Buy young, tender beans with firm and crisp pods.
Avoid wilted, flabby pods, serious blemishes, decay, or
thick pods, which indicate overmaturity.

Store covered in refrigerator for 3–5 days.

Finger Food: A whole steamed bean is tender and easy
to handle.

Green/Wax Beans

1 pound beans

1. Wash beans and remove ends and strings, if any.
2. Steam 20–30 minutes or bake in dish or foil for 30 minutes, at 325°F.
3. Purée with any equipment. Beans should require little or no thinning.

$ Beans, Lima

Nutrition: Incomplete proteins, B vitamins, carbohydrates.

Introduce cooked at eight months.

Buy well filled, clean, shiny, dark-green pods. Hard or discolored skin indicates overmaturity. Canned baby limas of grades A and B are the most tender and least starchy.

Store in pods in refrigerator 1–2 days.

Lima Beans

1 pound lima beans
½ cup liquid

1. Snap open pods and remove beans. Or cut off a strip from the inner edge of the pod and push out the beans.
2. Boil lima beans, not pods, for 20–30 minutes or steam beans for 25–35 minutes.
3. Purée with strainer or food mill to remove skin for the smoothest purée. A blender or processor will result in a coarser texture.
4. Thin with about ½ cup of cooking liquid, juice, or milk.

YIELD: 1½ cups purée or 12 food cubes.

Beets

Nutrition: Fair amounts of most vitamins and minerals, good carbohydrates in sugar. The green tops are highly nutritious. (See *Greens*.)

Introduce cooked at eight months, raw at nine months. Beets will cause bowel movements and urine to have a red color, and this is harmless.

Buy beets that are firm and round, with a rich red color and fairly smooth surface. Badly wilted or decayed tops may indicate long storage, but the roots are still usable if they are firm.

Do not buy long or large beets with round, scaly areas around the top; these are signs of toughness, fibers, and a strong flavor. Wilted and flabby beets have been too long in storage and are not fresh.

Canned and frozen beets are also available. They are called *Harvard* beets when they are packed in a thick, sweet vinegar sauce, and these should not be used.

Store beets, after removing root tips and most of the green tops, in the refrigerator, covered, for 1–2 weeks.

Cooked Beets

1 pound beets (4–6)

1. Wash beets, do not peel. Leave 1 inch of stem.
2. Boil for 35–60 minutes or steam for 40–65 minutes or bake for 40–60 minutes, at 325°F. (The older and larger the beet, the longer the cooking time.)
3. Rub off the skins and remove the stems from the beets.
4. Purée with any equipment.

YIELD: 1¾ cups purée or 8 cubes.

VARIATION

Purée equal amounts of beets and pineapple.

Raw Beets

2 medium beets
½ teaspoon vegetable oil (corn, safflower)
1 teaspoon lemon or orange juice

1. Wash beets and remove a thin paring.
2. Grate or purée in a blender or processor, adding juice and oil to improve the consistency.

YIELD: ½ cup or 3 food cubes.

$ Broccoli

Nutrition: Excellent source of vitamins A and C. Good source of calcium and potassium. The leaves contain the highest amounts of nutrients and should be cooked with the broccoli or saved and used as *greens*. It is one of the most valuable vegetables.

Introduce cooked only at seven months. Some babies may react with gas to broccoli. If so, postpone it for another month and try again in small amounts. If your baby has this reaction to broccoli, also postpone the introduction of the leafy green vegetables.

Buy broccoli that has a firm, compact cluster of the small dark-green flower buds. None should have opened enough to show the yellow flower. The stems should be thin and free of decay.

Do not buy broccoli with spread bud clusters, yellowish-green color, or wilted. These are all signs of overmaturity and too-long storage. Avoid thick stems since these will be tough. Soft, water-soaked spots on the bud clusters are signs of decay.

Frozen broccoli is available in several styles. The chopped variety is nutritious and more economical for use in baby food.

Store broccoli covered, in the coldest part of the refrigerator for up to two days.

Finger Food: The small bud clusters of cooked broccoli are tender and easy to handle.

Broccoli

1 pound fresh or 10-ounce package frozen broccoli
⅓ cup liquid (evaporated milk is good)

1. Cut off lower end of stalk. Do not remove leaves. Wash well. Slit the stalks if they are thick.
2. Steam 10 minutes. Remove cover for first few minutes for a milder flavor or bake for 20 minutes in dish or foil, at 325°F.
3. Purée with strainer or food mill for the smoothest texture. Add liquid. A good blender or processor will also produce a smooth purée. Add liquid while blending.

YIELD: 1½ cups or 8 food cubes.

Brussels Sprouts

Nutrition: Brussels sprouts have a fair amount of vitamin C and potassium.

Introduce cooked only, at nine months. This vegetable is part of the cabbage family (they look like very small cabbages) and may cause gas.

Buy: They are in good supply from October through December. Look for a bright-green color with tight outer leaves.

Do not buy sprouts with yellow or yellowish-green leaves, or those which are loose, soft, or wilted. These are signs of overmaturity and too-long storage. Small holes or ragged leaves indicate worm injury.

Store, covered, in the coldest part of the refrigerator for 2 days.

Finger Food: Whole small sprouts are an interesting food.

Brussels Sprouts

1 pound fresh or 10-ounce package frozen Brussels sprouts

¼ cup liquid (evaporated milk is good; it dilutes the taste)

1. Wash and remove any damaged leaves.
2. Steam for 10–12 minutes or bake for 15 minutes in covered dish or foil, at 325°F.
3. Cool and purée with any equipment, adding liquid.
YIELD: 2 cups or 10 cubes.

Cabbage

Nutrition: Cabbage, both red and green varieties, is a fair source of vitamin C, and is high in vitamin K.

Introduce cooked only at nine months. Cabbage contains a high amount of roughage and may produce gas. If your baby has had reactions to broccoli or green leafy vegetables, he may also have a reaction to cabbage.

Buy firm, hard heads of cabbage that are heavy for their size. The outer leaves should be a good red or green and without serious blemishes.

Do not buy new cabbage with wilted or decayed or yellow outer leaves. Worm-eaten outer leaves often indicate that the worm injury extends into the rest of the cabbage. If the leaves on cabbage are discolored, dried, or decayed, or the stems of the leaves are separated from the base, the cabbage is overaged.

Canned cabbage is usually pickled and not suitable for a baby.

Store cabbage covered, in the refrigerator, for up to 2 weeks.

Cabbage

1 pound cabbage

1. Remove any wilted leaves and wash.
2. Steam cabbage for 15 minutes. Remove cover for first few minutes for a milder flavor.
3. Purée with any equipment.
YIELD: 2 cups or 10 food cubes.

VARIATION

Lemon Cabbage. Add 1 tablespoon lemon juice.

Carrot/Cabbage

The flavor of carrots sweetens the cabbage taste.

½ pound carrots
½ pound cabbage
2 tablespoons evaporated milk (undiluted)

1. Scrub carrots. (Do not peel.)
2. Steam whole carrots 15 minutes. Add cabbage and steam another 15 minutes.
3. Purée, adding evaporated milk.
YIELD: 2 cups or 10 food cubes.

Carrots

Nutrition: Carrots are a highly nutritious vegetable, high in vitamin A, carbohydrates, and potassium. They are a fair source of vitamin C.

Introduce cooked at six months, raw at eight months. Cooked carrots actually supply more carotene, which the body turns into vitamin A. They are easily digestible and babies love the flavor. Carrot purée may be useful in the treatment of diarrhea.

Buy carrots which are smooth, well colored, and crisp. The smaller the carrot, the more tender and milder flavored. However, the deeper the color, the more vitamin A.

Canned baby carrots are especially tender.

Do not buy carrots with large green areas at the top, since the trimming will be wasteful. Also avoid carrots which are flabby or wilted or show spots of decay. These have been in storage too long and have lost much of their nutritional value.

Store carrots, covered, in the refrigerator for one week. Remove root tips and tops before storing.

Cooked Carrots

1 pound carrots (4–5)
¼ cup liquid (milk, orange juice)

1. Prepare carrots by scrubbing well with a brush.
2. Steam whole for 20–30 minutes (you can shorten the time by slicing the carrots) or bake in covered dish or foil for 35 minutes at 325°F.
3. Cool and rub off skin if preparing for a young baby or when first introducing. Otherwise the skin can be puréed with a blender or processor.
4. Purée, adding liquid, with any equipment. A strainer or food mill will also remove the skin.

Raw Carrots

Introduce raw carrot in small amounts by mixing it with a fruit. (See Raw Apple/Carrot Purée.)

Cauliflower

Nutrition: Cauliflower is a good source of vitamin K.
Introduce cooked only at nine months. It may cause gas. If so, wait a month or two, then offer again.

Buy cauliflower heads that are white, compact with clean tops or curd. It is in season from September through January. *Frozen* grade B cauliflower may look slightly gray or brown, but it is usable.

Do not buy heads where the curd is spread, shows severe wilting or discolored spots. These are signs of aging or overmaturity. Also avoid curd with a smudgy or speckled appearance, which are signs of insect injury, mold growth, or decay.

Store cauliflower, covered, in the refrigerator for 3–5 days.

Finger Food: Small cooked flowerets are easy to handle.

Cauliflower

1 pound fresh or 10-ounce package frozen cauliflower
⅓ cup liquid (milk or cooking water)

1. Remove any spots on head, base, or stem. Wash thoroughly and cut in chunks.
2. Steam for 10–18 minutes. Remove cover for first few minutes for a milder flavor, or bake in covered dish or foil for 20 minutes, at 325°F.
3. Purée, adding liquid, in strainer, food mill, processor, or blender.

YIELD: 1½ cups or 8–10 food cubes.

VARIATION

A small amount of grated cheese will add a good flavor.

Celery

Nutrition: Celery is a good source of sodium and cellulose. It contains a large amount of liquid and is a good vegetable to mix with a more solid one such as carrots or peas.

Introduce cooked at seven months, raw at nine months. Cold, raw celery stalks are an excellent teething food.

Buy celery that is fresh and crisp. The surface should be shiny with light or medium green color. Good celery is available year round.

Do not buy wilted celery with flabby upper branches or leaf stems. These are signs of overlong storage, toughness, and lower nutritional value. Also avoid celery with hollow or discolored centers in the branches. A sign of this internal discoloration is gray or brown on the inside surface of the large branches. In general, the larger the stalks, the less tender.

Store celery, covered, in the refrigerator for 3–5 days.

Cooked Celery

1 pound celery

1. Remove any leaves and trim the roots. Separate the stalks and wash well. Scrape off any discolorations. If a blender or processor is used, remove the strings from the large outer stalks or cut in short pieces; otherwise the strings may tangle in the blades.
2. Steam 30–35 minutes or bake in covered dish or foil for 35 minutes, at 325°F.
3. Purée with food mill or strainer for the smoothest purée, since the strings will be removed. A blender can also be used.

YIELD: 2 cups purée or 10 food cubes.

VARIATION

Celery/Carrots: Use ½ pound carrots, ½ pound celery.
Celery/Peas: Use ¾ pound celery, ⅓ cup peas.

Corn

Nutrition: Corn is a good source of carbohydrates and phosphorus. Yellow corn is better than white corn.

Introduce cooked only, at seven months.

Buy fresh corn in season during May through September. Look for fresh husks with good green color, silk ends without decay or worm injury, and stem ends that are not too discolored or dried. The small kernels are usually the most tender and juicy.

Do not buy husks that are yellowed, wilted, or dried, or corn with stems that are discolored or dried out. These are signs of too-long storage. Corn with very large kernels or of dark-yellow color is overmature and will be starchy and tough.

Frozen whole corn and kernels are available and are useful for baby food if good fresh corn is out of season.

Canned corn is available in several styles. The creamed corn is packed in a thick, creamy sauce made from corn, salt, sugar, water, and often starch. Here you are paying for preparation and ingredients that are not necessary or desirable in baby food. Only use this style when nothing else is available.

Corn is also canned in a clear liquid or in a vacuum pack with little or no liquid. The latter is usually the more tender. Only grade A canned corn should be used in purée-ing, since it is the sweetest, most tender, and juicy.

Canned corn does not require cooking, but if you are puréeing the hulls, it will be more tender if you simmer it for a while. Use a food mill to prepare a smooth purée and remove hulls.

Store fresh corn in the husks, uncovered, in the refrigerator for 1–2 days.

Finger Food: Cook corn, then, with a sharp knife, cut off only the tops or slice down the middle of each row of the kernels. Your baby will love holding the cob and sucking the corn from the kernels.

Corn

4 ears fresh corn or 10-ounce package frozen
3 tablespoons milk

1. Remove husk, all silk, and any bad spots.
2. Steam corn 10 minutes or boil for 7–10 minutes.

3. Cool and, with a sharp knife, cut the kernels off as close as possible to the cob.

4. You will prepare the *smoothest* purée by using a strainer or food mill to remove the hulls of the kernels. A high-speed blender or processor will also prepare a purée that most babies can digest.

YIELD: 1½ cups or 8 food cubes.

Cucumbers

Nutrition: Cucumbers contain only fair amounts of vitamins and minerals. However, they have a high liquid content and can be puréed with other vegetables as a thinner.

Introduce raw only at nine months.

Buy firm cucumbers with good green color and fairly thin.

Do not buy cucumbers that are overgrown, large in diameter, with dull color, or turning yellowish. Other signs of toughness and bitter flavor are withered or shriveled ends.

Store cucumbers, washed and covered or in crisper, in the refrigerator for 3–5 days.

Cucumbers

¼ medium cucumber

1. Peel. Cut in half lengthwise and scoop out the seeds with a spoon.
2. Purée only in a blender.

YIELD: ¼ cup or 1 food cube.

Note: Cucumber does not store or freeze well. It is best combined with another vegetable for a single serving.

Eggplant

Nutrition: Eggplant has only fair amounts of nutrients.

Introduce cooked only at nine months.

Buy firm, heavy eggplants with smooth, dark-purple skin.

Do not buy those which are poorly colored, soft, shriveled, or show decay with soft, dark-brown spots.

Store at cool room temperature (60°F.) for 2–3 weeks. At room temperature, only one week. Do not store in refrigerator.

Eggplant

  1 medium eggplant

1. Wash, do not peel.
2. Steam for 10–15 minutes or bake for 15–25 minutes, at 325°F.
3. Purée with any equipment.
YIELD: 2 cups or 10 food cubes.

$ Greens

Nutrition: The various leafy green vegetables are some of the best sources of all the vitamins and minerals, especially iron. They are also very inexpensive and easy to prepare as baby food. The various greens include:

Spinach—potassium, vitamin A, magnesium
Kale—vitamins A, C, magnesium
Collards—vitamins A, C, and riboflavin, niacin
Turnip greens—vitamins A, C, iron, B-complex
Beet greens—vitamin A, iron, magnesium
Chard—iron, magnesium, potassium, sodium, vitamin A
Mustard greens—high iron, potassium, vitamin A, B-complex
Broccoli leaves—vitamins A, C, potassium
Dandelion greens—high iron, potassium, vitamins A, B-complex
Parsley—vitamins A, C
Watercress—vitamins A, C

Introduce cooked at eight months, raw at nine months. If your baby has reactions of gas or rashes to any of these greens, postpone them a month. It is important to keep trying, since they are so nutritious. Parsley, watercress, and dandelion greens have a strong flavor, so introduce them in very small quantities, mixed with eggs, white sauce, or a favorite vegetable.

When your baby reaches the trying stage of eating paper, give him some large pieces of raw leafy greens, such as spinach or lettuce, to chew on. He may not actually eat any, but at least they are better than paper.

Buy greens that are fresh, young, tender, free from blemishes, with a good green color. Beet greens and some chard will have a reddish-green color. The spring months are the best time to buy young greens.

Frozen greens are also available and can save preparation and cleaning time. Use the grade A for the most tender greens.

Do not buy leaves with coarse, fibrous stems, yellow-green color, softness, or wilting. If greens show signs of insect damage, the insects may be hidden in the leaves and are very difficult to wash away.

Store greens in plastic bags in the refrigerator for 1–2 days.

Cooked Leafy Greens

1 pound fresh greens
1 tablespoon butter (optional) or yogurt
3 tablespoons milk or fruit juice

1. Wash the leaves thoroughly. Cut off any blemished areas. If the leaves have large or tough center stems, you may discard them without losing nutritional value. These stems will produce a coarser purée.
2. Steam most greens for 5–15 minutes depending on the thickness of the leaves. You may leave the cover off for the first few minutes for a milder flavor. Boil strongly flavored greens, such as dandelion, for 20 minutes in an uncovered pot.

3. Purée with blender for the smoothest texture, adding the butter and milk or juice. *Do not use cooking water*. In a processor, purée the greens without adding liquid.

YIELD: 1¾ cups or 9 food cubes.

A 10-ounce package of frozen greens will yield 1¼ cups purée; use only 2 tablespoons liquid.

VARIATION

If your baby objects to cooked greens, try introducing them in small amounts in **Vegetable Soufflé** and **Vegetable Custard**. (See also **Eggs**.)

Scrambled Raw Greens

When your baby is eating eggs, you can use them as a way of introducing raw greens. The main problem is the texture of the greens, since they tend to stick to his mouth and are difficult to swallow. Mixed with eggs, they go down quite easily. This can be a Protein/Vegetable serving.

¼ cup raw greens (cooked can also be used)
1 egg
1 tablespoon milk

1. Wash and prepare raw greens as for cooking.
2. Put egg, milk, and greens in processor or blender (the Mini-Blend jar is perfect) and purée. The mixture will be bright green.
3. Scramble the eggs to a soft consistency.

YIELD: 2 servings or ½ cup.

VARIATION

Raw chopped greens may also be added to cereal, or mixed with cooked egg yolk. Chop the greens in a blender or processor with a small amount of water. Mix in the greens and use a little liquid to thin the cereal or egg yolk.

See also: **Jellied Vegetables**
Vegetable Custard
Vegetable/Egg Yolk Custard

Kohlrabi

Nutrition: Good source of vitamin C and potassium. This is a little-used vegetable that is part of the cabbage family, although the edible portion looks like a turnip. The tops may also be used as greens.

Introduce cooked at nine months.

Buy small or medium-size roots with smooth surfaces and fresh tops.

Do not buy large vegetables, since they will be more fibrous and tough or those with blemishes or cracks.

Store kohlrabi, covered, in the refrigerator for up to 1 week.

Kohlrabi

1 pound kohlrabi
3 tablespoons liquid (evaporated milk is good)

1. Wash and remove skin. Cut into large pieces.
2. Steam for 30–40 minutes or bake in covered dish or foil for 1 hour, at 325°F.
3. Purée with any equipment, adding liquid.
YIELD: 1½ cups or 8 food cubes.

$ Legumes: Dried Peas, Beans, Lentils

Nutrition: The legumes (dried peas, beans, and lentils) are very economical sources of protein (incomplete), and contain high amounts of iron, phosphorus, calcium, magnesium, potassium, and the B-complex vitamins. They are also low in fat. Soybeans are a source of complete protein and are included in the "Protein Foods" chapter.

The various legumes include: *peas* (green, split, black-eyed, cow, and yellow); *beans* (navy, kidney, pinto, lima); *lentils*.

They are similar in nutrition and can be substituted for a serving of cereal grains. Cooked peas and beans are very thick and are good to combine with juicy fruits and vegetables. They can also be thinned with milk, to supplement their incomplete protein, or combined with a small amount of complementary or complete protein foods and served as a low-cost meat substitute. See **Inexpensive Protein** in chapter 10 for specific recipes and combinations. Another means of supplementing their protein is to soak these dried legumes in skim milk instead of water, then cook them slowly in the milk. As you can see, they are a very good buy in terms of their nutritional cost.

Introduce cooked at eight months. They can be served as a finger food if cooked until very soft.

Buy: *Dried* peas, beans, and lentils keep well and can be bought in large quantities. *Canned cooked* beans are also available in different varieties—baked beans, limas, or kidney beans—often with sauces. This is the most convenient way of using these beans since they require little, if any, cooking but they are much more expensive than preparing your own. For an older baby, they can be mashed directly from the can. Remember to read the labels—if they are packed in a salt brine, *drain the beans and do not use the liquid*. U.S. grade B canned beans are adequate and economical.

Store dried peas, beans, and lentils in tightly covered cans or plastic bags at cool room temperature for up to 2 years. Cooked purées will keep in the refrigerator for 3 days and can be frozen for 1 month.

Cooking: You may feel that dried peas, beans, and lentils require lengthy cooking time. They do, but little of your time and effort is involved. A timesaver is to cook a large quantity, then freeze them. If you have a good blender, you can also shorten the cooking time in half by first grating the dried legumes.

The packaged soup mixes of dried peas, beans, noodles, and vegetables are convenient and require a shorter cooking time. Remember to omit the seasoning packet and reduce the amount of cooking water to about half of that stated on the package; you are not preparing soup.

Cooking Times

30 minutes: split peas, lentils, black-eyed beans, or peas

1 hour: whole peas, lima beans

1½ hours: navy pea beans, Great Northern beans, garbanzos (chick peas)

2 hours: black beans, cranberry beans, kidney beans, pinto beans

$ Pea/Bean/Lentil Purée

1 cup any legume
3 cups water or skim milk
1 tablespoon butter or oil
¾ cup milk

1. Rinse legumes briefly. Soak in water or milk overnight. Or you may bring them to a boil for 2 minutes, cover, and allow them to sit for 2 hours. (This cooking is unnecessary if you are using a pressure cooker.)

2. Add the butter or oil to prevent foaming over.

3. Simmer with the cover partly ajar to prevent foaming over. (See **Cooking Times,** above.)

4. When cooking some beans, the skins will float to the top. You should skim these off for the smoothest purée.

5. Purée with any equipment, adding ¾ cup milk.

Note: If you are cooking beans or peas for the rest of your family, do not add salt until the last few minutes of the cooking. If it is added at the start of the cooking, the beans will take much longer to soften. For the same reason, do not add acid foods, such as tomatoes, until the end of the cooking time.

YIELD: 2½ cups or 12 food cubes.

Lettuce

Nutrition: The dark-green leafy lettuce has fair amounts of vitamin A and iron. The iceberg variety has very little nutritional value.

Introduce cooked at seven months, raw at nine months. As with the other green leafy vegetables, lettuce can be used as a substitute when your baby shows a desire for chewing paper.

Buy romaine or leaf lettuce, which is dark green and crisp. *Do not buy* lettuce with considerable discoloration or decay of the outer leaves. Avoid wilted lettuce, which is a sign of overlong storage and lower nutritional value.

Store lettuce in plastic bag, in refrigerator, for 1–2 days.

Use lettuce raw or cooked as a green leafy vegetable. (See **Greens.**)

Mushrooms

Nutrition: Mushrooms are very high in niacin and have fair amounts of other vitamins and minerals. They have a high liquid content and are good in combinations with other vegetables or meats.

Introduce cooked only at nine months.

Buy young mushrooms that are small to medium. The caps should be either closed around the stem or slightly open with pink or light-tan gills. The surface of the cap should be white, creamy, or light brown depending on the variety.

Canned mushrooms are available, with the "stems and pieces" style less expensive.

Do not buy mushrooms with wide-open caps, dark gills, or pitted and discolored caps. These are all signs of overripeness and decay.

Store in plastic bag, in the refrigerator, for 1–2 days. They are very perishable, often expensive, but freeze well. So if you come across a sale, prepare a purée and freeze at once.

Finger Food: This is one of the few vegetables that are *not* a good finger food. The small pieces tend to be tough but slippery. This encourages the baby to swallow the pieces whole, and they are not digested.

Mushrooms

    1 pound fresh mushrooms
    2 tablespoons wheat germ, rice, or instant cereal

1. Prepare mushrooms by washing thoroughly. Leave the stems, but cut off tough ends.
2. Steam the caps and stems in the top of a double boiler for 5–10 minutes (do not use a steamer, or you will lose the juice), or sauté in a little butter or oil for 5–10 minutes, or bake in covered dish or foil for 15 minutes, at 325°F.
3. Purée mushrooms and juice with blender or processor for the smoothest texture. Add thickener. A food mill may also be used, then add the liquid and thickener.

YIELD: 2½ cups or 12 food cubes.

Okra

Nutrition: Okra has only fair amounts of vitamins and minerals.

Introduce cooked only at eight months.

Buy: Fresh okra is the immature seed pod of the okra plant and should be small, no more than 4 inches long. On tender pods, the tips will bend with a slight pressure. They should have a bright green color and be free from blemishes. Frozen okra can also be used.

Canned okra is usually pickled and salted and is not suitable for a baby.

Do not buy fibrous pods with stiff tips, hard bodies, or pale, faded green color.

Store fresh okra, covered, in the refrigerator for 3–5 days.

Okra

1 pound okra

1. Wash and scrub the pods thoroughly. Cut off the stem end. If the pods are large, cut them in half. Do not peel.
2. Steam okra for 15–20 minutes or just until tender (when okra is overcooked, it will become gummy), or bake in covered dish or foil for 30 minutes, at 325°F.
3. Purée with any equipment.

VARIATION

Okra produces a thin purée, so it is good combined with vegetables such as carrots, or in stews.

Onions, Leeks

Nutrition: Onions and leeks contain fair amounts of many nutrients. They have a high liquid content and are good to combine with less juicy vegetables or stews.

Introduce cooked only at nine months. If you want to purée a family dish which contains a small amount of onions for flavoring and the other ingredients have been introduced, you can try it as early as seven or eight months.

Buy onions that are firm and dry. They should be fairly free of green sunburn spots or blemishes. Bermuda and Spanish onions are the sweetest and mildest flavored. Leeks should have crisp green tops.

Canned onions are usually packed in a salt brine, and should not be used.

Do not buy vegetables that are wet, with soft spots or necks. These are either immature or decayed inside. Also avoid onions with thick, hollow, woody centers in the neck, or with fresh sprouts.

Store onions at cool room temperature for 2–3 months.

They should either be spread out or piled in open mesh containers.

Moisture or high temperature will cause sprouting or decay.

Onions

> 1 pound onions
> 2 tablespoons wheat germ, cooked rice, or instant cereal

1. Prepare onions under water to prevent your eyes from watering. Wash and remove outer peel and any blemishes.
2. Steam whole 30–40 minutes, sliced 10 minutes, or bake in covered dish or foil, whole for 30 minutes, sliced 10 minutes. (Overcooking will produce a strong flavor.)
3. Purée with any equipment, add thickener.

YIELD: 2 cups or 10 food cubes.

Parsnips

Nutrition: Good source of carbohydrates and potassium, fair amounts of other minerals and B vitamins.

Introduce cooked at eight months.

Buy parsnips that are small to medium size, well formed, smooth, firm, and free from major blemishes. They look like white carrots and are sweetest during late winter.

Do not buy large parsnips which will have tough, woody centers, or badly wilted or flabby ones that will be tough and fibrous.

Store parsnips, covered, in the refrigerator for up to 1 week.

Parsnips

> 1 pound parsnips
> ¼ cup liquid (evaporated milk or apple juice is good)

1. Scrub well with brush.
2. Boil whole parsnips in water to cover for 10–20 minutes, or bake 45 minutes in covered dish or foil, at 325°F.
3. Plunge in cold water and rub off skins.
4. Purée with any equipment, adding liquid.

YIELD: 2 cups purée or 10 food cubes.

VARIATION

Baked Apple/Parsnips. Prepare ½ pound parsnips; combine and bake with 1 cup chopped raw apples or applesauce.

$ Peanuts, Other Nuts

Nutrition: Peanuts and other nuts are excellent sources of protein (incomplete), fat, linoleic acid (essential fatty acid), magnesium, phosphorus, niacin, folacin, and vitamin E. They also have fair amounts of other minerals and the other B vitamins. As with legumes, the protein of nuts is improved when it is combined at the same meal with an animal protein. Milk is the most practical source and can be used as a thinner in preparing the nut butter.

Introduce at eight to nine months. Although peanut butter is a nutritious staple for many toddlers, I thought twice about giving it to my baby. Properly thinned, she loved it!

Buy: There are many commercial peanut butters on the market, so read the labels carefully to find one with no additives, sugar, or salt. It is amazing what can be added to such a simple food—mono- and diglycerides, hydrogenated vegetable oil, dextrose, sugar, and salt. Avoid the peanut "spreads," which contain a lower amount of peanuts. All the commercial peanut butters will require thinning with milk or they will never get past the roof of your baby's mouth. The consistency is probably the major reason we never think of feeding peanut butter to babies.

If you live near a health-food store, you will be able to buy raw unsalted nut butters that require little, if any, thinning; however, they are quite expensive. You will find

it most nutritious and economical to make your own peanut butter with raw or roasted peanuts. You must use a
good blender, and the Mini-Blend jar is ideal. A food
processor is even easier and faster. You can make a family-
size amount with a very smooth texture. Your baby will
prefer both the consistency and the taste of homemade
peanut butter.

Do not buy nuts that are preserved with BHT, or are
"dry roasted."

Store unopened commercial peanut butter for 9 months
at cool room temperature; opened peanut butter for up to
6 months in the refrigerator. Homemade peanut butters
do not have preservatives and will not keep as long. These
may be kept for 2 months in the refrigerator. If you thin
with milk, only store for 1–2 weeks. Whole peanuts should
be kept in a tightly covered can, in the refrigerator, for up
to four months. These butters may also be frozen for 4–6
months.

Peanut/Nut Butters

1 cup peanuts or other nuts (raw or roasted)
2–3 tablespoons milk or safflower, corn, or olive
oil

1. If you must use roasted salted peanuts, rinse them to
remove the salt.
2. Purée the milk or oil and the peanuts in the blender
at a medium speed. If you do not use a Mini-Blend
jar, you must stop and push the mixture down as it blends.
In a processor, finely chop nuts, then add liquid as
necessary.

YIELD: ¾ cup.

VARIATION

Peanut Butter Custard
Peanut Butter Cookies
Peanut Butter Clay

$ Peas

Nutrition: Peas supply good amounts of iron, B vitamins, especially niacin, and carbohydrates.

Introduce cooked peas at six months.

Buy pea pods that are crisp, green, and unspotted, with a velvety surface, and well filled with peas.

Do not buy pods which are swollen, light in color, or spotted with gray. These will contain tough and poorly flavored peas. Immature peas will have dark green, or wilted flat pods. Wilting or flabbiness is also a sign of overlong storage.

Canned and *frozen* peas are available in several sizes and grades. *Grade A* or *fancy* peas will have the tenderest skins and sweetest taste. These will produce the smoothest purée. *Grade B* or *extra standard* peas will be more mealy, but have a good flavor. *Grade C* should not be used for baby food. Canned peas that have been graded for size will be more expensive; but the smaller the peas, the more tender they will be. Tenderness is important since peas are one of the first vegetables introduced.

Store fresh pea pods, covered, in refrigerator for 1–2 days. Like corn, peas will lose sweetness and tenderness as they are stored. Remove from pods just before using.

Peas

2 **pounds peas (in pods)**
3–4 **tablespoons liquid (milk or cooking water)**

1. Just before cooking, shell peas.
2. Steam 10–20 minutes.
3. For the smoothest purée, use food mill or strainer, which will also remove the skins. Add liquid. A blender or processor will prepare a coarser purée.

Peppers

Nutrition: Peppers are very high in vitamin C and are fair in other vitamins and minerals. They have a high liquid content and are good combined with a thicker vegetable, or in stews.

Introduce cooked at eight months, raw at ten months.

Buy either green or red sweet peppers that are shiny and heavyweight, and have firm walls or sides.

Do not buy those that have thin walls, are lightweight, and are wilted or flabby. (The vitamin C will have been reduced due to overlong or improper storage.) Also avoid peppers with soft watery spots which are signs of decay.

Store peppers, washed and covered, in the refrigerator for 3–5 days.

Cooked Peppers

They have a high juice content and are good combined with thick vegetables such as potatoes, or in stew. Allow about 10 minutes of cooking when combining with other recipes. Use only the outer shell.

Raw Pepper

Since the main value of peppers is vitamin C, and this vitamin is destroyed by heat, peppers should be used raw.

1. Prepare by removing stem, seeds, and membranes.
2. Purée in blender or processor in equal amounts with other raw, hard vegetables such as carrots.

Potatoes, White

Nutrition: High carbohydrates and potassium, good source of vitamin C if cooked in skins.

Introduce cooked at seven months.

Buy a variety of potatoes, depending on your cooking method. The *new* potatoes are good for boiling and should not be baked. They are available in late winter and early spring. They should be well shaped, firm, and without green sunburn discoloration. Some amount of skinned surface is normal. *General-purpose* potatoes are better for boiling but can be baked. *Baking* potatoes are used for baking in the skin. These types of potatoes are available year round and should be firm, well shaped, free from blemishes, sunburn, and decay spots.

Do not buy potatoes with large cuts or bruises which must be cut away or those with green sunburn spots. Sprouted and shriveled potatoes have been kept too long in storage and they are lower in nutritional value.

Canned and frozen potatoes are available in many styles. Avoid those canned styles that are packed in a salt brine. Dehydrated or "instant" potatoes can be used as an instant food, but they have large amounts of additives and should not be served often.

They are a very thick, bland vegetable and are good in combination with leafy greens.

Store potatoes, unwashed, in a dark dry place with good ventilation and a temperature of 45°–50°F. for 2–3 months. Exposure to light will cause greening or lower eating quality. High temperatures will speed sprouting and shriveling. Potatoes stored at room temperature should be used within 1–2 weeks.

Mashed Potatoes

1 pound potatoes
½ cup liquid (milk is good)

1. Wash well and scrub with brush. Remove eyes and blemishes. Do not peel.
2. Boil in water to cover, in covered pot, for 20–40 minutes, or steam 30–45 minutes, or bake in skin or wrapped in foil for 40–60 minutes, at 400°F.
3. Rub off skin (boiled) or scoop out (baked). Purée with fork, strainer, food mill, or mixer. Add liquid and a little

butter. *Do not* mash in blender. In a processor, use shredding disk; then metal blade if necessary for a smoother purée. *Do not overprocess*.

YIELD: 2 cups purée or 10 food cubes.

VARIATION

Add a little grated cheese for flavoring.

Stewed Apples and Potatoes

> 6 medium potatoes (1½ pounds), peeled
> 1 cup milk
> 2 medium cooking apples, cored, peeled, diced

1. Cut potatoes into thin slices, or chop.
2. Place potatoes and milk in pan.
3. Bring to a boil, cover, and simmer for 20 minutes.
4. Add apples and cook for another 15 minutes. Add more milk if the mixture is very thick.
5. Purée with any equipment. It should be soft enough for even a fork or spoon.
6. To serve as a family dish, just add a little salt and pepper.

YIELD: 4 cups or 20 food cubes.

Squash, Summer

Nutrition: High in potassium, good amounts of vitamins A and C, and niacin.

Introduce cooked only at seven months. This is a juicy vegetable, so it is good combined with more solid vegetables or in stews.

Buy any of the varieties—yellow are *crookneck, straight neck*, greenish-white *patty pan*, or green *zucchini, Italian marrow*. Look for squashes that are well developed, firm, with glossy skin.

Do not buy overmature or aged squashes which have

dull skins and a hard surface. These will have enlarged seeds and dry, stringy flesh.

Canned and frozen summer squash is available and useful.

Store summer squash, covered, in the refrigerator for 3–5 days.

Summer Squash

1 **pound squash**
2 **tablespoons wheat germ (optional)**
2 **teaspoons butter or oil**

1. Wash well, remove slice from both ends. For the smoothest purée, cut in half lengthwise and remove seeds.

2. Steam 15–20 minutes or bake in covered dish or foil for 25–30 minutes, at 325°F.

3. Purée with any equipment. A strainer or food mill will also remove the seeds and skin. Wheat germ may be added as a fortifier thickener. A small amount of butter may be added for flavor, if your doctor approves.

YIELD: 1½ cups purée.

$ Squash, Winter

Nutrition: The winter squashes are high in carbohydrates, potassium, and vitamin A. They also contain some iron, magnesium, and riboflavin.

Introduce cooked only at six months.

Buy any variety that is in season. *Acorn* is green and available all year. Other varieties are *butternut, Hubbard, delicious,* and *banana,* which are in season from early fall to late winter. Buy squash that has a hard, tough rind, and is heavy for its size. Variations in skin color do not affect the flavor.

Do not buy squash with cuts, sunken spots, or mold on the rind; these are signs of decay. A tender or soft rind indicates immaturity and poor eating quality.

Store winter squash at cool room temperature (around

60°F.) for several months. Keep them at room temperature for only 1–2 weeks. Do not store them in the refrigerator.

Instant Use: Canned and frozen squash is already cooked and mashed. The only preparation might be the addition of a little milk.

Winter Squash

1 **pound squash**
1 **tablespoon milk (optional)**
1 **tablespoon butter (optional)**
2 **teaspoons brown sugar or honey (optional)**

1. Wash well. Cut acorn squash in half; other varieties, cut in large pieces. Remove seeds and stringy centers. Do not remove skin.
2. Steam for 25–30 minutes or bake in moderate oven for 45–55 minutes. (Place halved squash cut side down on dish or foil; put pieces of squash in covered dish or wrap in foil to shorten the baking time.)
3. Scoop out of skin and purée with any equipment. Add milk for a thinner purée. Add butter or brown sugar for a family dish.

YIELD: 1 cup purée or 5 food cubes.

$ Sweet Potatoes, Yams

Nutrition: Sweet potatoes and yams are high in carbohydrates and vitamin A. They contain fair amounts of other vitamins and minerals.

Introduce cooked only at seven months.

Buy well-shaped, firm sweet potatoes with smooth, bright-orange skins that are free from signs of decay. Yams have white to reddish skins and are more moist when cooked. However, they are a tropical vegetable and are difficult to find fresh. Frozen yams and sweet potatoes are available in several styles, including cooked and mashed. Canned sweet potatoes should be bought in a vacuum pack without any syrup. The canned solid pack may have a small amount of liquid.

Do not buy sweet potatoes with worm holes, cuts, or any injury which penetrates the skin. These defects will increase the spoilage. Even if you cut away the decayed spot, the rest of the flesh will have a bad taste. Sweet potatoes decay easily, so look for such signs as wet, soft spots; discolored or shriveled ends; or sunken, discolored spots on the sides.

Store sweet potatoes at cool room temperature (around 60°F.) for a month or two. Keep them for only 1 week at room temperature. Never store them in the refrigerator.

Instant Use: Some styles of canned and frozen sweet potatoes are already cooked and mashed. It is only necessary to thin with milk.

Sweet Potatoes

1 pound sweet potatoes
⅓–½ cup liquid (milk, orange, or apple juice is good)
1 tablespoon butter (optional)

1. Scrub and wash potatoes. Trim roots and any bad spots. Do not peel.
2. Steam 30–35 minutes or bake for 40 minutes at 400°F. or 60 minutes at 350°F.
3. Scoop potato out of skins and mash with food mill, mixer, or strainer, adding liquid, then butter. *Do not use* blender. In a processor, use shredding disk; then metal blade for a smoother purée if necessary. *Do not overmix*.

YIELD: 1½ cups purée or 8 food cubes.

Baked Sweet Potatoes and Apples

¾ cup cooked sweet potatoes
½ pound apples or 1 cup applesauce
¼ cup liquid (milk or fruit juice)

1. Preheat oven to 350°F.
2. Remove skin and slice sweet potatoes. Prepare apples: Remove skin and core. Slice.
3. Mix sweet potatoes and apples in buttered baking dish and pour liquid over.
4. Bake covered for 30 minutes.
5. To purée, mash with fork.

YIELD: 2 cups or 10 food cubes.

Note: This is a good family dish.

Turnips, Rutabagas

Nutrition: Fair amounts of carbohydrates, vitamins, and minerals.

Introduce cooked only at eight months.

Buy turnips (white flesh) and rutabagas (yellow flesh) year round. Look for small or medium-size firm vegetables that are heavy for their size. If the tops are attached on turnips, they should be green and fresh. These greens are high in nutritional value and should be used. (See Greens.) *Do not buy* large vegetables which tend to be fibrous and tough, or those with skin punctures or signs of decay.

Frozen turnips and rutabagas are available and convenient.

Store turnips at cool room temperature (60°F.) for up to five months. Keep them only one week at room temperature.

Turnips/Rutabagas

1 pound turnips
2 tablespoons evaporated milk

1. Wash and remove skin. Cut into large pieces.
2. Steam 20–30 minutes or bake 35–45 minutes, at 350°F.
3. Purée with any equipment, adding milk. A small amount of butter may be added for flavor.

YIELD: 2 cups purée or 10 food cubes.

Tomatoes

Nutrition: Tomatoes contain good amounts of vitamins A and K. They contain about half as much vitamin C as oranges and can be used as a substitute, if your baby is allergic to orange juice. Remember to double the serving. Their high juice content makes tomatoes a good vegetable to combine with other foods as a thinner.

Introduce cooked at six months, raw at nine months.

Buy tomatoes either picked unripe or ripe; the latter will have better flavor and more nutrition. They are most plentiful from July to October. Look for tomatoes that are smooth, well formed, and reasonably free from blemishes. Marks around the top of a ripe tomato are harmless and sometimes indicate excellent flavor. Fully ripe tomatoes should yield to slight pressure and should have a rich red color. Underripe tomatoes will be hard and have a pink to light-red color.

Do not buy overripe and bruised tomatoes or those with green or yellow areas, or deep growth cracks near the stem scar. Also avoid decayed tomatoes with soft, water-soaked spots, depressed areas, or surface mold.

Store ripe tomatoes in the refrigerator for several days. Ripen tomatoes at room temperature for 3–5 days. Do not place them in the sun.

Instant Use: Both canned and raw tomatoes are good instant foods. With raw tomatoes, cut them in half, remove the seeds, and scrape out the flesh. Buy canned tomatoes that are packed without added water, salt, or preservatives. *Do not give tomato purée or paste to a baby, as these are concentrates.*

Finger Food: Small pieces of raw, peeled tomato are juicy and nutritious.

Greenish or very hard tomatoes can be kept for several weeks around 50°F.

Cooked Tomatoes

1 **pound tomatoes (4–5)**
3 **tablespoons wheat germ or instant cereal**
    or
2 **tablespoons whole wheat flour**
    or
2 **tablespoons cooked rice or cereal**

1. Wash tomatoes. If a blender or fork will be used, remove the seeds and skins. (An easy way is to dip the tomatoes briefly in boiling water, then plunge them in cold water.) However, a strainer or food mill will remove the skins and seeds. This seems the easier preparation.
2. Steam 5 minutes in a pot with a tightly fitting lid or in the top of a double boiler, or bake in a covered dish or foil for 8 minutes at 325°F. (Do not use a steamer/blancher or you will lose the juice.)
3. Purée with fork, strainer, food mill, processor, or blender, depending on your preparation, and whether you want to remove skins.
4. Add one of the thickeners. (If flour is used, heat until thickened. If rice is added, purée with the tomatoes.)
YIELD: 1½ cups or 8 food cubes.
Note: This is the only vegetable purée that can be canned in the same way as fruit. (See **Home Canning,** chapter 5.)

Raw Tomatoes

This is very economical in season and very nutritious, since all the vitamin C is preserved.

1 **pound ripe tomatoes (4–5)**
3 **tablespoons wheat germ or 2 tablespoons rice or cereal**

1. Prepare and purée as for cooked tomatoes. Omit the cooking step.

2. Do not thicken with flour. Use rice, cereal, or wheat germ. You can also freeze the purée without thickening, then use the individual cubes as a thinner for meats, etc.

3. Store in refrigerator for 2–3 days, or freeze in food cubes.

YIELD: 1½ cups or 8 food cubes.

General Vegetable Recipes

The easiest way to prepare vegetables is to serve them plain or in combinations. For variety, with strong-tasting vegetables or those with consistency problems, such as greens, you may do a little extra work and use one of the following recipes for variation. Where an egg or cereal is used, remember to increase the serving so that it counts as an all-in-one meal of vegetable, protein, and/or cereal. These recipes can be prepared for the rest of the family and used as a vegetable dish.

Good vegetables to prepare this way are: **asparagus, broccoli, carrots, cauliflower, leafy greens, mushrooms, peas, winter squash, and sweet potatoes.**

Vegetable Soufflé

   ½ **cup cooked or canned vegetable, mashed**
   ½ **cup Medium White Sauce (see Index)**
   2 **eggs, separated**
   ⅛ **teaspoon cream of tartar**

1. Preheat oven to 325°F.
2. Mix vegetables, white sauce, and egg yolks. (With a blender you can do this at the same time you are mashing the vegetables.)
3. Cool mixture if necessary.
4. Beat egg whites. Add cream of tartar. Beat until stiff.
5. Fold into vegetable mixture.
6. Bake 40 minutes in greased casserole, or individual dishes. The mixture can also be steamed in the top of a double boiler for 1½ hours.

7. Serve at once. This may be kept for 1–2 days—the texture will not be the same, but the baby probably won't know the difference.

YIELD: 3–4 servings.

Vegetable Custard

1 teaspoon butter or margarine
1 teaspoon whole-wheat or enriched flour
¼ cup hot milk
1 tablespoon nonfat dry milk
    or
⅓ cup Medium White Sauce
1 egg, beaten
½ cup mashed vegetable

1. Preheat oven to 350°F.
2. Grease 2 custard cups.
3. Melt butter, blend in flour, wheat germ, or cereal.
4. Gradually add hot milk and nonfat dry milk.
5. Stir sauce until thickened.
6. You can substitute ⅓ cup white sauce for steps 3–5.
7. Stir a small amount of hot sauce into egg, then mix egg with rest of sauce.
8. Add vegetables.
9. Pour into custard cups and place in pan of hot water that comes up to level of mixture.
10. Bake 30 minutes or until a knife comes out clean. The custard may be stored, covered, in the refrigerator for 2–3 days.

YIELD: 2–3 servings.

Easy Vegetable Custard

Follow the above recipe; however, substitute for the white sauce any of the following: ¼ cup milk, ¼ cup cooking or canning liquid plus 2 tablespoons nonfat dry milk, ¼ cup fruit juice. Skip steps 3–5.

Vegetable/Egg Yolk Custard

This is a good supper dish that counts as a serving of vegetables and egg yolk, if you double the amount given. You can make this as soon as your baby has been introduced to egg yolk, and it is also very useful if he shows an allergy to egg whites.

> ¼ cup vegetable purée (asparagus, broccoli, carrots, leafy greens, peas, and sweet potatoes are good; see specific vegetable for preparation of purées)
> 1 egg yolk, beaten
> ¼ cup milk (whole or skim)
> ½ teaspoon honey or brown sugar

1. Preheat oven to 350°F.
2. Blend together vegetable, egg yolk, milk, and honey.
3. Pour into 2 custard cups and place in pan of water.
4. Bake for 30 minutes or until a knife comes out clean. (The cups may also be placed in a pan of simmering water for 10 minutes.)
5. Refrigerate for up to 3 days.
YIELD: 2 servings.

Jellied Vegetables/Fruit

You can combine almost any food or raw grated vegetable or fruit with gelatin to improve the "swallowability" or add variety. It is an especially good way to serve leafy green vegetables, raw carrots, and raw beets, and is very easy to make with a blender.

> ½ envelope plain gelatin (the dessert gelatins can also be used, but they contain sugar and preservatives)
> ½ cup boiling water or vegetable cooking water
> ⅓ cup fruit or vegetable juice, or cold water
> 1 cup cubed fruit or vegetables
>   or
> ¾ cup puréed fruit or vegetables

1. Dissolve gelatin in hot water.
2. In blender or processor, combine cold water or juice with the vegetables until they are finely puréed. Or finely grate raw vegetables.
3. Drain the vegetables and add ⅓ cup of the liquid to the gelatin. If completely puréed, add purée at this point.
4. Chill until the mixture is very thick (about ½ hour).
5. Fold in the fruit or vegetables.
6. Pour into mold and chill until firm.
7. Cover and store in refrigerator for 4–5 days. Do not freeze.
YIELD: 1½–1¾ cups.

Medium White Sauce

This sauce can be used to improve the texture of leafy green vegetables, or in custards and soufflés.

    1½ tablespoons butter, margarine, or vegetable oil
    2 tablespoons whole-wheat or enriched flour*
    1 cup hot milk
    ⅓ cup nonfat dry milk (optional)

1. Heat oil or butter.
2. Blend in flour until smooth.
3. Gradually add hot milk and stir until blended and thickened. Add dry milk if desired.
4. Keep for 2–3 days.
YIELD: 1 cup.

Mayonnaise

You can use a small amount of mayonnaise to improve the texture or flavor of raw vegetables, the green leafy vegetables, and meat purées. It is also a way to add fat to your baby's diet if he is drinking skim milk.

---

* Instant White Sauce can be made by substituting 4 tablespoons dry infant cereal for the flour. You can mix it with oil without heating.

2 egg yolks, beaten
2 tablespoons lemon juice
1 cup oil (corn, safflower, olive)

 1. Put the egg yolks and lemon juice in a processor, blender, mixer, or bowl (use an egg beater).

2. Blend on a low speed, slowly adding the oil.

3. Cover and store in the refrigerator for up to 2 weeks.

10

Protein Foods

At least two servings of a good source of complete proteins should be included in your baby's daily diet. They also supply some vitamins and minerals, especially iron, that are lacking in milk. Included in this group are Meats (beef, lamb, veal, pork), Organ Meats (liver, kidney, brains, sweetbreads), Poultry, Fish, and Eggs. Soybeans are also a good source of high-quality protein. Some of these protein foods are less expensive than others and some are easier to prepare as baby food. However, as long as you balance your selection, you can count any of these foods as an equal serving of a protein food.

Meats:
Beef, Lamb, Veal, Pork

Nutrition: Meat is one of the essentials in your baby's diet. Veal is meat from young cattle. It is grayish pink with very little fat. Beef comes from mature cattle, lamb from young sheep, and pork from young hogs. The different meats, or cuts of meat, contain nearly the same high amount of complete protein. Meat is especially valuable as a source of iron, with beef and veal supplying the highest amounts.

Introduce: When your baby is eight months old you can introduce lean meat purées of veal, beef, and lamb. Pork and ham are usually given a month later. After meat is introduced, your baby should be eating several servings weekly.

Buy: Since meat is probably the most expensive but necessary food that you will feed your baby, it is important to know how to get the best value for your money. According to law, all meats and meat products which are shipped between states must be inspected for wholesomeness and proper labeling, and to make certain the meat has not been adulterated or contaminated. Each state must supply the same inspection service for meat sold only within that state. The inspection seal is a circle with the words: "U.S. Inspected and Passed by Department of Agriculture." Only buy meat that carries the seal. (See *U.S. Grades* in chapter 2.)

The government has also published this handy chart so that you can easily compare the serving cost of different meats and cuts of meat at various prices. Inflation keeps raising the price per pound, but you can easily adjust this table. For example, if you are considering paying $1.89 a pound for stew meat, you can find out the cost per serving by adding $.28 (at $1.39 a pound) to $.10 (at $.49 a pound). The cost per serving is now $.38 a pound.

The government also supplies a voluntary grading service which is widely used for beef. The grade shield is marked on the wholesale cut and may appear on the meat you buy or on the label. If you are not sure of the grade, ask the butcher. The main basis for the grade is the tenderness which results from liberal marbling, or fat, in the meat. *There is no difference in wholesomeness or nutrition among the grades.* You can use the less expensive grades for a considerable saving of money in buying meat for purées.

The most expensive grades are **USDA prime** and **USDA choice**; the latter is the grade sold by most supermarkets.

Cost per Serving of Red Meat and Poultry

Retail cut	Servings per pound	Price per pound											
		69	89	109	129	149	169	189	209	229	249	269	289
		Cost per serving											
BEEF:													
Sirloin Steak	2½	28	36	44	52	60	68	76	84	92	100	108	116
Porterhouse, T-bone, Rib Steak	2	35	45	55	65	75	85	95	105	115	125	135	145
Round Steak	3½	20	25	31	37	43	49	55	61	67	73	79	85
Chuck Roast, bone-in	2	35	45	55	65	75	85	95	105	115	125	135	145
Rib Roast—boneless	2½	28	36	44	52	60	68	76	84	92	100	108	116
Rib Roast—bone-in	2	35	45	55	65	75	85	95	105	115	125	135	145
Rump, Sirloin Roast	3	23	30	36	43	50	56	63	70	76	83	90	96
Ground Beef	4	17	22	27	32	37	42	47	52	57	62	67	72
Short Ribs	2	35	45	55	65	75	85	95	105	115	125	135	145
Heart, Liver, Kidney	5	14	18	22	26	30	34	38	42	46	50	54	58
Frankfurters	4	17	22	27	32	37	42	47	52	57	62	67	72
Stew Meat, boneless	5	14	18	22	26	30	34	38	42	46	50	54	58
LAMB:													
Loin, Rib, Shoulder Chops	3	23	30	36	43	50	56	63	70	76	83	90	96
Breast, Shank	2	35	45	55	65	75	85	95	105	115	125	135	145
Shoulder Roast	2½	28	36	44	52	60	68	76	84	92	100	108	116
Leg of Lamb	3	23	30	36	43	50	56	63	70	76	83	90	96

PORK—FRESH:

Center Cut or Rib Chops	4	17	22	27	32	37	42	47	52	57	62	67	72
Loin or Rib Roast	2½	28	36	44	52	60	68	76	84	92	100	108	116
Boston butt—bone-in	3	23	30	36	43	50	56	63	70	76	83	90	96
Blade Steak	3	23	30	36	43	50	56	63	70	76	83	90	96
Spare Ribs	1⅓	52	67	82	97	112	127	142	157	172	187	202	217

PORK—CURED:

Picnic—bone-in	2	35	45	55	65	75	85	95	105	115	125	135	145
Ham—fully cooked:													
bone-in	3½	20	25	31	37	43	49	55	61	67	73	79	85
boneless and canned	5	14	18	22	26	30	34	38	42	46	50	54	58
shankless	4¼	16	21	26	30	35	40	44	49	54	58	63	68
center slice	5	14	18	22	26	30	34	38	42	46	50	54	58

POULTRY:

Broiler, ready-to-cook	1⅓	52	67	82	97	112	127	142	157	172	187	202	217
legs, thighs	3	23	30	36	43	50	56	63	70	76	83	90	96
breasts	4	17	22	25	32	37	42	47	52	57	62	67	72
Turkey, ready-to-cook:													
under 12 lbs.	1	69	89	109	129	149	169	189	209	229	249	269	289
12 lbs. and over	1⅓	52	67	82	97	112	127	142	157	172	187	202	217

The next grades are **USDA good,** which has even less fat, and **USDA standard** with the least amount of fat. These two lower grades will cost less and contain more lean meat. What an opportunity for a bargain! After the meat is braised and puréed your baby will never know how tender the original piece of meat was.

You can also save money in your choice of the cut of meat that you use. The boneless chuck roasts, the various round roasts, and stewing meat are easy to prepare and are very tender when braised. You should look for the cuts with the least amount of fat and take advantage of sales. Remember that stewing chuck meat has at least the same amount of protein, possibly even more, than prime sirloin steak.

Ground meat, if you do not have a blender, is easier to purée with a food mill. Select a lean piece of boneless meat—beef, veal, or lamb—and ask the butcher to grind it. Even if the whole cut is more expensive than the packaged preground meat, you will still get more value for your money, since ground meat can legally contain as much as 30 per cent fat. If you must buy preground meat, make sure it is bright red, and is as lean as possible. Dark-red or brownish-red meat is not fresh.

Another type of meat that is easy to purée without a blender is the **precooked meat** that is sold sliced in many delicatessens. **Roast beef** and **baked or boiled ham** are usually available. These meats are quite expensive, but they can be puréed with a grater or food mill—quite handy when you are short of time or are traveling. They also make good finger foods since the thin slices are very tender. The ham, because of its high salt content, should not be served too frequently.

Do not give your baby the **precooked luncheon meats.** They contain salt, additives, and fillers, and are also expensive in terms of nutritional cost.

Frankfurters will be discussed in the chapter on **Finger Foods.**

Bacon, a salted meat which contains a high percentage of saturated fat, is very expensive for a small amount of protein and should not be counted as a serving of protein.

The meat purées that you make at home will be much

less expensive than the commercial purées. However, the major advantage in making your own purées is that you know exactly what you are feeding your baby.

Store: Since meat is expensive, you should store it properly. *Uncooked* meat should be stored in the coldest part of the refrigerator. Meat can be kept in the store wrapper for 1–2 days; just put a couple of holes in it for the air to circulate. If the surface of the meat is dry, the bacteria will grow less quickly. Large cuts of meat can be wrapped loosely and stored up to five days. However, ground meat spoils quickly and should be used within 1–2 days. Cured or smoked meats can be kept for one week. Uncooked meat can easily be frozen if it is wrapped properly. Remove any excess fat and wrap the meat tightly in plastic or foil freezer wrap. Label and date the packages if you plan to freeze them for a long period. Freeze the meat quickly, at 0°F. or lower. Here are suggested times for different meats and cuts.

Lamb, beef (roasts and steaks): 12 months
Veal, pork (roasts): 8 months
Veal, lamb, pork (chops or cutlets): 4 months
Cured or smoked meats (such as ham): 2 months
Ground and stew meat of any kind: 3 months

Meat should be thawed in its wrappings, in the refrigerator, before cooking. Meat may also be cooked frozen; allow twice as much cooking time.

Cooked meats should be covered, refrigerated promptly, and can be kept in the refrigerator for 2–3 days. Cooked purées can be frozen up to 2–4 months without losing quality. (See chapter 5.)

Meat Purée

You can use any meat that you have cooked for your family, or you can cook a month's supply of meat, 3–4 pounds, only for use as baby food. (**Each pound of meat will yield about 1½ cups of purée or 8–10 food cubes, depending on the cut of meat you use.**) Always cook meat at low to moderate temperature for as short a time as possible. If you overcook meat or use a high heat, the meat will shrink and become tough and tasteless. When meat is done properly, it will be tender and easy to purée. Pork and veal must be thoroughly cooked until well done. If you are using the less tender cuts, or lean grades, you should always cook the meat with the *braising* or *stewing* method.

Braising is cooking the meat with steam and a small amount of liquid or in the meat's own juices.

1. If you are using the oven, preheat to 350°F.

2. Cut away as much fat as you can.

3. Brown the meat evenly in a heavy pan. If the meat is very lean, use a little oil. Flouring the meat will cause it to brown better, but it is not necessary. The browning seals in the meat juices and helps prevent shrinkage. (You can also wrap any meat tightly in aluminum foil and braise it in the oven. It will cook in its own juice.)

4. Add a small amount of liquid (½ cup for a roast).

5. Cover the pan tightly and cook in the oven or simmer on the top of the stove. You can also use your steamer for braising.

6. Add water if the liquid cooks away before the meat is done.

7. See **Puréeing Meat.**

TIMETABLE FOR BRAISING MEATS

Beef roasts	3–5 pounds	3–4 hours
Beefsteak	1–1½ inches	2–2½ hours
Short ribs	2–2½ pounds	2–2½ hours
Veal shoulder	3–5 pounds	2–2½ hours
Veal chops	½–¾ inch	45 minutes
Lamb chops	½–¾ inch	30–45 minutes
Lamb shanks	1 pound each	1½–2 hours
Lamb shoulder	3–5 pounds	2–2½ hours
Pork chops	½–1 inch	45–60 minutes
Pork roast	3–5 pounds	3–4 hours

Near the end of the cooking time, you can poke the meat to test for tenderness. If it looks stringy, the meat is getting overcooked. You can easily braise a small amount of *cut-up* meat or chops. Just remove the fat and place the meat in aluminum foil and place in a 350° oven for 45–60 minutes. This is practical if your oven is already in use.

Stewing is similar to braising. However, more liquid is used and the meat is cut into pieces or cubes. Here is a recipe for an all-purpose stew in which you may use pieces of veal, beef, or lamb. Stews are a good all-in-one meal; just serve 2–3 food cubes each feeding and omit other vegetables.

All-Purpose Meat Stew

⅓ cup flour
1½ pounds boneless stew meat, cut in 1-inch cubes
2 tablespoons fat or oil
3 cups liquid (water, vegetable or fruit juice)
4 medium potatoes
5 medium carrots
10-ounce package frozen peas (or any other green vegetable)

1. Heat fat or oil in the bottom of a heavy saucepan.
2. Coat meat in flour and brown in fat.
3. Add water and cover tightly.
4. Simmer about 1½ hours.
5. Add potatoes and carrots. Simmer 15 minutes.
6. Add frozen peas and simmer for 5 minutes.
7. See **Puréeing Meat.**

YIELD: 4–5 cups of purée or 20–25 food cubes.

VARIATION

Any vegetable can be substituted and ½ cup of rice may be substituted for the potatoes. Follow the cooking times for other vegetables in chapter 9, "Vegetables."

Ground Meat

You can also cook ground meat of any type to use in meat purées. It has the advantage of faster cooking and it can be puréed easily in a food mill or strainer, if you do not have a blender.

1. The easiest way to cook ground meat is to place it in a heated saucepan.

2. Cook over low heat, stirring to break up the meat.

3. Cook ground meat until it is thoroughly cooked, but not browned. If it is crunchy, it will not make a smooth purée. Be sure to cook pork thoroughly.

4. Drain off fat.

PURÉEING MEAT

Cooking meat for use in baby food is very easy. The difficulty comes in puréeing the meat to a very smooth consistency, so that a young baby can swallow it. If you have a high-speed blender or food processor, you can easily purée any cut or grade of meat, whether it is roasted, broiled, stewed, or braised. If you don't have a blender, try to use a neighbor's to make a month's supply at a time.

Other alternatives are a food mill or grater. You can use a food mill to purée meat that has been braised until very tender. The meat will have a fairly coarse mixture, and it is time-consuming. Ground meat can be puréed to a smooth texture with a food mill. You can grate small amounts of chilled meat in a hand grater, such as the Mouli. This will make a very smooth purée and is an economical way to use leftovers such as steak.

In general:

- Thin the meat purée with the meat cooking juices and the juice that runs out when cutting the meat. If stewing or braising, cook the liquid down. You can remove excess fat from the cooking liquid by chilling it quickly in the refrigerator or freezer, then skimming off the fat that has solidified on the top.
- You can also use vegetable juice as a thinner, or add a juicy vegetable or fruit to the meat while it is cooking.
- **For a purée with a smooth consistency, one cup of cooked meat requires about ¼ cup of liquid.** A little butter or mayonnaise can be added for a smoother consistency, if your doctor approves their use.

- When using a food processor, purée meat with little or no liquid, then thin. The purée may be slightly coarse, but should be fine for most babies. A food processor will not purée gristle. It is easier to remove it before processing the meat; otherwise you can pick it out of the purée.
- Cool the purée quickly and freeze into food cubes immediately. Or, store in refrigerator for 2 days.

$ Organ Meats: Liver, Kidney, Brains, Sweetbreads

Nutrition: Organ meats are some of the most nutritious and *economical* meats that you can easily prepare. Your baby will probably love the taste, even if you do not. So serve with a smile!

Liver (calves, beef, lamb, pork, and chicken) and *kidneys* are some of the highest sources of iron, phosphorus, sodium, vitamin A, thiamine, riboflavin, and niacin. They contain the same amount of high-quality protein as meat.

Sweetbreads are high in protein but lower in the other nutrients. *Brains* contain only ½–⅓ the protein in meat or the other organ meats, and lower amounts of the other nutrients. Unless you prepare brains or sweetbreads for your family, their nutritional value is not high enough for the effort (and on my part, the mental anguish) involved in their preparation. There are other organ meats, such as tripe, tongue, and heart, that I choose to ignore completely.

Introduce beef liver or kidney at eight months, other organ meats at nine months.

Buy fresh meats and plan to cook them the same day.

Store uncooked meat, loosely covered, in the coldest part of the refrigerator. *Uncooked* meats can be frozen for 2–3 months. The *cooked* purées can be frozen for 1 month, or refrigerated for 2 days.

Liver Purée

Liver is one of the easiest protein foods that you can prepare for your baby, and you do not need a blender to make a smooth purée. Beef or lamb liver costs quite a bit less than calves' liver and is fine for baby food. You should always keep a supply of frozen cubes on hand and you can serve it two or three times a week. It is especially valuable for its high iron content.

A *warning:* Steamed or braised liver has a very strong odor, so make it on a day when you aren't having company and can open a window!

> 2 pounds liver
> 1 cup liquid (milk or vegetable juice, or cooking liquid)

1. Rinse the liver under cold water.
2. If you are using a blender or processor to purée, remove the outer skin and any large veins.
3. Steam liver for 10 minutes, covered, in steamer; or in a pot with a little water, or broil liver for 3–4 minutes on each side.
4. Purée, adding the liquid to thin. A food mill, processor, or blender will give the smoothest purée. Cooked liver is also one of the few meats that can be scraped with a spoon or dull knife to prepare a purée. Chicken livers can be mashed with a fork.

YIELD: 3 cups or 15 food cubes.

VARIATION

Liver stew: Combine equal amounts of liver, carrots, and green beans or broccoli to make a complete dinner dish. You can steam them all together; just follow the individual cooking times.

Kidney/Carrot Stew

Kidneys are more difficult to prepare than liver, and they also give off a very strong odor when cooking. But babies like them. They are inexpensive and highly nutritious, so take an hour one day and make enough for a month.

> 1 pound kidneys
> 4 medium carrots, scrubbed
> ½ cup liquid (milk, juice, or cooking liquid)

1. Preparing the kidney is the most work. Remove the outer membrane, split the kidney lengthwise through the center, and remove the inner fat and tubes.
2. Soak it in cold water for 1 hour, drain.
3. Place kidneys in a pot, cover with cold water, and simmer for 1 hour.
4. Drain the water. Add enough new water to cover.
5. Add carrots.
6. Simmer for another 15–30 minutes until tender.
7. Purée, adding liquid to thin. A blender, processor, or food mill will produce a smooth purée, but the food mill takes a longer time. A hand grater will produce a coarser texture.

YIELD: 2½ cups or 12 food cubes.

VARIATION

The kidney can be prepared without any vegetable, or you can add any other vegetable; tomatoes are good.

Sweetbreads or Brains

I am including general cooking instructions in case you do want to prepare them for your baby. They are considered delicacies. The recipe is untested due to my own squeamishness.

1. Wash under cold running water. Soak in salted water for 15 minutes and drain.

2. Remove the membrane on brains with the tip of a knife.

3. Add 1 teaspoon salt and 1 tablespoon vinegar or lemon juice to a quart of water.

4. Bring water to a boil. Drop in brains or sweetbreads and cover.

5. Simmer brains 15–20 minutes. Simmer sweetbreads 25–35 minutes.

6. Rinse thoroughly in cold water.

7. Hold the sweetbreads under cold water and slip off the membrane. Cut out the dark veins and thick connective tissue.

8. Purée as for liver and kidneys, thinning if necessary.

Poultry

Nutrition: Poultry, either chicken or turkey, offers the same amount of high-quality protein as meat and can be substituted often. It is also an excellent source of niacin, with good amounts of thiamine, riboflavin, and linoleic acid. Turkey supplies the most iron. Some types of poultry, which are very adequate for use in baby food, can be considerably less expensive than meat.

Introduce chicken and turkey at seven months.

Buy any poultry that carries the U.S. Department of Agriculture inspection seal. Federal inspection of poultry is compulsory and it is your guarantee of wholesomeness, both while the bird was alive and during processing. The grading is voluntary. However, most of the poultry sold carries the *U.S. grade A*. The lower grades are not usually available to the consumer and are used in processed foods where the appearance is not important. If you can buy the lower grade, you will be able to save money, and the cooked poultry will be fine for baby-food purées. Any *poultry product*, frozen or canned, must also carry the U.S. "Inspected for Wholesomeness" seal on the label.

You can use any type of poultry—roasters, fryers, or broilers—which you usually buy for your family meals.

However, you can save money by using the lower-priced mature chickens or turkeys that may be labeled "Mature," "Old," or "Stewing." These terms refer to the age of the bird when killed and not the freshness when sold. These older birds are not tender enough to be broiled, fried, or roasted, but they are perfect for stewing or braising.

If you want to save time, buy the frozen boned chicken and rolled-turkey roasts. However, you are paying a premium for the preparation, as they are more expensive. Look for sales on these. Also, dark meat is as nutritious as white meat and may be less expensive.

As a rule, whole chickens are more economical than cut-up parts. Breast sections should not be priced more than 40 per cent higher than the whole chicken. Leg and thigh sections should not cost more than 30 per cent higher. For example, if the whole chicken is $.49 per pound, the breast sections should be $.69 per pound, and the leg and thigh sections only $.65 per pound. If they are priced higher, you will save money by buying the whole chicken, and it is just as easy to use in preparing baby food. Large turkeys are usually more economical than smaller ones. The self-basting variety is very costly for the little time you save and up to 6 per cent of the weight can be injected vegetable oil used in the basting.

Store uncooked poultry in the coldest part of the refrigerator and use within 1–2 days. Do not store in butcher paper, but rewrap it in waxed paper or plastic, first removing the giblets.

Frozen uncooked poultry, tightly wrapped, can be kept at 0°F. for as long as 12 months for chicken and turkey, and 3 months for livers and giblets.

Cooked purées can be stored, tightly covered, in the coldest part of the refrigerator for two days. You may also freeze it in food cubes or store for 1–2 months.

To thaw frozen poultry, either raw or cooked, place it unwrapped in the refrigerator or in cold water. *Do not thaw it at room temperature*. If you allow additional cooking time, you can cook poultry still partially frozen. Frozen food cubes should be heated while frozen, just before a feeding. Thawed poultry spoils quickly, so do not save leftovers.

Chicken/Turkey Purée

The easiest way to cook poultry for baby food, either whole or in parts, is to *braise* or *stew*. Always cook the poultry completely; that is, do not partially cook it one day and finish it the next day. As a rule, **you will obtain 1 cup of cooked poultry (without the bone) from each 1½ pounds of a whole chicken or turkey.** For each 1 pound of a boneless turkey roast, you will obtain 1 cup of cooked turkey. (Since there is some indication that chemical steroids, used in poultry food, tend to accumulate in the skin, you should remove most of the skin before cooking.)

To **braise** poultry, you will cook it in a small amount of liquid in a tightly covered pot.

1. For oven braising, preheat the oven to 325°F.

2. Put the poultry in a heavy, covered roasting pan. You may need to add additional liquid during cooking. Place in oven or simmer on top over a moderate heat.

3. Allow 45 minutes per pound for whole birds up to 4 pounds.

For larger birds, cook about ½ hour per pound.

- You can also braise small parts such as drumsticks or breasts in the oven by tightly wrapping the pieces in *aluminum foil*. They will cook in 30–45 minutes.
- If you have a *large steamer,* you can use it to braise small birds or parts. Braising is really the same method as steaming. Depending on the size of the poultry, the cooking time should be 30–60 minutes.
- You can test for doneness by piercing a fleshy part and noting the color of the juice that runs out. If it is at all pink, the poultry is not done. You may also be able to tell by pressing the flesh and moving the drumstick. However, these are rather subjective tests with which I have never been too successful. Just be sure the juice and the flesh show no sign of pinkness. The flesh should also be separating from the bones.

Stewing is a good way of tenderizing the more mature poultry. You can leave the chicken whole or cut it into parts. Remove the skin.

1. Place poultry in a deep pot. Add enough water to half cover the whole bird or, if cut up, to completely cover the parts.

2. Cover the pot tightly and simmer: 2–3 hours for a 3–4 pound stewing chicken; ½ hour per pound for a larger chicken or turkey; 45–60 minutes for a broiler fryer.

3. Check for doneness. It should be well separated from the bones, thus saving you time and effort.

Note: When you have stewed the poultry, you will have a considerable amount of cooking liquid with a mild flavor and some nutrients. Cool, skim off fat, and freeze it as food cubes. You can then use it as thinner, or serve it to your baby as soup if he is sick or unable to eat solids.

Meal-In-One Poultry Stew

Cooked poultry can be combined with vegetables, cereals, rice, etc., or you can save pots and time by adding vegetables or rice to the poultry while it is stewing. Just check the cooking time for the individual vegetable. You can also thin the cooked poultry with a juicy vegetable such as tomatoes, raw or cooked. If you use equal amounts of poultry, a yellow vegetable, and a green vegetable, you will have a balanced stew to use as a complete all-in-one meal.

For example:

> 1½ pounds poultry
> 10-ounce package frozen greens (last 15 minutes)
> ½ cup of rice (last 45 minutes)
> 3–4 medium carrots (last 30 minutes)

YIELD: About 4 cups of purée, or 20 food cubes.

PURÉEING POULTRY

If you have braised or stewed the poultry, it should be falling away from the bones. Just pull it off, making sure you remove all the small bones.

- **For each 1 cup cooked chicken, purée with about ⅓ cup liquid.** Use the cooking juices or vegetable juice.
- You can use a food mill, processor, or blender for a very smooth purée.
- To prepare small amounts with a coarser texture, you can chill the poultry and use a hand grater.
- You can add a small amount of butter, or oil, to improve the texture—about 2 teaspoons for 1 cup purée if your doctor approves.

Fish

Nutrition: Fish is one of the most valuable foods that are also easy to prepare and to purée. It can be an inexpensive source of high-quality protein, containing the same amount as the more expensive meats. Salt-water fish is also one of the few good sources of iodine. Other nutrients that are found in good amounts in fish are vitamins A and D (higher in fatty fish), thiamine, riboflavin, niacin, calcium, phosphorus, and iron (although a smaller amount than in meat).

Introduce *lean* fish at eight months, *fatty* fish at nine to ten months, and *shellfish* after your baby is one year old. Although fish is not commonly served as a baby food in America, it is widely used in Europe and other areas. One reason might be that we eat considerably less fish than meat and poultry. Most babies love the soft texture and the mild flavor of fish, so try to feed your baby fish at least twice a week as a protein dish.

Fish, especially shellfish, may cause an allergic reaction in some babies, usually in the form of a rash. Introduce fish in a very small amount, about a teaspoon, and wait four days to make sure there is no reaction. If there is, wait a month and try it again.

LEAN FISH

Bass, black	Perch	Smelts
Carp	Pickerel	Snapper
Catfish	Pike	Sole
Cod	Pollack	Spot

LEAN FISH

Flounder	Redfish	Suckers
Fluke	Red Snapper	Sunfish
Grouper	Robolo (snook)	Tautog
Haddock	Rockfish	Walleyed pike or perch
Hake	Rosefish	Weakfish (sea trout)
Herring, lake	Sheepshead	Whiting (silver hake)
Kingfish		

FATTY FISH

Alewife	Mullet	Shad
Bonito	Pompano	Striped Bass
Butterfish	Porgies	Sturgeon
Eels	Salmon	Tuna
Halibut	Sablefish	Whitefish
Herring, sea	Sardines	Yellowtail
Mackerel	Sea Bass	

SHELLFISH

Shrimp	Crayfish
Lobster	Scallops
Crab	

Buy fish either whole, as steaks, or in fillets, fresh or frozen. If your family eats fish, you can use whatever type of fish that you usually cook. If you are buying fish only to prepare as baby food, the steaks and fillets will be the easiest type to use.

Fresh fish. Whole fresh fish should have clear, bright eyes; reddish gills, shiny scales, firm flesh that is not separated from the bones; and a fresh, mild odor. If you notice a distinct fishy smell in any type of fresh fish, do not buy it. Steaks and fillets should be moist, white, and free from brown, yellow, or dried spots. If you plan to freeze the uncooked fish, make sure that it was not already frozen and defrosted. You should not refreeze thawed fish. You can test by placing the fish in water; if fresh it will float, if thawed the fish will sink.

Frozen fish is available whole, in steaks, and fillets. Look for the *U.S. grade A* or *B* on the package. The

"U.S." means that the fish was processed and packed under continuous in-plant inspection by the U.S. Department of the Interior. This inspection and grading is done on a voluntary basis, and many products may be packed without this control which is your guarantee of a wholesome product.

If, when you open or thaw the frozen fish, it has a cottony look, darkened or yellow areas, a fishy smell, or an excess of liquid, do not use the fish, but return it to the store. The signs indicate that the fish has been thawed and refrozen.

Frozen fish products such as sticks, portions, etc., should not be used as food for your baby, since they usually contain various additives and fillers.

Store fish carefully, since it does spoil easily. The faster you use fresh fish, the better the taste and texture.

Fresh fish should be stored, tightly wrapped in plastic or foil, in the coldest part of the refrigerator for 1–2 days. Do not store in butcher wrap or newspaper.

Frozen uncooked fish should be tightly wrapped in freezer wrap and kept frozen at 0°F. for 4–6 months.

Cooked fish should be tightly covered and stored in the refrigerator for no longer than two days.

Cooked frozen fish purées can be kept for up to 1 month.

Thaw frozen fish in the refrigerator or under cool running water. You can always cook fish frozen or partially thawed.

Cooking fish. Fish is one of the easiest foods to prepare. The main thing to remember is not to overcook fish since it will become tough. Fish is done when the color changes from translucent, or watery, to white, and the flesh flakes easily and separates from the bones.

- Prepare the fish as baby food as soon as possible after cooking, and freeze the purée at once.
- The best way to cook fish for baby food is to bake, poach, or steam it. If your family eats fish prepared by these methods, just make some extra for the baby. (Do not give a young baby fried fish.)

• **One pound of fish fillet yields about 1½ cups purée or 8 food cubes.** Prepare and freeze a month's supply at one time.

Baked Fish

1. Preheat oven to 350° F.
2. Place the fish on a buttered pan or aluminum foil. Dot with butter. You can also wrap the fish in foil, but this is actually steaming it.
3. Bake dressed whole fish (about 3 pounds) for 30–45 minutes; fillets or steaks (about 2 pounds) for 20–25 minutes. It is not necessary to turn the fish.
4. See **Puréeing Fish.**

Poached Fish

This method is good for thin fillets, steaks, and small whole fish. It is quick, easy, and the cooked fish is very digestible.

1. If you have a steamer, it is perfect for poaching, or use a shallow pan. In the steamer or pan place enough court bouillon, water with a little lemon juice, or milk to cover the fish.
2. Bring the liquid to a boil and reduce heat to a simmer.
3. Lower the fish into the steaming basket (or place in the pan of cooking liquid).
4. Cover and simmer for 5–15 minutes, depending on the thickness of the fish.
5. You can boil the liquid down and use it as a thinner.
6. To steam the fish, use only enough water to cover the bottom of the steamer and keep it boiling for 10–15 minutes.
7. Test for flakiness.
8. See **Puréeing Fish.**

Meal-in-one Fish Stew

Fish can be combined with most vegetables to make an all-in-one stew. If you are steaming vegetables, just add the fish during the last 10–15 minutes. Cooked fish can also be used in custards and soufflés, but you needn't bother just for the baby.

PURÉEING FISH

Although fish is easily and quickly cooked, you must be especially careful to remove all bones before you prepare it as a purée. Even fillets, which are considered boneless, should be checked.

* When the fish has been thoroughly flaked and the bones removed, you can purée it with a blender, processor, or food mill for the smoothest purée; or simply mash it with a fork for coarser texture. Fish is an easy food to chew, so it is a good way to start introducing coarser texture. Larger flakes can be used as one of the first *finger* foods.
* **For each 1 cup of fish, purée with about ¼ cup liquid,** either milk, cooking juice, or vegetable juice.

$ Soybeans

Nutrition: Although soybeans are a vegetable, they supply almost the same amount of high-quality complete protein as meat or poultry, and can be counted as a serving of a protein food. They are also high in linoleic acid, iron, potassium, thiamine, and fat. As you can see, soybeans are quite a nutritional bargain at around $.39 a pound—and that is the *dry* weight. Although we do not usually consider them as desirable a food as sirloin steak, your baby will never know the difference.

Introduce at seven months. They are easily digested and are a very *un*allergenic food. If your baby is drinking skim milk, serve soybeans to supply some fat to his diet.

Buy: If you cannot find soybeans in your local supermarket, try the nearest health-food store. Buy them in quantity, since they keep well.

Store dry soybeans in tightly covered cans or plastic bags, at cool room temperature for up to 2 years. Cooked purées will keep in the refrigerator for up to 3 days and can be frozen for 2 months.

Soybean Purée

1 cup dry soybeans
3 cups water
1 tablespoon butter or oil
¾ cup liquid (milk or tomato juice is good)

1. Rinse the soybeans, then soak them in water overnight. You can also bring them to a boil for 2 minutes, cover, and allow them to sit for 2 hours. The presoaking or cooking is not necessary if you are using a pressure cooker.

2. Add the butter or oil to help prevent the beans from foaming while cooking. Do not add salt.

3. Return the pot to a moderate heat and simmer about 2 hours. Leave the cover ajar to prevent foaming and spilling.

4. When the skins float to the top, you can skim them off to prepare the smoothest purée.

5. Purée with any equipment, adding ¾ cup liquid to thin.

YIELD: 2½ cups or 12 food cubes.

VARIATION

If you do not thin the mashed soybeans, you can use the purée as a nutritious thickener for juicy fruits and vegetables.

$ Eggs

Nutrition: Eggs should be one of the staples of your baby's diet. They are nutritious, inexpensive, and easy to cook and purée. Eggs contain a good amount of complete protein, iron, riboflavin, vitamins B_6, B_{12}, and A, and are one of the few foods that contain natural vitamin D. They also supply saturated fat, which is important to your baby's diet if he is drinking skim or nonfat dry milk. The *yolk* has most of the fat, iron, and vitamins A and D in the egg. The *white* contains half the riboflavin and protein of the whole egg. So if you want to use only the egg yolk, you can double the amount and come out ahead nutritionally. At $.90 a dozen for large eggs, the cost comes to about $.60 per pound. Very economical for a high-protein food!

Introduce: The cooked egg yolk can be introduced in small amounts at seven months. The cooked egg white is a possible source of allergy and should not be introduced until your baby is eight months old. Always use the cooked egg yolk or white when first introducing; raw yolk can then be used in beverages. Most doctors recommend that a baby eat 1 egg per day, but no more than 7 to 9 per week. You may use it occasionally as the second daily protein serving. Some doctors limit eggs because of their cholesterol content, but others criticize this as unnecessary. If your baby is drinking skim milk, eggs are an important source of fat and cholesterol. (See "Nutrition," chapter 1.)

Buy: The grade, size, and color of an egg do not affect its nutritional value. The important thing to look for in buying eggs is freshness. In some areas, the last date of sale must be stamped on the carton. Another guarantee of freshness is the *grade AA* or *fresh fancy* which shows that the eggs have been produced under the U.S. Department of Agriculture's Quality Control Porgram. This grade must be dated with the last day of sale, which is ten days after the eggs were inspected. The main difference in the grades is the appearance of the eggs. *Grade*

AA or *A* eggs have a better appearance and are good for frying or poaching. Since your baby won't be concerned with the appearance and will be eating his eggs well cooked and mixed, you can save money by buying the *grade B* eggs. Just be sure they are fresh!

The *size* on the egg carton refers to the minimum weight for the dozen eggs and ranges from 30 ounces for *jumbo* eggs to 18 ounces for *small* eggs. If you are buying eggs specifically to feed your baby, the *medium-size* egg should be adequate for one feeding without wasteful leftovers. You can easily figure out which size is the most economical by the **$.07 rule: If the difference in price between two sizes of eggs is less than $.07, buy the larger size.**

The nutritional value of brown and white eggs is exactly the same. Since most people prefer the white eggs, you may find the brown eggs less expensive.

Besides freshness, the important sign to look for in buying eggs is a clean, uncracked shell. If the shell is cracked or dirty, the egg might contain bacteria that cause food poisoning, salmonella.

Store: *Whole eggs* in the refrigerator with the large end up. Do not wash them or you will remove the protective coating. They should be used within 1 week, or else they may develop off-flavors and lose some of their thickening ability.

Whole hard-cooked eggs in the shell for up to 1 week.

Cooked yolks and/or *whites* should be covered and can be saved for 2–3 days.

Raw yolks should be covered with water in a tightly lidded container and stored for 1–2 days.

Raw whites should be tightly covered and stored for 1–2 days. If your baby is eating only yolks, you can use these whites in cakes, meringues, soufflés, and whipped in many desserts. You can also beat an egg white and use it as an inexpensive facial mask!

Frozen raw eggs (whole, yolk, or whites) may be stored for 6 months. If you are freezing the whole egg, first mix the white and yolk together. Do not freeze raw or cooked eggs in the shell.

Cooked egg yolks may be frozen in food cubes for up to one month. Other cooked egg dishes should not be frozen.

USING EGGS

You can prepare eggs in many ways and this is one area in which you can really use your ingenuity.

Both the egg yolk and the white are useful as a way of smoothly binding together many nutritious foods that would be difficult for your baby to swallow, such as leafy green vegetables, wheat germ, etc. Almost any food can be combined with eggs.

As a binder you can cook eggs in the form of custards, soufflés, or just plain scrambled—the easiest.

If you are using only the egg yolk, remember to substitute 2 yolks for each whole egg that a recipe calls for. Yolks only can be substituted for whole eggs in any custard recipe and in most baked goods. The main exception is a soufflé, which depends on the beaten egg white for its lightness.

- Eggs will separate easily if they warm to room temperature.
- When you are cooking any dish with eggs as the main ingredient, use a low to moderate heat, to prevent the egg from becoming tough or hard.
- You will also find hard-boiled egg yolks useful as a highly nutritious thickener for juicy fruits and vegetables, or when you have overthinned a purée.
- Finally, you can combine a small amount of eggs, with their complete protein, with many inexpensive foods that contain incomplete proteins, such as dried peas, beans, lentils, cereals, noodles, and rice.

The following recipes cover the basic and easiest ways to prepare eggs that your baby will enjoy eating.

Egg Yolk Purée

This is the easiest food to cook and mash. There should be no reason for you to buy the commercially prepared egg yolks. It is also a food on which you can save considerable money by preparing yourself. The yolks of two *large* eggs, thinned to the same consistency, make the same amount of purée (3⅓ ounces) as in a jar of commercial egg yolks. The cost of the eggs, at $.89 a dozen, is $.16 (and you will still have the whites to use), as compared with an average cost of $.57 for a jar of egg yolks. Now, see how easy it is to prepare your own!

    4 large eggs
    ¼–⅓ cup liquid (milk, fruit, or vegetable juice)

1. Wash eggs.
2. Place eggs in a pan and cover with cold water.
3. Bring water to a simmer and cook for 15–20 minutes. Do not let the water boil.
4. Plunge the eggs, in the shell, immediately into cold water.
5. Cut the eggs in half and remove the yolks.
6. With a spoon or fork, mash the yolks with the liquid. If you are using the yolk as a thickener, store or freeze it without thinning. Use a blender or processor for larger amounts.
7. The purée may be frozen for up to one month, or covered and stored in the refrigerator for 2–3 days.

YIELD: 1 cup purée or 5 food cubes.

(You can use the hard-cooked white in sandwiches, salads, and casserole dishes; or serve it to an older child.)

VARIATION

Egg Yolk/Wheat Germ Purée

Mix 1 tablespoon wheat germ with 2 tablespoons milk or fruit juice, and allow to soften for 10 minutes.

Mix together with the cooked egg yolks and rest of liquid.

(For a single egg yolk, use about 1 teaspoon wheat germ and 2 teaspoons liquid.)

Scrambled Eggs

You may scramble the whole egg or only the yolk. The size of the egg to use for 1 serving depends upon your baby.

> 1 medium egg (or 2 egg yolks)
> 1 tablespoon milk (vegetable or fruit juice)

1. Melt a small amount of butter or oil in a pan.
2. Beat the egg and milk. (If you want to save a dish, you can do it quickly in the pan.)
3. Cook the egg slowly, stirring until it is loosely cooked. (If the egg is cooked too long, it will be dry and difficult to swallow.)
4. Serve at once. It should not be necessary to thin the eggs.
5. Leftover scrambled eggs become hard and should not be saved. Do not freeze.

VARIATION

Meal-in-One Eggs

You can add up to ¼ cup of almost any purée to a *medium* egg while you are beating it, or you can purée a food with the egg. Try fruit, vegetable, or meat purées, grated cheese, cottage cheese, leftover cooked cereal or rice, etc.

This is also a good way to feed your baby the highly nutritious *wheat germ*. Soften 1 teaspoon wheat germ in 2 teaspoons milk for a few minutes before beating it with the egg and milk. For a balanced meal, combine a *cereal grain* and *fruit/vegetable* with the eggs.

Smooth Eggs

This is an easy way of preparing an egg dish with the consistency of custard.

> 2 eggs (or 4 yolks)
> ½ cup milk
> 2 teaspoons butter or oil

1. Mix the eggs and milk together.
2. Melt the butter (or oil) in the top of a double boiler.
3. Add the egg mixture, cover.
4. Cook 10–15 minutes without stirring.
5. Cool and store in the refrigerator for up to 3 days.
YIELD: 3 servings.

Basic Baked Custard

Custard takes more effort to make, and since the main ingredient is milk, it should not be counted as a serving of eggs. You may wish to make a custard for a family dessert, and the baby will also enjoy it as a good supper dish. You may find that custard is useful as a way of feeding your baby some valuable foods such as green leafy vegetables, wheat germ, etc.

> 2½ cups milk (whole, skim, or evaporated)
> 4 eggs (or 8 egg yolks)
> 1 teaspoon vanilla extract
> ⅓ cup brown sugar or honey or 2 tablespoons molasses

1. Preheat oven to 350°F.
2. Bring milk to boiling point and remove from heat.
3. Beat the eggs, adding vanilla and sweetening.
4. Pour a little hot milk into the eggs, and mix.
5. Pour the egg mixture into the rest of the milk, stirring until it is mixed.
6. Pour custard into cups or casserole and place in a

pan of hot water that reaches to the level of the custard. The water will cook the custard evenly.

7. Bake in oven for about 40 minutes or until a knife inserted in the center comes out clean. If you overcook the custard, it will pull away from the sides of the cup, leaving liquid around it, and the custard will have a harder texture.

8. Cool, cover, and store in the refrigerator for up to three days.

YIELD: 4–6 servings.

VARIATIONS

Stirred Custard

1. Follow the recipe for **Baked Custard** until you have mixed the eggs and milk together.

2. Pour the custard into the top of a double boiler and cook over simmering water for about 5 minutes or until the spoon is well coated. Stir constantly.

3. The custard will have a smooth, creamy texture.

Wheat Germ Custard

Add 1 tablespoon wheat germ to the milk before heating it. Proceed as for **Baked** or **Stirred Custard**.

Anything Custard

You can add ¼–½ cup of almost any purée—vegetable, fruit, cereal, meat, fish, etc.—for each whole egg used in a custard. Mix the purée (or chopped food) with the eggs before mixing with the milk or liquid. Proceed as for **Baked Custard**. See also **Vegetable Custard, Easy Vegetable Custard, Vegetable/Egg Yolk Custard,** and **Fruit Custard**.

Soufflés

A soufflé is a very light custard that often uses a *White Sauce*. The lightness is obtained by beating the egg whites separately and folding them carefully into the egg mixture. A soufflé takes even more time and dishes than a custard, and it must be eaten immediately. Most likely, the only time that your baby will eat a soufflé is when you have made one for the rest of the family. As with custard, you can add almost anything to a soufflé. (See **Vegetable Soufflé**.)

Yogurt

Nutrition: Yogurt contains all the valuable nutrients in milk—complete protein, calcium, riboflavin, and others. If you make your yogurt with milk that has been fortified with vitamins A and D, they will also be present in the yogurt. Some brands of commercial yogurt are also fortified with vitamins A and D. In addition, the bacteria in yogurt stimulates the body to produce vitamin K, which is important in blood-clotting and liver functions. Breast milk contains an adequate supply of vitamin K, but cow's milk contains less. If your baby is bottle fed, yogurt can be an important supplement in his early diet.

Introduce plain yogurt as early as four to five months. It is easily digested and is easy to swallow. The fruited varieties can be used after the specific fruit has been introduced. When your baby is accustomed to the taste and consistency of yogurt, you can use it, mixed with meats and vegetables, as a way of introducing new tastes and textures.

Buy commercial yogurts without preservatives or fillers. See the **Yogurt** section in the chapter **Instant Food** for a full discussion of commercial yogurt. The purest yogurt will contain only fresh milk, nonfat dry milk, and yogurt cultures.

Store yogurt in the refrigerator for 1 week to 10 days. It will develop a stronger flavor the longer it is kept. *Do not freeze.*

Homemade Yogurt

Yogurt is one of the easiest foods that you can make yourself. It will have a milder, less acid taste than the commercial yogurts. You can also save quite a bit of money! An 8-ounce container of plain yogurt costs around $.50. You can make yogurt, using nonfat dry milk, that costs $.10 for the same 8 ounces. Now see how easy it is!

1 quart milk (any kind—whole, skim, goat, soy, etc.)
½ cup nonfat dry milk powder
¼ cup plain yogurt (commercial or homemade)

1. Mix the milk and milk powder together in a pot.

2. Bring the milk to a boil and remove from heat at once. This will destroy any bacteria already in the milk. Be careful not to allow the milk to scorch the pot.

3. Cool the milk to about 105°–110°F. You can use the same wrist test that is used in warming a baby's bottle. A few drops of milk on the inside of your wrist should feel warm.

4. Mix a spoonful of milk into the yogurt, then stir the yogurt into the milk, blending well.

5. Now you must find a warm place for the yogurt to sit for about 5 hours. There are several choices, but the main principle is to keep the yogurt at a temperature of around 105°–110°F. so that the yogurt bacteria will grow. Too hot or too cold a temperature will kill the bacteria and you will have only sour milk. But if you are off by a few degrees, it will just take longer for the yogurt to set. So you needn't be too worried about thermometers and exact degrees.

- If you can easily replace the light bulb in your oven with a 100-watt bulb and can leave the light on with the door closed, you will have a good temperature.

- I have had good results by simply warming the oven at 150°F. for 5 minutes then turning it off. After 2–3 hours you may check to see whether it needs another minute or so of warming. The oven should feel warm, but not hot when you open the door. You can always use a thermometer, of course.

- Probably the simplest and oldest way of making yogurt is to mix it in a heavy warmed casserole, cover, and wrap it in a blanket for 12 hours or until set. A wide-mouthed thermos can also be used for a small amount.

- There are commercial yogurt makers that you can buy for about $12, but they really are not necessary.

6. Using the oven method, the yogurt should set in about 5 hours. The longer you allow it to set, the more sour the yogurt will be. Do not stir.

7. Chill the yogurt before dividing into smaller containers or transferring.

Here is an even easier method which can save cleaning a pot. In step 1, bring 1 quart of water to a boil. Pour the water into yogurt container and add 1¾ cups nonfat dry milk. Proceed with step 3. (Since nonfat dry milk is already sterile, you do not need to boil it.)

Note: You can feed your baby the yogurt cold or slightly warmed. Another way you can use yogurt is to mix it with foods that are difficult to swallow, such as green leafy vegetables, wheat germ, etc. When you are first introducing meat, you can mix it with a little yogurt as you are feeding your baby. The meat purée will be easier for him to swallow.

VARIATIONS

There are many ways that you can add flavor and variety to your homemade yogurt.

Before heating the milk, add ¼ cup honey or brown sugar or 2 tablespoons molasses.

After heating the milk and cooling, add ⅓ cup of any cooked fruit (prunes, apricots, peaches), puréed or chopped, or even some vegetable purée such as squash. You can also add ½ cup of fresh chopped or puréed fruit.

Before serving, you can stir in any flavoring you happen to have around.

Yogurt Cheese

You can make a tasty cream cheese by hanging yogurt in cheesecloth and allowing it to drain several hours.

Cheese

Nutrition: Cheese contains the same nutrients as milk and is a valuable food. It does lack the iron that is in other protein foods. For example: a 1-inch cube of Cheddar cheese has the same calcium as ½ cup milk; and ½ cup cottage cheese = ⅓ cup milk.

As for protein, 1 ounce hard cheese (Cheddar, Swiss, or American) or ¼ cup cottage cheese equals the protein of 1 ounce lean meat, fish, or poultry.

If your baby is drinking milk, there is no need to add large amounts of cheese to his diet. You will find small amounts of cheese useful as an easy way of improving the quality of protein in such low-cost foods as noodles, cereal, rice, dried peas, beans, and lentils.

Introduce all types of cheeses around seven to eight months.

Buy firm cheese—Swiss, American, Cheddar, etc.—that has not been diluted with various additives and fillers. See chapter 2 on *How to Read Labels*. In general, you should not buy any cheese that is labeled with the word "imitation," "spread," or "food."

Cottage cheese varies as to the types of additives, so read labels to buy the brand with the least amount. Sorbic acid is usually added as a preservative. Also, try to buy a brand that carries a government or state *grade* or *inspection* seal. In some areas the containers will be dated with the last day of sale, so look for it.

Store *firm cheeses*, tightly wrapped, in the refrigerator for 2–3 weeks. Any mold spots can be cut away. Hard cheese may also be frozen for several months. *Cottage cheese* should be kept in the refrigerator for up to 1 week. It should not be frozen.

USING CHEESE

- Grated hard cheese can be used as a protein supplement and as flavoring in many purées. It is especially good in rice and vegetable dishes.
- To grate, cut hard cheese into small cubes and grate in a processor, blender, or with a hand grater. Softer cheese will grate better if it is well chilled or placed in a freezer for 20–30 minutes. (One half pound cheese makes 1 cup grated cheese.)

- Always cook cheese at low to moderate temperatures and add near the end of cooking.
- For one way to use cottage cheese, see **Noodle and Cheese Pudding.**
- Creamed cottage cheese may be mashed with a fork or puréed in a processor or blender, and fed directly to your baby. It is a good *instant* food that is readily available.
- See Bibliography for pamphlet on how you can make your own cottage cheese.

$ Nonfat Dry Milk

Nutrition: Nonfat dry milk powder is an excellent source of complete protein and contains all the vitamins and minerals of fresh milk. Only the fat and water have been removed. At $.22 for the equivalent of a quart of milk, it is a very low-cost and convenient way to serve protein to your baby, especially as a supplement with the economical cereal grains and legumes.

Buy: The *U.S. extra grade* mark on the label indicates that the dry milk meets the government's standards of composition and wholesomeness. The label will also tell you whether vitamins A and D have been added as supplements.

Store: The unopened powder can be kept at cool room temperature for several months. The opened packages of powder should be kept dry and used within 2 weeks.

Using Dry Milk

- You can add dry milk as a fortifier in any recipe that contains liquid. It is especially good in any fruit or vegetable purées that are naturally thin or have strong tastes.
- Added to baked goods, it supplements the incomplete protein in the flour. *Use 2–4 tablespoons powder for each cup of liquid.*

- Remember that ⅓ cup powder supplies the same nutrients as 1 cup milk.
- You can also increase the amount of nonfat dry milk powder, when it is specified in a recipe, by up to 50 per cent.

$ Protein Economy

Protein is an essential part of everyone's diet and is especially important for a baby's growth. Yet prices of what we commonly think of as protein sources—beef, lamb, pork, veal, and fish—have risen astronomically. Fortunately, **poultry, eggs, soybeans,** and **milk** are still economical in terms of their "nutritional cost." The following list gives an idea of the protein values of various foods. Keeping in mind the different "completeness" of the proteins, these amounts of food will supply the same quantity of protein:

COMPLETE PROTEIN
1 cup milk (whole or skim)
1 ounce Cheddar, American, or Swiss cheese
1 ounce lean meat, fish, or poultry
1 egg or 2 egg yolks
⅓ cup cooked soybeans

INCOMPLETE PROTEIN
2 tablespoons wheat germ
2 tablespoons peanut butter
½ cup cooked legumes (peas, beans, lentils)

Supplementing protein. All the incomplete protein foods are inexpensive sources of protein. These include rice, pastas, legumes (peas, beans), and seeds (peanuts, sesame). You probably prepare many family dishes that stretch the more expensive meats by combining them with inexpensive rice, beans, or pastas. Turkey is an excellent complement since using turkey as only one fifth of a dish makes the protein value of the dish the same as if it were all beef. If you combine the incomplete protein foods in dishes with the inexpensive milk, eggs, cheese, or soybeans you have an even more economical source of complete protein. Most of these family dishes can be puréed for a baby if they are not highly seasoned. Some recipes included are:

Noodle and Cheese Pudding	Rice Pudding
Macaroni and Cheese	Sautéed Rice
Rice Cheese	Peanut Butter Custard
Rice and Wheat Germ Purée	Pea/Bean/Lentil Purée
Soybean/Rice Purée	

Complementing proteins. Incomplete protein foods each lack some of the essential amino acids that make up protein; however, the amino acids that are lacking in one food (such as legumes) are present in another food (rice). *You can obtain very inexpensive high-quality complete protein by combining complementary foods in the right amounts— either in the same dish or at the same meal!* It is even easier to combine these foods in purées; a baby has no built-in bias against sesame seeds with rice. For some interesting family dishes using complementary proteins, see Bibliography and look into some vegetarian-oriented cookbooks. The baby's portion can be removed before seasoning is added, but most recipes are not highly seasoned.

You should combine these foods in the following proportions, although you have some leeway, especially when you thin the purées with milk. The amounts given are for uncooked rice and legumes. In general, *1 cup dry legumes = 2 to 2½ cups cooked;* and *1 cup rice = 3½ cups cooked rice.* Sunflower seeds can be substituted for sesame seeds. Thin with milk, fruit, or vegetable juice until desired consistency.

COMPLEMENTARY PROTEIN PROPORTIONS

Rice (1⅓ cups)	+	Legumes (½ cup)
Rice (2½ cups)	+	Soybeans (¼ cup)
Rice (1 cup)	+	Sesame seeds (⅓ cup)
Cornmeal (1 cup)	+	Legumes (¼ cup)
Legumes (⅓ cup)	+	Sesame seeds (½ cup)*

* Use fewer sesame seeds and purée with milk.

COMPLEMENTARY PROTEIN PROPORTIONS

Sesame seeds (1 cup)	+ Peanuts (¾ cup) or Peanut butter (½ cup)
Milk (1½ cups)	+ Peanuts (1½ cups)
Milk (2 cups) or Cheese (⅔ cup)	+ Legumes (1 cup)
Milk (1 cup) or Cheese (¼ cup)	+ Rice (¾ cup)

$ Hummos

In this recipe for hummos, a Middle Eastern food, garbanzo beans, or chick peas, are combined with sesame seeds. It is a high-protein purée that can also be seasoned with garlic, lemon juice, salt, and pepper to be used as a vegetable dip.

> **1 cup dried garbanzos (chick peas)**
> **½ cup sesame seeds**
> **½ cup cooking liquid from beans**
> **1 cup milk, or ½ cup milk + ½ cup yogurt**
> **¼ cup oil**

1. Cook garbanzos in 3 cups water for 1½–2 hours (2 cups canned chick peas may be substituted; do not cook).
2. If using a food processor, blend garbanzos and sesame seeds until finely puréed, then add liquids. In a blender, add liquid first. The purée can be frozen for 3–4 months.
YIELD: About 2 cups.

$ Peanut Butter Pancakes

These pancakes have only a slight taste of peanuts; however, the combination of milk, eggs, flour, and peanuts provides a high *8 grams* of complete protein in just *1* pancake. They can be served as a finger food or puréed (1 tablespoon milk for each pancake).

2 eggs, beaten
¼ cup honey
½ teaspoon vanilla extract
½ cup peanut butter
¾ cup milk
1 cup whole-wheat flour
¼ cup dry milk powder
½ teaspoon salt
2 teaspoons baking powder

1. Beat eggs, honey, vanilla, and peanut butter together.
2. Add milk and mix.
3. Combine flour, milk powder, salt, and baking powder.
4. Add to egg and milk mixture and stir until smooth.
5. Fry on lightly oiled griddle.
YIELD: 8 pancakes.

11

Desserts

Desserts are not a necessity in your baby's diet. The highly sweetened or starchy ones, such as puddings, can even be harmful. I have included some basic recipes for nutritious desserts that your family will enjoy and that you can also feed your baby as fruit, cereal, protein, or dairy servings.

Fruit Milk Sherbet

This is a different way to serve fruit and is something the rest of the family will enjoy. There are egg whites, a possible allergen, in this dessert, so be sure that you have already introduced your baby to whole eggs, probably around eight months. Any fruit that has been introduced can be used; bananas, peaches, apricots, pears, plums, berries are especially good.

    1 teaspoon plain gelatin powder
    1 tablespoon water
    1½ cups fruit purée (use any basic recipe for purées
        in the Fruit chapter)
    2 tablespoons honey (optional, depending on tartness
        of fruit)
    ¾ cup milk (whole or skim)
    1 egg white

1. Soften the gelatin in the water. Blend into the purée.
2. Add honey, if used.
3. Add milk and blend thoroughly.
4. Pour into a metal ice cube tray without the dividers. Cover and freeze until it is frozen around the edges.
5. While the mixture is freezing, beat the egg white until stiff.
6. Pour the frozen mixture into a bowl or blender and blend slowly until it is smooth.
7. Fold in the egg white.
8. Return to the ice cube tray and freeze until it is solid.

YIELD: 2½ cups.

Note: All the steps may be done in a blender except for dissolving the gelatin and beating the egg white. A food processor may also be used unless there is so much liquid that it rises over the drive shaft and leaks out.

Citrus Fruit Sherbet

Once citrus juices have been introduced, this dessert is a good way of feeding your baby the entire fruit which contains additional nutrients. This recipe requires a high-speed blender to purée the pulp finely.

> 1 tablespoon brown sugar or honey (omit if a sweet
>   orange is used)
> 1 cup fruit juice
> 1 teaspoon plain gelatin powder
> 1 lemon or orange or ½ medium grapefruit

1. Melt sugar or honey in fruit juice. Dissolve in the gelatin.
2. Remove the fruit peel.
3. In a blender, liquefy the fruit. Add the juice and blend.
4. Pour into metal ice cube tray with the dividers removed.
5. Cover and freeze until fairly firm—about 1 hour.

6. Pour back into blender, and blend at a slow speed until smooth.

7. Return to ice cube tray and freeze until firm.

YIELD: 1½ cups.

Fruit/Egg Yolk Custard

This is a dessert that counts as a serving of fruit and egg yolk. It makes a good supper dish and can be given as soon as your baby has been introduced to egg yolk. You will find it especially useful if your baby shows an allergy to egg whites.

    1 piece fruit (banana, pear, or peach is good)
        or
    ¼ cup fruit purée
    1 egg yolk, beaten
    ¼ cup milk (whole or skim)

1. Preheat oven to 350°F.
2. Blend together the fruit, egg yolk, and milk.
3. Pour into 2 custard cups and place in pan of water.
4. Bake for 30 minutes or until a knife comes out clean. The cups may also be placed in a pan of simmering water for 10 minutes, if you do not have an oven available.
5. Refrigerate for up to 3 days.

YIELD: 2 servings.

Fruit Custard

This is a highly nutritious dessert for the entire family. It contains eggs, so wait until you have introduced the whole egg to your baby's diet.

    2 cups milk (whole or skim) plus ½ cup nonfat dry
        milk (optional)
    3 beaten eggs
    ½ cup fruit purée, raw or cooked (banana, peaches,
        plums, or apricots are good)

1. Preheat oven to 350°F.

2. If you have a blender, the milk, eggs, and fruit can be slowly blended at the same time. Do not use a high speed because you will have too much foam. Otherwise, mix them together until they are blended. This may be too much liquid for a processor. If so, purée fruit, then add to liquid in a separate bowl.

3. Pour the mixture into 8 custard cups. Place in pan of hot water that comes to the level of the custard.

4. Bake for 30 minutes or until a knife comes out clean.

5. Cover and refrigerate for up to 3 days.

YIELD: 8 servings.

$ Peanut Butter Custard

1⅓ cups milk (whole or skim)
⅓ cup peanut butter
2 eggs, beaten
3 tablespoons honey (optional)

1. Preheat oven to 325°F.

2. Add the milk gradually to the peanut butter, stirring until smooth.

3. Blend in the eggs and honey.

4. Pour into a small baking dish or custard cups. Place in pan of hot water to level of custard.

5. Bake for 30 minutes, until knife comes out clean.

6. Cover and refrigerate for up to 3 days.

YIELD: 2 cups.

Fruit Crunch

This is an easy family dessert that your baby can eat as a serving of fruit and cereal.

> 3 cups sliced fruit*
> ⅔ cup brown sugar (or less, depending on tartness of fruit)
> ½ cup quick-cooking rolled oats
> 3 tablespoons flour (whole wheat, unbleached, or enriched)
> 3 tablespoons melted butter or margarine or safflower oil

1. Preheat oven to 350°F.
2. Peel fruit if your baby does not eat skins and you are puréeing in a blender or processor.
3. Place fruit in an 8-inch-square baking pan.
4. Sprinkle with the sugar.
5. Combine the dry ingredients.
6. Mix the fat or oil with the dry ingredients until crumbly.
7. Sprinkle the mixture over the fruit.
8. Bake 1 hour.
9. Purée baby's portion in blender or processor for smoothest texture.

Apricot Whip

This dessert is high in iron and contains some protein. It is also a way to use leftover egg whites.

> 1 pound package dried apricots
> 2 teaspoons orange or lemon juice
> ¼ cup brown sugar
> 3 egg whites

1. Prepare the apricot purée as in **Stewed Dried Apricots.**
2. Add the juice and sugar, heating until the sugar is dissolved. Cool.
3. Beat the egg whites until stiff.

*Some good fruits are: apples, peaches, plums, nectarin͏   ͏ ͏ berries, and rhubarb (2 cups, or 12 ounces frozen, with 1 cup of any ot͏

4. Fold the apricot mixture into the egg whites.

5. Cover and store in the refrigerator for up to 3 days.

YIELD: 6 servings (adult).

VARIATION

You can also use other stewed dried fruits such as prunes or peaches.

Gelatin Desserts

Gelatin contains no vitamins or minerals, but it does supply a fair amount of protein. It also gives a thicker consistency to some thin or difficult to swallow foods. You can use it to give some variety to your baby's meals, either plain or combined with almost any puréed food. The gelatin dessert powders contain mainly sugar and a variety of preservatives, so do not use them. Instead, buy the envelopes of plain dry gelatin which are less expensive and just as easy to prepare. Here is a basic recipe.

½ cup cool water
1 envelope plain gelatin
1½ cups fruit or vegetable juice
1 cup puréed fruit, vegetables (optional)

1. Place cool water in a small pan. Sprinkle in gelatin and stir to dissolve.

2. Add juice and heat for a minute or so, stirring well.

3. Pour into 4 small cups and cool. If you are adding a purée, stir it in after the gelatin has begun to thicken, in about ½ hour.

4. Store in refrigerator for 3–4 days.

YIELD: 4 servings.

12

Beverages

Beverages are essential in your baby's daily diet. Milk is the most important, but fruits and vegetable juices also supply vitamins and minerals. Since there is a wide variety of milks and juices for you to choose from, I feel it is important for you to be aware of the differences. I have also included basic information on buying, storing, and using milk and juices.

Milk For Your Baby

You will probably be feeding your baby some form of cow's milk, even if you breast-feed during the early months. Milk is an almost complete food, inexpensive for the amount of nutrition, and indispensable for your baby's growth. By the time he is three months old he should be drinking 3 cups to 1 quart a day and should continue for the next few years. Milk contains high amounts of complete protein, calcium, phosphorus, and riboflavin. It is naturally low in vitamin D and loses most of the vitamin C during processing. The amount of butterfat depends on whether the milk is whole or skimmed.

Whole milk, whether it is pasteurized, homogenized, or evaporated, contains at least 3.25 per cent butterfat if it is stamped *U. S. Grade A*. This grade also indicates that the milk was processed under sanitary conditions and is wholesome. The fresh milk has been heated to kill harmful bacteria, and this pasteurizing also destroys the vitamin C. The butterfat in this milk will rise to the top, and the bottle must be shaken, before pouring, to distribute the fat.

- *Homogenized milk* is pasteurized fresh milk that has been processed to disperse the butterfat evenly through the milk. Read the label to see if a particular brand has been fortified with vitamin D.
- *Evaporated milk* is concentrated by removing half of the water. It is sterilized and sold in cans and is usually fortified with vitamin D. One advantage is that you can easily carry home a good supply and store the cans at cool room temperature for several months. It is also good to use when traveling, since it is readily available and of uniform composition throughout the world. It is also less expensive than fresh, whole milk.

    You can easily prepare whole milk by mixing equal parts of evaporated milk and water. It is very convenient to mix it directly in your baby's bottle. Remember to wash the top of the can before opening. You can cover the opened can and store it in the refrigerator for up to 5 days. You can also use evaporated milk in concentrated form to thin purées, especially strong-flavored vegetables; and also in fruit and vegetable drinks to supply some extra nourishment.

Skim milk is available in fresh, evaporated, and powdered form. It is whole milk that has had most of the butterfat removed. Since vitamin A is also removed with the fat, most skim milk is fortified with vitamin A. Otherwise, it has the same nutritional composition as whole milk.

- *Fortified skim milk* has vitamins A and D added, along with a small amount of nonfat milk solids.
- *Evaporated skim milk* has been concentrated by removing part of the water. It is sold in cans and is stored and used in the same way as evaporated whole milk.
- *Nonfat dry milk powder* is skim milk from which almost all the water has been removed. You can buy it in any store, packed in boxes or in premeasured 1-quart envelopes. The *U.S. Extra Grade* on the label indicates that the milk meets the government's standards of composition and wholesomeness. The label also indicates whether vitamins A and D have been added.

This form of milk is very inexpensive, around $.22 a quart as compared with $.60 or more for a quart of fresh liquid milk. This can mean a saving of at least $12 each month if your baby is drinking a quart a day.

I have found this milk very convenient, since I can carry home twenty quarts in one box, and never have to dash out on a late-night search for a bottle of fresh milk.

You can store the unopened powder at cool room temperature for several months. The opened package of powder should be kept dry and used within 2 weeks.

You will find it very convenient to carry a small amount, when you are traveling or visiting, and mix up a bottle wherever you find water—even a park or a gas station.

To obtain liquid milk, you will usually mix 1⅓ parts nonfat dry milk powder to 4 parts water. For example:

1 cup (8 ounces) = ⅓ cup powder + 1 cup water
1 bottle (8 ounces) = 3 ounces powder + 8 ounces water
1 quart = 1⅓ cups powder + 1 quart water

You can also use nonfat dry milk as a fortifier, to add nutrients to whole or skimmed milk, or in any recipes. Just add up to 50 per cent more powder, for instance:

1¾ cups powder to 1 quart water
2–4 tablespoons powder for each 1 cup liquid in a recipe

As a way of saving money and moderating the amount of cholesterol, you can also mix equals parts fresh milk and liquid nonfat dry milk. If your baby is already drinking whole fresh milk, you can use this mixture to gradually accustom him to skim milk. Once nonfat dry milk has been mixed, it must be stored as fresh liquid milk.

SKIM MILK OR WHOLE MILK?

There is, at present, a controversy among doctors and nutritionists as to whether or not a baby should be fed whole milk or skim milk, which has had the fat removed. Some doctors feel that by feeding a baby skim milk and limiting the amount of other foods that are high in saturated fat, they can reduce the possibility of atherosclerosis, or hardening of the arteries, in adult life. (See *Nutrition—Fats* and *Oils*.)

Dr. Fomon and other experts on infant nutrition object to such a drastic manipulation of an infant's diet for several reasons. They feel that a moderate intake of saturated fat, or food cholesterol, is necessary for proper development of the brain and nervous system and may also enable the body to handle cholesterol in adult life. Another essential nutrient in butterfat is linoleic acid, which is important in your baby's development. Skim milk also supplies only half the calories of whole milk, and calories are important for an underweight baby. Another point to remember is that breast milk *does* contain butterfat.

However, besides the cholesterol question, there are some reasons why you might prefer to feed your baby skim milk. Some babies have difficulty digesting the butterfat in whole milk, and the result is the very messy and smelly habit of "cheesing." This may not happen if you use skim milk. You should also be able to take advantage of the convenience and economy of nonfat dry milk.

One answer, until more conclusive research is done, is to plan a well-balanced diet for your baby. A young baby should be drinking whole milk. When your baby is eating solids, he will get an adequate amount of saturated fat in such foods as meat, liver, poultry, egg yolk, and butter, and you can then feed him skim milk as a regular beverage. You may also add to a bottle of skim milk 2 teaspoons of polyunsaturated safflower, corn, or olive oil, which will be equivalent in fat to whole milk and supply more of the essential linoleic acid.

If you are still feeding your baby whole milk, you should limit the amounts of high-cholesterol foods or saturated fat. In any case this is an important question for you to discuss with your doctor, in view of your baby's own individual needs.

Of course, you can always use powdered milk for convenience, when traveling or visiting, and still use whole milk as your baby's main milk. A baby will not have difficulty in switching from whole milk to skim, since it is the fat in whole milk that usually causes digestive trouble.

MILKS NOT FOR YOUR BABY

Raw cow's milk or **certified raw milk** is one instance where an unprocessed food should not be used. All the original nutrients are there, but so are all the bacteria which can cause various illnesses and intestinal troubles. Since you must boil it to make it sterile, you have the same loss of vitamin C as in pasteurized milk, so it hardly seems worth the trouble and risk.

Condensed milk is sold in cans, usually on the same shelf as evaporated milk. Be careful not to confuse them. Since this milk is highly sweetened, it is not suitable for your baby.

Filled, diet, and modified skim milk are various names for milk products that were developed for diet-conscious people who do not like the taste of skim milk. If the name confuses you, read the list of ingredients on the label. The different brands vary in composition but are usually some mixture of skim milk, nonfat dry milk, water, and vegetable fat.

While there is nothing harmful in these ingredients, the government has not set standards to ensure that these milks have the same nutritional composition as cow's milk.

The protein content may be higher or lower, and the vegetable fat is often coconut oil, which is a saturated fat that lacks essential fatty acids. They are usually more expensive than plain whole or skim milk.

If this type of milk is the only one available, your baby will not be harmed by an occasional bottle, but he should not drink this milk regularly.

Synthetic, nondairy, and imitation milk are also sold in dairy departments. These products have no relation to cow's milk. They are a combination of vegetable fat, sodium caseinate, soy solids, corn syrup, flavoring agents, emulsifiers, stabilizers, and water. Government standards have not been set for their nutritional value. Needless to say, do not give them to your baby.

Chocolate milk is also sold in dairy departments. It is sweetened and many babies are allergic to chocolate, so don't even try it in an emergency.

Instant breakfasts are a form of milk drink, packaged in cans or in powder form. They are really a combination of sugar, flavorings, and some vitamin supplements. In an emergency, if milk is just not available, you can give your baby the liquid *vanilla* flavor. The powder form depends on being mixed with milk for its nutritional value. So don't just mix it with water and give it to your baby as milk.

Buttermilk is made from skim milk, and bacterial cultures have been added, which gives it a sour taste. The name sounds healthful, but it is not suitable for your baby.

Goat's milk and soybean-based milk are often given to babies who show an allergy to cow's milk. However, they do not have the same nutritional composition, so you should never use them without the advice of your doctor.

HOW TO STORE MILK

Fresh milk, and evaporated or nonfat dry milk that has been reconstituted, should be carefully handled to retain nutrients and prevent spoilage. I've always felt so guilty when I've had to throw away a quart of spoiled milk.

- Always buy fresh milk that is as fresh as possible. In some areas of the country the cartons must be clearly stamped with the date of the last day that the milk can be sold. In areas which do not have this law, the cartons are usually stamped with a coded date, and you can ask the owner of the store to interpret it. If you are buying more milk than you will use immediately, select those cartons with the latest date. If you find milk in the case that is past the legal selling date, you should not buy it; instead, notify the manager of the store to have it removed from the shelf.
- Cans of evaporated milk and packages of nonfat dry milk powder are often stamped with the packaging date. Buy the most recent date if you are buying large amounts. Store unopened evaporated and dry milk at cool room temperature.
- Keep liquid milk tightly covered and store it in the coldest part of the refrigerator. Remember that the door, which may have a shelf for milk, is usually the warmest area of the refrigerator, and milk should not be stored there.
- Plan to use milk within 3–5 days.
- Do not allow containers of milk to stand in the light, since light destroys the vitamin riboflavin. If you have your milk delivered, supply a box for the milk to be left in, so that it does not sit in the light. Since your baby's bottle may often be out for as long as an hour during a feeding, you can preserve the riboflavin by using opaque plastic bottles, or the disposable bottles which are used inside a solid holder.
- Do not pour unused milk back in the original container once it has been removed, or mix old milk in with fresh milk.
- You may freeze milk for up to a month, but it must be used soon after thawing.

Homemade Fortified Milk

If your baby becomes balky at eating solids, here are some fortifiers that you can add to one bottle daily. You may even find a combination that you can give as an evening bottle to insure a wakeless night.

> 1 cup milk or formula
> 2 tablespoons nonfat dry milk powder
> 1–2 raw egg yolks* (raw egg white is difficult to digest)
> ¼ teaspoon molasses (laxative, iron)
> ½ teaspoon powdered brewer's yeast—(*not* baking yeast; B-vitamins)
> 2 teaspoons vegetable oil (vitamin E, linoleic acid)
> 2 teaspoons plain yogurt (vitamin K)

1. Blend the ingredients with an electric blender or egg beater.

2. Allow it to settle for a few minutes so that there are no air bubbles.

3. Use a nipple with an enlarged hole. You can enlarge the hole by piercing it with a hot needle in a pencil eraser.

Juices: Fruit and Vegetable

Fruit and vegetable juices supply vitamins and minerals while satisfying your baby's thirst. The juices sold especially for infants are very expensive and may be sweetened. Instead, you should serve your baby any of the canned and frozen juices on the market, or you can easily prepare juice from fresh fruits and vegetables.

Nutrition: Juice is most valuable in your baby's diet as a source of vitamin C. This vitamin, although adequate in human milk, is destroyed in cow's milk by the pasteurization process. You can give your baby a vitamin supplement, but daily servings of certain juices will supply an adequate amount of vitamin C, together with other nutrients. Fruits and vegetables have different amounts of vitamin C.

---

* Raw egg yolk should not be added until after cooked egg yolk has been successfully introduced.

- "An orange a day keeps the doctor away" should replace the old proverb about the apple. The citrus fruits—oranges, grapefruits, lemon—are your highest vitamin-C fruits. One *3-ounce serving* each day of one of these juices, either fresh, dehydrated, or frozen, will give your baby enough vitamin C. When these juices are canned some of the vitamin is lost, so you should increase the serving to at least *4 ounces*. The orange and grapefruit juices sold in bottles in the dairy section have been pasteurized and are the same as canned juices.
- Guava juice, available in cans, is as high as the citrus fruits in vitamin C.
- Canned tomato or papaya juice will supply an adequate amount of vitamin C, if you double the serving to *6 ounces* daily.
- Never heat fruit juice before serving, since heat destroys vitamin C.
- Other fruits are low in vitamin C and should be considered only beverages.
- Apricot nectar, papaya, and mango juices are very high in vitamin A.

Introduce orange juice, then other citrus juices at around four months. Orange juice is a possible allergy food, so when you first introduce it, dilute the juice with an equal amount of water. Begin with 1 ounce daily, then gradually increase to 3 ounces. If your baby does show an allergic reaction to orange juice, you can try guava or tomato juice or give him a vitamin C supplement. Other juices can be given as beverages at around the same time you would introduce the fruit or vegetable.

Buying: The federal Food and Drug Administration has set standards of identity for the various forms of fresh, frozen, and canned orange juice that require a high content of juice. Unless you live in a tropical climate or buy oranges in season, the frozen orange juice concentrates are the most economical source of vitamin C. Since the juice content is set by the government, you can take advantage of the lower-priced store brands or private labels.

Standards have also been set for canned pineapple,

tomato, and prune juice. Any sweeteners and preservatives must be stated on the label, so you can select the brands *without* additional sweeteners.

If you buy fruit juice, other than orange juice, that has been fortified with vitamin C, read the label carefully to check the amount of vitamin C in a serving that your baby is likely to drink. Remember that he should have 40–50 mg. of vitamin C daily.

Please notice that I have been using the word *"juice."* There are many beverages, both canned and frozen, which cannot be legally labeled "juice." These include the fruit *"punches," "nectars," "drinks,"* and *"ades"* and are clearly labeled with these descriptive words. **The nutritional cost of these beverages is very high:** you are paying for and filling your baby up with mainly water and sugar. *This is equally true of such citrus drinks as "orangeade" or "lemonade."* Even if vitamin C is added (and advertised in large letters), you are still missing the other vitamins and minerals in the original fruit and paying more. You would come out ahead, in terms of nutritional cost, if you diluted frozen orange juice concentrate, instead of the usual 3–1 dilution, with the same amount of water as in these drinks— **often as high as 9 parts water to 1 part juice.** There are no government standards for these drinks, and the label does not have to state the percentage of real juice. Carefully read *the ingredient list* on any canned or frozen juices. Do not be misled by "natural" on the label.

Other beverages that your baby should not drink are the *"instant breakfast-drink powders"* and the *"imitation orange juices."* Again, the label and list of ingredients are your warning. These drinks contain little or no real juice and instead are made up of a variety of fillers, artificial color, artificial flavor, vegetable oil, sugar, and preservatives. Some vitamin C is added, but they still lack the other nutrients found in orange juice. These imitation juices are usually sold in the same freezer section as frozen orange juice, so you must be careful not to confuse them. You can also buy dehydrated-juice crystals that are real juice and should not be confused with the breakfast-drink powders. If you are in doubt about a product, just read the list of ingredients.

Store canned juices at cool room temperature for several months. Before opening the can, shake it well and rinse the lid. The opened can can be covered and stored in the refrigerator for 2–3 days. The acid in citrus juices acts as a preservative and these juices keep the longest. Frozen juices can be kept solidly frozen for several months in a 0°F. freezer, or for 1 month in the freezer compartment of a refrigerator. Do not refreeze thawed juices; use them within 3–4 days. Fresh citrus juices can be refrigerated for 3–4 days or frozen. Other fresh fruit and vegetable juices should be prepared just before serving and should not be saved.

Straining: Until your baby is drinking from a cup you will have to strain citrus juices so the pulp will not clog the nipple of the bottle. Even enlarging the hole in the nipple will not help. You might as well strain a 2- or 3-day supply to save cleanup. If you serve the "nectars," or a banana milk shake, you can enlarge the hole in the nipple with a hot needle held with a pencil eraser. As soon as your baby is drinking from a cup, you can serve him citrus juices with the pulp (which contains nutrients), and any other fruit or vegetable juice you have liquefied in your blender.

Here are a few easy recipes for preparing fresh juices. For detailed buying and storing information, see "Fruits" (chapter 8) and "Vegetables" (chapter 9).

Fresh Orange Juice

The best juice oranges are the Valencia, Hamlin, and Parson Brown. Select oranges that have smooth skins and are heavy for their size. Oranges with russet or greenish skin color are often less expensive, but just as nutritious as the oranges with a bright-orange color.

1 medium juice orange

1. Wash the orange.
2. Cut in half and squeeze the juice with either a hand or electric juicer or if you have a good blender: peel the

orange, cut in half, and liquefy. This is a good method if you are making a large quantity and do not have an electric juicer.

3. Strain the juice for bottle feeding.
4. Do not add any sweetener.
YIELD: 3 ounces or 2 food cubes (1 serving).
Note: It will save you cleanup time to make a large batch and freeze it in food cubes.

Fresh Grapefruit Juice

½ medium grapefruit

1. Prepare as for orange juice.
YIELD: 3 ounces or 2 food cubes (1 serving).

Fresh Lemon Juice

2 lemons
½ teaspoon brown sugar or honey

1. Prepare as for orange juice. Add sweetening.
YIELD: 3 ounces or 2 food cubes (1 serving).

All-Purpose Fruit Juice

You can prepare almost any fruit as a juice with a processor or blender. Here is a general recipe with suggestions for some specific fruits.

½ cup chopped fruit
¾ cup liquid* (water, fruit juice, or milk)

1. Select ripe fruit. Take advantage of seasonal prices or sales.
2. Wash the fruit. Peel and remove seeds. (If you are

* For very juicy fruits such as berries, decrease the liquid to ½ cup. Do not combine milk with citrus fruits.

straining the juice, do not bother to peel thin-skinned fruits such as peaches, apricots, pears.)

3. Place fruit and liquid in blender and blend on high-est speed until the fruit is liquefied. In processor, purée fruit first, then add liquid.

4. Strain for use in a bottle. Or use a nipple with an enlarged hole. As soon as your baby starts drinking from a cup, leave the pulp in to make a thick, nutritious drink.

5. Serve at once; do not store.

Note: Do not add sugar. Fruits contain natural sugar.

YIELD: 1 cup juice.

VARIATION

Combine thick fruits with juicy fruits such as *banana/orange*. Experiment with any fruit you may have on hand or left over from a family meal. This is a good way to use up a piece of very ripe fruit that you might otherwise throw away.

All-Purpose
Raw-Vegetable Juice

There are fewer vegetables that can be prepared and served as juices because of their generally stronger tastes; however, they do make highly nutritious drinks. Carrots are an excellent source of vitamin A; spinach and green leafy vegetables contain high amounts of vitamins and minerals; and beets are high in natural sugar; however, do not serve more than 8 ounces a day. See "Vegetables" (chapter 9) for specific information on any vegetable you prepare as a juice. Here is a general recipe for use with a blender or processor.

    ½ cup chopped vegetable
    1 cup liquid (water, milk, or fruit juice)

1. Wash the vegetable. Peel if necessary.

2. Place vegetable and liquid in blender and liquefy on highest speed. In processor, purée vegetable first.

3. Strain and serve at once. Do not store.
YIELD: 1 cup.

VARIATION

This is another way of preparing vegetable juice if you do not have a blender. You can also make a large amount and freeze it.

    2 cups chopped vegetable
    1 quart water

1. Wash and peel vegetable if necessary. Chop or cut in small pieces.
2. Place in pot. Cover tightly and simmer for 1 hour.
3. Cool and strain. Store in refrigerator for 2–3 days, or freeze in food cubes.
YIELD: 3½ cups.

VARIATIONS

You can combine many fruits and vegetables to make a variety of nutritious drinks. Here are some suggestions, but use your imagination and whatever you may happen to have on hand—either fresh, frozen, or canned.

Carrot/Orange	Tomato/Green leafy
Carrot/Pineapple	Carrot/Apple
Pear/Green leafy	Beet/Pineapple
Orange/Green leafy	Carrot/Celery

Fresh Carrot Juice

This is one of the first vegetable juices that you can serve your baby when he is three to four months old. It is also an old-fashioned treatment for diarrhea. You will need a blender or processor to prepare this juice. Limit servings to 1 per day.

1 medium carrot
¾ cup water (or skim milk)
1 tablespoon nonfat dry milk powder (optional)

1. Wash carrot. Cut in half.
2. Place carrot and water or dry milk in blender or processor. Blend on highest speed.
3. Strain and serve at once. Do not save.
YIELD: 6 ounces juice.

Boiled Carrot Juice

This is really the same as raw carrot juice, but you will not need a blender and you can make enough for several servings. Limit to 1 serving a day.

1 pound carrots (4–5 medium)
1 quart water (or 2 cups water plus 2 cups skim milk)
½ cup nonfat dry milk powder (optional)
1 tablespoon brown rice (optional)

1. Wash carrots and cut in small pieces, or chop.
2. Place all ingredients in a pot. Cover tightly.
3. Bring to a boil. Simmer for 1 hour.
4. Cool and strain. Do not force the carrots through: you want a juice, not a purée.
5. Serve in a bottle with an enlarged nipple hole.
6. Store the juice, tightly covered, in the refrigerator for 2–3 days. Or, freeze in food cubes.
YIELD: 3½ cups.

13

Instant Baby Food: How to Live Off the Land

The foods that are described in this chapter form the basis of easy baby-food cookery. In fact, they can all be used without any cooking or can be purchased already cooked in stores or restaurants. You can feed your baby some foods directly from the container. Other foods require only a fork or spoon to prepare the smoothest purée. A few foods may require the use of a blender, food mill, or strainer to prepare a smooth purée, but can still be mashed to a coarse texture with a fork or spoon. Since you are preparing your own baby food, you can quickly accustom your baby to eating coarser textures. You can always try a food; a hungry baby can become very adept at swallowing!

The small food mills that are sold specifically for processing baby food are very convenient to carry when traveling. Some prepare a finer purée than others, but they will all process almost any food into at least a "junior" texture. Once your baby is eating most table food and coarser textures, you can prepare "instant" food from your regular family meals with this type of food mill. I tried a portion of a quiche that was very much enjoyed by a visiting baby!

Instant foods can be particularly valuable when you are traveling or visiting, since there is no need to carry or store specially prepared food for your baby. To make your life even easier, train your baby to eat any food cold. These foods may be found in any small store, restaurant, or home kitchen. You should also keep some of these foods on hand for quick use if you happen to run out of your frozen supply of food cubes, or if you do not have adequate freezer space to take advantage of the food-cube method.

You should keep a list of the more successful ones for use by baby sitters and for your own quick reference. Use your imagination in finding new instant foods that I have missed; just keep in mind the basic good buying principles as described in chapter 2—"How to Save Money." For more detailed information, look up any specific food in the preceding recipe chapters. The instant foods are also organized according to their basic food group, i.e., **cereal grains, fruits, vegetables,** and **protein foods;** so you can easily select a well-balanced menu.

Cereal Grains

Dry infant cereals are easy to carry and prepare. They are usually mixed 1 part cereal to 5 parts cold milk or formula.

Instant cereals can usually be ordered in any restaurant. The smoothest ones will be the cream of wheat or rice. If your baby has been introduced to whole-grain cereals, order oatmeal, Ralston, or Wheatena.

Graham crackers or other soft enriched or whole-grain crackers can be soaked in milk and mashed to a soft purée. Bread can also be soaked. Avoid those which use BHT as a preservative.

Rice pudding is usually available in restaurants and can be mashed with a fork or spoon.

Fruits

Fresh fruit is one of your most convenient instant foods. It is easy to carry and is available in any store or restaurant. As soon as possible, you should introduce raw fruit to your baby. Bananas can be served as early as six weeks, and other raw fruits at four to five months of age. You will be able to easily prepare a very smooth purée with only a spoon from any of the following fresh fruits. You will not even need a feeding dish.

Apples	Mangoes
Apricots	Nectarines
Avocados	Papayas
Bananas	Peaches
Cantaloupe	Pears
Guavas	Plums

1. Select ripe fruit.
2. Wash the fruit. Do not peel; the skin will serve as the dish.
3. Cut the fruit in half, or cut as large a slice as your baby will eat. Peel one side of a banana.
4. Remove the pit or seeds.
5. As you feed your baby, mash spoonfuls of fruit by scraping the cut side with the front or back edge of a spoon. This method is easy and will make a smoother purée than mashing with a fork.

Whole fruit keeps well, but when mashed, it turns brown quickly. So only mash as much as you will use in one feeding. The unpeeled part of the fruit can be wrapped and will keep at room temperature until the next feeding. You can also store it in the refrigerator for 1–2 days.

Canned or stewed fruits are also convenient as instant fruits. You can keep a supply on hand in your pantry. Try to buy the brands that are packed in water, or in their own juice, or in "light syrup." The heavier the syrup the more sugar it contains. Always drain the fruit before puréeing, since it should not require any thinning. Some good fruits are:

Applesauce: Use the plain variety. The applesauce that is combined with other fruits often contains artificial color, flavor, or other additives, and is more expensive. You can serve applesauce to your baby without puréeing.

Baked apples: Mash with a fork or spoon for a smooth purée.

Jellied cranberry sauce: Can be mashed with a spoon for a smooth purée. Do not feed your baby the whole type, which contains skins.

Pears: Can be mashed with a fork for a smooth purée.

Peaches, apricots, fruit salad, prunes can be mashed with a fork for a coarser purée.

Pineapple requires a blender to prepare a purée.

Vegetables

There are many vegetables that you can keep on hand or order in a restaurant as instant food.

Mashed potatoes require thinning with a little milk. The "instant" or dehydrated potatoes should be used only as a last resort, since they may be lower in nutrients and usually are loaded with additives and fillers.

Canned yams or sweet potatoes are already cooked and can be mashed with a fork, adding a little milk. Buy the vacuum-pack instead of the type that is packed in sugar syrup.

Beans, baked or kidney, and peas can be puréed to a coarse texture with a fork, and thinned with a little milk. Or use a blender for a smooth purée:

Peanut butter: Thin with an equal amount of milk.

Winter squash (acorn, butternut, etc.): The frozen squash is cooked and mashed. It only requires thawing, since it is already puréed. You can usually order this squash in a restaurant.

Fresh ripe tomatoes: Cut in half, remove the seeds, and scrape with a spoon.

Any canned vegetable: Since they are already cooked, you only need to purée them in a blender or food mill. (See "Vegetables" in chapter 9.) Most can be mashed with a fork to a coarse texture. Drain the canning liquid, then add a small amount for thinning if necessary. If the canning liquid is not salted, you can serve it as a nutritious beverage.

Protein Foods

EGGS

One of the best and most convenient instant protein foods! They are included as an instant food since a boiled egg is so easy to make, stores well, and can be easily carried when traveling. You can always order an egg in any restaurant.

Egg Yolk

- Keep the boiled egg in the shell until ready to use. It can be kept at room temperature for 1 day, or refrigerated for 1 week.
- Cut it in half and remove the yolk.
- Mash the yolk, adding about 1 tablespoon milk or juice to thin.

Scrambled Eggs

Order or prepare an egg so that it is loose, or softly scrambled. Mash it with a fork or spoon, adding a little milk.

Egg custard can be ordered in most restaurants and can be fed directly to your baby.

LIVER

Either chopped chicken liver or a pâté can be thinned to make a very smooth purée. It is available in most delicatessens and restaurants. Since these pâtés are rich and highly seasoned, use them only as a last resort to feed an older baby. You can also order sautéed or broiled chicken livers in many restaurants and mash them with a fork, adding a little milk. The beef and calf's liver is usually too tough to prepare with a fork, but you can scrape some off with a spoon or dull knife.

Prepared spreads such as deviled ham, chicken, and liver can be purchased in small cans. These can easily be thinned to make a smooth purée, but they are also highly seasoned and often contain additives.

PRECOOKED MEAT AND POULTRY MEALS

There are many canned and frozen prepared dishes that contain meat, poultry, cheese, vegetables, rice, pastas, beans. While they are more expensive than the same dishes that you can prepare yourself, they are easily stored and very convenient. For a quick meal, just open the can (or defrost) and put the food through the blender.

Some dishes such as spaghetti or macaroni and cheese can also be mashed with a fork or food mill to a coarser purée. These dishes can often be ordered in a restaurant.

The amount of protein depends on the type of dish and the specific brand; however, most contain more protein and other solids than the corresponding commercial baby-food dinners.

Read the labels carefully and buy those which list protein foods first, as the major ingredient. Avoid those brands which contain many additives and fillers. Remember that these foods should only be served occasionally when convenience is important.

Stews (usually the highest in protein)

TV dinners (choose one with a plain meat and two vegetables)

Chicken and noodles

Spaghetti and meatballs

Macaroni and cheese

Chile con carne (for an older baby)

Do not use the frozen chicken or meat pot pie, since they contain very small amounts of protein.

Leftovers can be stored in the refrigerator for 2 days. The canned foods can be frozen in food cubes for up to 1 month. *Do not* refreeze the frozen foods.

DAIRY FOODS

These dairy foods can also be used as sources of protein, and they contain the same nutrients as milk. They are very convenient and readily available instant foods.

Yogurt can be one of your baby's earliest foods. There is a wide variety of brands and flavors.

- Buy the brands that do not contain fillers and additives. The simplest list of ingredients is: fresh milk, nonfat dry milk, and yogurt cultures.
- You should introduce *plain* yogurt first, then *prune whip*.
- Older babies will enjoy the various fruit flavors. The Swiss-style yogurts have small pieces of fresh fruit which are easily mashed.
- Do not feed your baby the *chocolate* or *coffee* flavors.
- You can feed your baby yogurt directly from the container, at refrigerator temperature.
- Unused yogurt must be stored in the refrigerator and can be kept up to 1 week.
- See chapter 10 for instructions on how you can easily make your own yogurt.

Cottage cheese is easy to prepare.

- Use the creamed variety or add a little milk. Mash with a spoon for a smooth purée. It is also good when mixed with a little fruit such as applesauce.
- Avoid those brands which contain fillers and preservatives.
- Cottage cheese spoils easily, so try to buy by the date, or taste it yourself before feeding it to your baby.
- You can store it in the refrigerator for up to 1 week.

Ice milk or cream is readily available and is a favorite of most babies.

- Ice milk is more easily digested by young infants.
- Introduce *vanilla* first and then fruit flavors. Remember to mash or remove any large pieces of fruit.
- Do not feed your baby *chocolate* or *nut* flavors.
- Sherbet is mostly water and sugar.

Puddings, if they are homemade, can be served occa-

sionally as an instant food. The canned and frozen puddings are highly sweetened and contain a high percentage
of fillers and additives, so don't bother feeding them to
your baby.

14

Finger Foods

Sooner or later, often around eight months, your baby will decide that he wants to feed himself. He will subtly indicate this by grabbing for the spoon, hitting the spoon away, or simply refusing to eat. By this time you will probably be more than happy to give him the opportunity to feed himself. Unfortunately, this desire may come before he can handle a spoon well enough to consume an adequate meal. The result can be a hungry, cranky, and frustrated baby and a mess of splattered purées for you to clean up.

One way to handle this difficult stage is to serve your baby a well-balanced selection of finger foods that he can pick up, chew easily, and swallow without choking. Don't worry about discouraging his willingness to eat with a spoon. You can always give him a spoon and serve a thick purée. (See **Self-Feeding** section in chapter 3.) He is more likely to become discouraged if he becomes frustrated in trying to get enough to eat. He may then give up entirely and you will end up feeding him for much longer than is necessary. Instead, as your baby picks up his finger foods, he will be gaining valuable eye, hand, and muscular coordination; and will also be eating the foods that are so necessary for his growth. This stage can be a happy and healthy one for both of you!

Some General Suggestions

- For your own convenience, serve finger foods that fit in with the meals you are preparing for the rest of your family.
- Just as you planned to keep on hand a store of purées, plan to have a ready supply of finger foods, frozen, canned, or fresh.
- For specific nutritional, buying, storage, and preparation information, look up any food in the recipe chapters.
- The consistency of any finger food should be firm enough for your baby to pick up, yet tender enough for him to chew and swallow easily. A cooked food is the proper consistency as soon as you are able to pierce it easily with a fork.
- Begin with small pieces of very tender food. As the baby grows and becomes more adept at chewing, you can add more solid finger foods.
- Be careful if your baby is teething very young. Just because he has teeth doesn't mean he knows how to chew food. He is more likely to bite off a piece, try to swallow it whole, and start choking.
- Avoid small pieces of firm food such as meat, raw peas, or hard vegetables that may cause choking.
- If your baby is swallowing food whole and it is not being digested, it will show up whole in his bowel movements. In that case, you should cut the food into smaller pieces and make sure it is very tender.
- There is one thing that you should buy which will save you considerable cleanup time. It is a plastic "catchall" bib and it means just that. The bottom of the bib is folded up to form a pocket so that the pieces of food that do not make it to your baby's mouth, or that he decides to reject, drop into the pocket instead of on the floor.

You can easily make this bib by folding up the bottom of any plastic or cloth bib about 2 inches, then sewing or stapling the edges or you can fasten the edges with paper clips, which can then be removed for easy cleaning. Remember, when you fasten the edges, you must allow the pocket to buckle out so that the food will be caught.

One additional word of warning. Your baby may discover that it is fun to drop these finger foods from his high chair and watch them land on the floor. This may be educational, but it is also a nuisance for you to clean up. So watch out for this game and tolerate it according to your own patience. Since your baby will usually do this when he is no longer hungry, the simplest thing is to just take him out of his chair and declare the meal finished.

The following section lists some easy and nutritious finger foods according to their basic food group—**Cereal Grains, Fruit, Vegetables,** and **Protein Foods.**

Cereal Grains

The cereal-grain foods are economical sources of incomplete protein, carbohydrates, minerals, and the B vitamins.

Dry, Ready-to-Eat Cereals: These are some of the easiest finger foods, and, since you are faced with an overwhelming selection, here are some general rules:

- Do not buy the sugar-frosted, honey-coated, or chocolate flavored cereals.
- Do not buy the flaked cereals: your baby could choke on them.
- Buy those cereals with a definite shape that your baby can easily pick up.
- There is some controversy over the nutritional value of some of these ready-to-eat cereals. You should read the labels carefully and buy only those that are "enriched."

- When you first introduce these cereals, soften them with a little milk, a few at a time. They will be easier to swallow.

Pasta: You can now buy spaghetti and macaroni in many different shapes which your baby can easily pick up. Even if he swallows them whole, they will be well digested.

- Always buy brands that are "enriched."
- Some good shapes are shells, wheels, twists, and small elbow macaroni. The long, thin spaghetti and noodles are very difficult to manage.
- You can serve these pastas plain, or with a little butter, tomato sauce, or melted cheese as in **macaroni and cheese.**
- You can take advantage of the prepared spaghetti and macaroni dishes, either frozen or canned. Again, read the labels and buy the brand that is enriched and contains the fewest additives and fillers.

Baked Goods: The first breads your baby can eat are either very moist, soft breads, or very hard baked goods that he can teethe on. If a bread or a cracker has a medium, crumbly consistency, he may choke on it.

- Always buy crackers, cookies, and breads that are baked with enriched, unbleached, or whole-grain flour. (See "Cereal Grains" in chapter 7.)
- You can harden almost any bread by baking it in a very low (150°–200°F.) oven for 15–20 minutes. Your baby will enjoy teething on a variety of hard breads, and they are less expensive and messy than the teething sticks sold for babies.
- Stale bagels are also an excellent teething food.

Here are some easy and nutritious recipes for both moist and hard breads. You will be able to serve them to your baby and the rest of your family.

Banana Bread Sticks

¼ cup brown sugar
2 eggs
½ cup vegetable oil (safflower, corn)
1 cup banana, mashed (add whole if using a processor)
1¾ cups flour (whole wheat, unbleached, enriched)
2 teaspoons baking powder
½ teaspoon baking soda

1. Preheat oven to 350°F.
2. Beat sugar, eggs, and oil together.
3. Stir in bananas.
4. Mix dry ingredients together—flour, baking powder, baking soda.
5. Add dry mixture to banana mixture, stirring only until smooth.
6. Pour into greased loaf pan.
7. Bake for about 1 hour or until firmly set. Reduce oven to 150°F.
8. Cool, remove from pan. Cut into sticks.
9. Spread out on cookie sheet or foil and bake until the sticks are hard and crunchy. Or, serve as a moist bread.
YIELD: About 2 dozen, depending on size of sticks. Store sticks in tightly covered container in a dry place.

VARIATIONS

Date Bread Sticks
Add ½ cup of finely chopped or puréed dates (good for iron).

Nut Bread Sticks
Add ½ cup finely chopped nuts.

Fruit Bread Sticks
Substitute other fruit purées such as apricot, peach, etc., for the banana.

Carrot Bread Sticks
Substitute ¾ cup finely grated raw carrots for the banana.

$ Date-Oatmeal Bread

This is a moist bread that is highly nutritious. If you have a blender or processor you can easily mix all the wet ingredients and chop the dates.

>   1½ cups flour (enriched or unbleached)
>   ½ teaspoon baking powder
>   1 teaspoon baking soda
>   ¾ cup quick-cooking oatmeal
>   1 egg
>   1 cup sour cream
>   ½ cup brown sugar
>   ½ cup dark molasses
>   ⅓ cup chopped dates

1. Preheat oven to 350°F.
2. Grease a loaf pan.
3. Combine flour, baking powder, soda, and oatmeal in mixing bowl.
4. Blend together the egg, sour cream, sugar, and molasses. (If you are using a blender, add dates while blender is on.)
5. Mix in the chopped dates.
6. Pour mixture over dry ingredients and mix well.
7. Turn into the loaf pan and bake 45–55 minutes.

$ Peanut Butter Cookies

This is a healthful cereal/protein snack.

>   1 cup shortening (melted butter or vegetable oil)
>   1 cup peanut butter (preferably homemade)
>   1 cup brown sugar
>   2 eggs
>   1 teaspoon vanilla extract
>   ½ cup nonfat dry milk
>   2½ cups flour (whole wheat, unbleached, or enriched)
>   ¾ teaspoon baking soda
>   ½ teaspoon baking powder

1. Preheat oven to 375°F.

2. Beat shortening and peanut butter until creamy. It will be easier if the peanut butter is at room temperature.

3. Gradually add the sugar, beating until mixed.

4. Beat in the eggs and vanilla.

5. Blend in the remaining ingredients.

6. Shape into balls about 1 inch in diameter.

7. Place about 2 inches apart on an ungreased baking sheet.

8. Flatten each cookie with tines of a fork.

9. Bake 10–15 minutes. Turn oven off and leave door slightly open. Allow cookies to cool in oven until quite hard.

10. Store in a tightly covered container in a dry place.

YIELD: 4 dozen cookies.

Oatmeal Cookies

These old favorites count as a healthful cereal serving; good for an easy snack.

1 cup flour (whole wheat, unbleached, or enriched)
1¼ teaspoons baking powder
½ teaspoon baking soda
½ cup melted butter or vegetable oil
½ cup brown sugar, packed
½ teaspoon coffee cake spice (optional)
1 egg
¾ teaspoon vanilla extract
1½ cups quick-cooking rolled oats
¼ cup wheat germ (optional)

1. Preheat oven to 350°F.

2. Mix together flour, baking powder, soda.

3. Beat butter or oil with sugar and spice until creamy.

4. Beat in egg and vanilla.

5. Blend in flour mixture, oats, and wheat germ. (If using a processor, mix in the oatmeal by hand.)

6. Chill.

7. Shape dough into balls about 1 inch in diameter.

8. Place 2 inches apart on an ungreased baking sheet.

9. Bake for 10–15 minutes. Turn off oven, leaving oven door slightly open and allow cookies to cool. They should be quite hard.

10. Store in a tightly covered container in a dry place.

YIELD: 3–4 dozen cookies.

Sesame Crackers

This is a simple recipe that combines complementary foods to obtain more complete protein.

> 1½ cups whole-wheat flour
> ¼ cup soy flour
> ¼ cup sesame seeds
> ½ teaspoon salt
> ¼ cup oil
> ½ cup water

1. Preheat oven to 350°F.

2. Stir flours, sesame seeds, and salt together.

3. Add oil and blend well.

4. Add only enough water to make it easy to roll—the consistency of pie dough.

5. Roll dough to ⅛ inch thick and cut into shapes or sticks.

6. Bake on ungreased baking sheet until crisp.

YIELD: 3–4 dozen crackers.

Fruits

Fruits are some of the easiest and most nutritious finger foods that you can serve your baby. You can look up the specific fruit in chapter 8 for detailed information; however, here are some general suggestions.

- To prepare **fresh fruit,** remove skin, seeds, and cut into small pieces, or long thin sticks. To conserve nutrients, prepare fruits just before serving.

- To remove skins, dip fruit in boiling water, then rub off skin under cold water. Or use a paring knife.
- Apples are an exception, since they are hard enough for your baby to choke on. Instead, remove the skin of a small apple, and let him gnaw on the whole apple. Even if your baby only has a few teeth, he will be able to scrape away most of the apple. This is also an excellent food with which to keep his teeth clean.
- When your baby is one year old, you can serve, unpeeled, such fruits as pears, nectarines, and plums. Remember that the skins contain nutrients.
- Frozen sticks of bananas are also a good finger and teething food. They are not as messy when eaten frozen, and the cold will be very soothing to his gums.
- **Frozen and canned fruits** can also be served. Try to buy those brands that are packed in their own juice instead of sugar syrup. You should also buy the *grade A* fruits for use as finger foods, since they will have better shape and are usually more tender.
- **Dried fruits,** such as pitted prunes, apricots, apples, peaches, and dates are excellent finger foods and good sources of iron. Either buy the moist variety or soak them in water overnight to soften them. Stewed dried fruit that is sold in jars is very convenient to use; however, it is heavily sweetened and should not be served too often.

The following fruits are convenient to serve as finger foods. Unless noted, they should be introduced peeled and cut into small pieces.

*Apples**	*Cantaloupes*
Apricots	*Nectarines*
Avocados	*Peaches*
Bananas	*Pears*
Berries†	*Plums, prunes*
Cherries†	*Mangoes*
Oranges, grapefruit (sections)	*Papayas*
Grapes†	

* Serve whole to prevent possible choking.
† Do not serve until your baby is able to digest the skins, at around one year.

Fruit Leather

You can buy this ready made, but it will contain unspecified amounts of sugar and water. It is very easy to make at home and is a nutritious soft "chewing" food for your baby. It is also a good grown-up snack.

1. Combine any of the following fruits:

> **Apricots—fresh, canned (drained), dried (soak overnight in water)**
> **Peaches**
> **Apples—raw (peeled or unpeeled)**
> **Prunes—canned (drained), dried (soak in water)**
> **Bananas**

2. Process in blender or processor into a very thick purée. If using raw fruit, add a little lemon or orange juice to prevent browning.

3. Spread on a lightly oiled cookie sheet.

4. Allow to dry until the consistency of leather! The length of time depends on the amount of heat. You can dry the fruit in an oven that was preheated to 200°F. and then turned off, or you can replace the oven light with a 100-watt light bulb as when making yogurt. A sunny spot in the house will take longer and the fruit may pick up some general dust. Don't leave the fruit outside to dry in the sun unless you can devise a foolproof way of keeping insects off—they're one source of protein your baby doesn't need!

5. Store, tightly wrapped, in refrigerator for 2–3 weeks.

Vegetables

Vegetables are essential in your baby's diet and you can use many as convenient finger foods. For more detailed information, look up the specific vegetable in chapter 9. Here are some general suggestions:

- You will have to cook most vegetables. Whenever possible, cook them in their skins and in large pieces or whole. You will conserve nutrients and it will be easier to peel and cut the vegetables after they are cooked.
- The best way to cook most vegetables is to steam them only until they are tender and can be pierced with a fork.
- Cooked vegetables can be served cut in small pieces, long thin strips, or whole.
- Tomatoes are the only raw vegetables that a young baby can eat as a finger food. Dip them in boiling water to remove the skins easily and spoon out the seeds.
- **Raw vegetables** are not suitable for finger food because most are quite hard. If your baby has even a few teeth, he might bite off a piece of the vegetable and choke on it.
- While your baby is teething, but does not yet have teeth, you can give him thick sticks of cold, raw vegetables to chew on. Some good ones are *carrots, celery, kohlrabi,* and *turnips.* You can prepare a few sticks at a time and keep them crisp and handy in a glass of water in your refrigerator.
- You might also try giving your baby raw leafy greens or lettuce, when he is at the stage of chewing paper. He may even obtain some vitamins!
- **Frozen vegetables** can be treated like fresh vegetables. You will save money and time if you buy the large bags of cut vegetables and use only a few pieces for each meal. The *grade A* will be the most tender.
- **Canned vegetables** are very convenient to use as finger foods, since they do not require cooking and can be served directly from the can. *Grade A* vegetables will be the most tender and juicy.

The following vegetables, either canned, frozen, or fresh, are good to serve as finger foods:

Asparagus
Beans, green or yellow
Beans, baked
Broccoli (flowerets)
Carrots
Cauliflower (flowerets)
Corn on the cob (make a slice down the middle of each
    row of kernels, so your baby will not eat the skins)
Corn (kernels for a baby over one year)
Leafy greens
Lima beans
Peas (young, small ones with tender skins)
Soybeans (cook until they are very soft)
Summer squash
Tomatoes

Protein Foods

Your baby will require two daily servings of high-quality protein food for good growth and energy. Yet, many protein foods are difficult for a baby to chew and swallow. Your baby may reject, at first, even the tenderest pieces of meat or poultry. However, there are finger foods with which you can satisfy your baby's need for protein. Here are some suggestions for foods that are both nutritious and convenient to prepare. For specific buying and storing information, look up the food in chapter 10.

$ Eggs

Eggs are almost a complete food—high in iron, protein, vitamins, and fat. They are your best protein finger food, since they are inexpensive, you can prepare them easily and quickly, and even a toothless baby will be able to swallow them. Eggs can be served as often as once a day. You can also combine eggs with other foods, that cannot easily be prepared as finger foods. Here is the basic recipe for preparing eggs, along with some variations.

All-Purpose Omelet

1 egg or 2 egg yolks (the size egg depends on how much your baby will eat)
1 tablespoon liquid (milk, fruit, or vegetable juice)

1. Lightly grease a small frying pan, using vegetable oil, butter, or margarine. Heat the pan over low heat.
2. Beat the egg and liquid together.
3. Pour the egg mixture into the pan. Allow it to sit for about a minute, or until the bottom has set.
4. Fold the omelet in half, then in half again. You want the pieces of omelet to be thick enough for your baby to easily pick up.
5. Allow it to cook another minute or until it is firm. Do not overcook, because the omelet will become dry and hard.
6. Cut it into small pieces and serve.
7. Leftover omelet can be wrapped and stored in the refrigerator for 1 day. Do not freeze cooked omelets.

VARIATIONS

You can add almost any food to an omelet, either finely chopped or puréed. You can make all-in-one meals by combining a vegetable, rice or cereal, and the egg. As you can see, it is a good way to use leftovers from family meals. Whatever combination of food that you use in your omelet, you must add enough egg for a firm consistency. **Usually 1 egg for each added ¼ cup of food will be enough.** A blender or processor is very convenient for blending these omelets. Here are some suggestions:

Wheat-Germ Omelet
Beat 1 tablespoon wheat germ with the egg and liquid. Allow it to sit for 5 minutes before cooking. This is a cereal/protein serving. (You can also use cooked cereal or rice.)

Meat, Poultry, Fish Omelet

Place 2 tablespoons cooked meat in blender with egg and liquid. Purée. If you do not have a blender, use very finely chopped meats, poultry, or fish. This is really a double protein serving.

Fruit/Vegetable Omelet

Beat in ¼ cup of any fruit or vegetable purée with the egg. Or use a blender to purée everything together. This is especially good for serving your baby leafy greens.

Meats and Poultry

These are the most difficult foods for your baby to chew and swallow, no matter how tender they are. The best way to initially feed your baby beef, veal, pork, lamb, chicken, or turkey is to first cook and purée the meat, then prepare it either in **All-Purpose Croquettes** or as **Meatballs**. An older baby will enjoy spareribs or drumsticks.

All-Purpose Croquettes

This is a good finger food that can be made from leftovers, and frozen for future use. It is most easily prepared in a processor.

> 3 cups cooked vegetables, fish, meat, rice, etc. (try to use equal amounts)
> 2 tablespoons lemon juice (optional)
> 1 cup white sauce or 1 cup milk with a beaten egg
> 2 slightly beaten eggs
> 1 cup wheat germ or whole-wheat bread crumbs

1. Chop all cooked ingredients to desired texture, or purée, adding lemon juice, white sauce, or milk and egg. It should have a stiff consistency.
2. Shape into small balls or sticks, using about 2 tablespoons for each. You should have about 20 pieces.
3. Dip in beaten egg and then roll in wheat germ.

4. Sauté until brown. You can also bake them at 375°F. for 10–15 minutes.

5. Spread out on a flat sheet and freeze at once. Place in bag and store in freezer in meal-size servings for 2–4 months.

YIELD: About 20 servings.

Note: You can also use your family's favorite croquette recipe—just make smaller pieces.

Meatballs

This is a good finger food that you can feed your baby in place of the controversial frankfurter or hot dog. You can use various ground meats or poultry. You can place solid cubed meat with the other ingredients in a processor for one-step mixing.

> 2 pounds ground meat
> 2 eggs, beaten
> ¼ cup rolled oats
> ½ cup wheat germ

1. Mix all ingredients together.
2. Shape into small balls or sticks, each the size of 1 serving.
3. Brown in lightly greased pan.*
4. Add about ½ inch of water or vegetable juice. Cover the pan tightly and simmer over low heat for 30 minutes. You can also place the covered pan in a 350°F. oven.
5. Drain and cool.

YIELD: About 20 servings or meatballs. You can freeze them for 3–4 months.

VARIATION

Instead of the oatmeal and wheat germ, use bread crumbs, mashed potatoes, rice, or cooked cereal.

---

* Instead of browning and simmering, you can easily cook meatballs in a steamer. Steam about 20 minutes for most meats, 30 minutes for pork. Check water level and add more if necessary.

Spareribs

This is a good teething and finger food. As soon as your baby has even a few teeth, he will be able to gnaw the bone clean. You can use either pork spareribs or breast of lamb, which is very inexpensive. You can cook them by either roasting or braising. Pork must be *thoroughly* cooked. If they are very meaty and the meat comes off in too-large pieces, you can trim some off.

Roasted Spareribs

1. Preheat oven to 325°F.
2. Place spareribs in shallow pan, cover with foil, and roast for ½ hour. Pour off fat. You can also precook the ribs by simmering them, in water to cover, for ½ hour. The object is to remove most of the fat.
3. Increase the oven heat to 400°F., and roast the ribs, uncovered, for 1 hour or until fork-tender. You can baste them with a little honey or molasses if desired.

Braised Spareribs

1. Cut into single ribs.
2. Brown the ribs in hot butter or oil in a frying pan.
3. Add enough water, tomato, or apple juice to almost cover the ribs.
4. Cover the pan and simmer over low heat about 1½ hours. Add more liquid as necessary.

Store the cooked spareribs in the refrigerator for up to 3 days, or freeze in individual servings for up to 2 months.

Steamed Drumsticks

Your baby may be able to eat steamed chicken legs or drumsticks as soon as he has teeth. You can begin by cutting most of the flesh away and letting him chew on the meat next to the bone.

1. Preheat oven to 350°F.

2. Wrap each drumstick in aluminum foil, or place in baking dish with a little water and cover tightly.

3. Bake in oven for 30 minutes or steam the drumsticks in a steamer for 30 minutes or until tender.

4. Store them in the refrigerator for 2–3 days, or freeze them separately for up to 4 months. You can then reheat in the foil.

$ Liver

Liver is one highly nutritious meat that most babies can chew as finger food. You can use either beef, calf, or chicken liver. It is very easy to prepare.

1. Place the whole pieces of liver in a pot with a small amount of boiling water, or use your steamer.

2. Cover and simmer over low heat for 5–10 minutes. Do not overcook the liver, because it will become tough. You can even serve it slightly pink.

3. Cut out any veins or outside membrane and slice into very thin pieces.

4. Do not freeze cooked liver because it will become tough when reheated. If you are buying liver only for your baby, you can cut the raw liver into single servings and freeze it up to 3 months.

Other Meats

Bacon may be served as a finger food. However, you must remember that it is mostly fat, with very little meat, so you should not count it as a serving of a protein food. It is also a highly salted food and should not be served too often.

Delicatessen meats, such as boiled or baked ham and roast beef, can be served as *"instant"* finger foods, if they are sliced very thin. They are expensive, but very convenient, and your baby really eats very little. Do not use luncheon meats, salami, or bologna, except as a last resort. They contain many additives and artificial flavorings and color. Besides, they are an even more expensive source of protein than plain ham or roast beef.

Hamburgers, medium broiled, can be cut in small pieces. Be careful how you buy ground meat. (See **Meats,** chapter 10.)

Frankfurters also can be used as finger foods, but, please, only as a last resort. The controversy over this old stand-by food concerns the many chemical additives and artificial flavorings and colors that are used, and also the low percentage of meat or protein. The current Department of Agriculture "recipe" for frankfurters includes 30 per cent fat, 15 per cent poultry, 10 per cent water, 2 per cent corn syrup, and 3.5 per cent cereals and nonfat dry milk. "*All-meat*" frankfurters do not contain any poultry products, and the "*all-beef*" contain only beef as their meat ingredient. However, both of these higher-priced types of frankfurters can contain nonfat dry milk, cereals, and starch. You are paying a high price for these ingredients and, actually, the lower-priced frankfurters can be just as nutritious. If you do serve them to your baby, read the list of ingredients and buy the brand with the smallest number of additives and fillers. To prepare, cook them and remove the skins.

Fish

Fish is a good protein finger food that is soft enough for your baby to chew and swallow. Read the **Fish** section in chapter 10 for details on the types of fish and ways of preparing. You can serve your baby small flakes of the cooked fish or use the following recipe for fish sticks. If your family eats fish, separate a few flakes for your baby. Do not freeze the cooked fish flakes because they will become tough. When your baby is one year old, you can try serving him the canned tuna and salmon flakes.

Steamed Fish Sticks

This is a good protein food that your baby can feed himself. You will find they make a delicious hors d'oeuvre served with horseradish. This is most easily prepared in a processor.

> **3 pounds whitefish, pike, etc. (frozen fillets are easy to use)**
> **2 small onions**
> **2 eggs, beaten**
> **3 tablespoons cracker meal or wheat germ**
> **½ cup water or vegetable liquid**

1. Finely chop or grind the raw fish fillets.
2. Chop the onions.
3. Mix the fish, onions, eggs, and cracker meal until well blended, adding a small amount of water.
4. Form the chopped fish mixture into sticks about the size of a short frankfurter. You may also shape into balls. You should have about 30 pieces.
5. In the bottom of your steamer basket, or any pot you use for steaming, place a few slices of carrot, onion, and celery. This is used to raise the fish above the water and add a mild flavor, but the vegetables are not really necessary if you have a steamer.
6. Place the fish sticks on top of the vegetables, cover tightly, and steam over a low heat for 2 hours. Add water as necessary.
7. Cool, arrange the sticks on a flat sheet, and freeze. You can store them in meal-size servings for up to 2 months. They will also keep in the refrigerator for 3–4 days.

YIELD: About 30 pieces.

Cheese

Cheese is a protein food that contains the same nutrients as milk. It is not a source of iron, as are the other protein foods. However it is a convenient finger food that is readily available. Your baby will enjoy chewing the sliced semifirm cheeses such as American, Swiss, Muenster, and Cheddar.

When buying cheese, read the labels carefully to avoid

those types which contain additives, artificial flavor and color, or fillers. Remember that the words "imitation," "flavored," "cheese food" indicate that the product is not pure cheese.

$ Peanut Butter

Peanut Butter Clay

In this recipe you are combining complementary peanuts and milk for a complete protein food and a good nutritional "buy." It has the consistency that one-to-two-year-olds love to play with, but doesn't make much of a mess. For a toddler you can add chopped raisins, dates, or dried apricots and let him help roll it into shapes.

>   1 cup peanut butter (or 1 cup peanuts + ¼ cup milk)
>   5 tablespoons nonfat dry milk
>   1–2 tablespoons honey (optional)

1. Blend all ingredients together. Add more dry milk as needed to make the mixture stiff enough to handle easily. This should be done by hand or in a processor.
2. Chill "clay," then form into shapes or balls.
3. Store in refrigerator for up to a month or freeze in freezer bag or box for several months.

Appendix A
Nutritive Values of Foods

The following table is compiled from:
United States Department of Agriculture
Home and Garden Bulletin No. 72, *The Nutritive Values
of Foods*
Agriculture Handbook No. 8, *Composition of Foods*.

I have found that knowing the nutritional composition of
foods is very useful for understanding their nutritional
cost. These values are a basis for comparing the kinds and
amounts of nutrients in different foods or different forms of
the same food. For example, lamb liver is as high, if not
higher, in the important nutrients as steak; however, it is
considerably less expensive. Just look through and check
the foods that you usually serve, then pick out the ones
that are economical.

You do not need to use these values in planning your
baby's daily diet, although you might want to compare the
nutrients he consumes in a typical day with the advisable
daily intakes that are described in chapter 1.

The values for calories and nutrients are the amounts
present in the edible part of the items, unless noted
otherwise. For many of the prepared items, values have
been calculated from the ingredients in typical recipes. If
a food is fortified with one or more nutrients, the information is on the label. The values shown in this table are
based on products from several manufacturers and may
differ slightly from those in a specific product.

NUTRITIVE VALUE OF FOODS

(A dash in the columns for nutrients shows that no suitable value could be found although there is reason to believe that a measurable amount of the nutrient may be present)

| Food, approximate measure, and weight (in grams) | Water | Food energy | Protein | Fat | Fatty acids | | Carbo-hydrate | Cal-cium | Iron | Vita-min A value | Thia-min | Ribo-flavin | Niacin | Ascor-bic acid |
| | | | | | Satu-rated (total) | Unsatu-rated lin-oleic | | | | | | | | |
	Grams	Per-cent	Calo-ries	Grams	Grams	Grams	Grams	Grams	Milli-grams	Milli-grams	Inter-national units	Milli-grams	Milli-grams	Milli-grams	Milli-grams
MILK, CHEESE, CREAM, IMITATION CREAM; RELATED PRODUCTS														
Milk:														
Fluid:														
Whole, 3.5% fat....1 cup 244	87	160	9	9	5	Trace	12	288	.1	350	.07	.41	.2	2
Nonfat (skim) ......1 cup 245	90	90	9	Trace	—	—	12	296	.1	10	.09	.44	.2	2
Partly skimmed, 2% nonfat milk solids added ...1 cup ... 246	87	145	10	5	3	Trace	15	352	.1	200	.10	.52	.2	2
Canned, concentrated, undiluted:														
Evaporated, unsweetened ...1 cup 252	74	345	18	20	11	1	24	635	.3	810	.10	.86	.5	3
Condensed, sweetened .....1 cup 306	27	980	25	27	15	1	166	802	.3	1,100	.24	1.16	.6	3
Dry, nonfat instant:														
Low-density (1⅓ cups needed for reconstitution to 1 quart) .....1 cup 68	4	245	24	Trace	—	—	35	879	.4	120	.24	1.21	.6	5
High-density (⅞ cup needed for reconstitution to 1 quart) .....1 cup 104	4	375	37	1	—	—	54	1,345	.6	130	.36	1.85	.9	7
Buttermilk														
Fluid, cultured, made from skim milk .....1 cup 245	90	90	9	Trace	—	—	12	296	.1	10	.10	.44	.2	2

Cheese; Cream; Imitation cream products; Malted milk; Milk desserts

Food, approximate measure, and weight (grams)	Water (%)	Food energy (cal.)	Protein (g)	Fat (g)	Saturated (total) (g)	Unsaturated oleic (g)	Unsaturated linoleic (g)	Carbohydrate (g)	Calcium (mg)	Iron (mg)	Vitamin A (I.U.)	Thiamin (mg)	Riboflavin (mg)	Niacin (mg)	Ascorbic acid (mg)
Cheese:															
Cheddar ......1 ounce (28 g)	37	115	7	9	5	3	Trace	1	213	.3	370	.01	.13	Trace	0
Cottage, large or small curd:															
Creamed ......1 cup (245 g)	78	260	33	10	6	3	Trace	7	230	.7	420	.07	.61	.2	0
Uncreamed ......1 cup (200 g)	79	170	34	1	1	Trace	Trace	5	180	.8	180	.06	.56	.2	0
Cream ......1 ounce (28 g)	51	107	2	11	6	3	Trace	1	18	Trace	440	Trace	.07	Trace	0
Parmesan, grated ....1 tablespoon (5 g)	17	25	2	2	1	1	Trace	1	68	Trace	60	Trace	.04	Trace	0
......1 ounce (28 g)	17	130	12	9	5	3	Trace	1	383	.3	360	Trace	.25	Trace	0
Swiss ......1 ounce (28 g)	39	105	8	8	4	3	Trace	1	262	.3	320	.01	.11	Trace	0
Pasteurized processed cheese															
American ......1 ounce (28 g)	40	105	7	9	5	3	Trace	1	198	.3	350	Trace	.12	Trace	0
Swiss ......1 ounce (28 g)	40	100	8	8	4	3	Trace	1	251	.3	310	Trace	.11	Trace	0
Pasteurized process cheese food,															
American ......1 tablespoon (14 g)	43	45	3	3	2	1	Trace	1	80	.1	140	Trace	.08	Trace	0
......1 ounce (28 g)	49	80	5	6	3	2	Trace	2	160	.2	250	Trace	.15	Trace	0
Cream:															
Half-and-half (cream and milk) ......1 tablespoon (15 g)	80	20	1	2	1	1	Trace	1	16	Trace	70	Trace	.02	Trace	Trace
Light, coffee or table....1 tablespoon (15 g)	72	30	1	3	2	1	Trace	1	15	Trace	130	Trace	.02	Trace	Trace
Sour ......1 tablespoon (12 g)	72	25	Trace	2	1	1	Trace	1	12	Trace	100	Trace	.02	Trace	Trace
Imitation cream products (made with vegetable fat):															
Creamers:															
Powdered ......1 teaspoon (2 g)	2	10	Trace	1	Trace	Trace	0	1	1	—	Trace	0	0	—	—
Liquid (frozen) ......1 tablespoon (15 g)	77	20	Trace	2	1	1	0	2	2	Trace	¹10	0	0	—	—
Malted milk:															
Dry powder, approx. 3 heaping teaspoons per ounce ......1 ounce (28 g)	3	115	4	2	—	—	—	20	82	.6	290	.09	.15	.1	0
Milk desserts:															
Custard, baked ......1 cup (265 g)	77	305	14	15	7	5	1	29	297	1.1	930	.11	.50	.3	1
Ice cream:															
Regular (approx. 10% fat) ......1 cup (133 g)	63	255	6	14	8	4	Trace	28	194	.1	590	.05	.28	.1	1
Rich (approx. 16% fat) ......1 cup (148 g)	63	330	4	24	13	8	1	27	115	Trace	980	.03	.16	.1	1
Ice milk ......1 cup (131 g)	67	200	6	7	4	2	Trace	29	204	.1	280	.07	.29	.1	1

Food, approximate measure, and weight		Water	Food energy	Protein	Fat	Fatty acids		Carbohydrate	Calcium	Iron	Vitamin A value	Thiamin	Riboflavin	Niacin	Ascorbic acid
						Saturated (total)	Unsaturated linoleic								
	Grams	Percent	Calories	Grams	Grams	Grams	Grams	Grams	Milligrams	Milligrams	International units	Milligrams	Milligrams	Milligrams	Milligrams
Yoghurt:															
Made from partially skimmed milk ..... 1 cup	245	89	125	8	4	2	Trace	13	294	.1	170	.10	.44	.2	2
Made from whole milk. 1 cup	245	88	150	7	8	5	Trace	12	272	.1	340	.07	.39	.2	2
EGGS															
Eggs, large, 24 ounces per dozen:															
Raw or cooked in shell or with nothing added:															
Whole, without shell .. 1 egg	50	74	80	6	6	2	Trace	Trace	27	1.1	590	.05	.15	Trace	0
White of egg .... 1 white	33	88	15	4	Trace	—	—	Trace	3	Trace	0	Trace	.09	Trace	0
Yolk of egg .... 1 yolk	17	51	60	3	5	2	Trace	Trace	24	.9	580	.04	.07	Trace	0
Scrambled with milk and fat .... 1 egg	64	72	110	7	8	3	Trace	1	51	1.1	690	.05	.18	Trace	0
MEAT, POULTRY; RELATED PRODUCTS															
Bacon (20 slices per lb. raw), broiled or fried, crisp .... 2 slices	15	8	90	5	8	3	1	1	2	.5	0	.08	.05	.8	—
Beef, cooked:															
Cuts braised, simmered, or pot-roasted .... 3 ounces	85	53	245	23	16	8	Trace	0	10	2.9	30	.04	.18	3.5	—
Hamburger (ground beef), broiled:															
Lean .... 3 ounces	85	60	185	23	10	5	Trace	0	10	3.0	20	.08	.20	5.1	—
Regular .... 3 ounces	85	54	245	21	17	8	Trace	0	9	2.7	30	.07	.18	4.6	—
Roast, oven-cooked, no liquid added:															
Relatively fat, such as rib .... 3 ounces	85	40	375	17	34	16	1	0	8	2.2	70	.05	.13	3.1	—

Steak, broiled: Relatively lean, such as heel or round ....3 ounces	85	62	165	25	7	3	Trace	0	11	3.2	10	.06	.19	4.5	—
Relatively fat, such as sirloin ......3 ounces	85	44	330	20	27	13	1	0	9	2.5	50	.05	.16	4.0	—
Relatively lean, such as round ....3 ounces	85	55	220	24	13	6	Trace	0	10	3.0	20	.07	.19	4.8	—
Beef, canned: Corned beef ....3 ounces	85	59	185	22	10	5	Trace	0	17	3.7	20	.01	.20	2.9	—
Corned beef hash ....3 ounces	85	67	155	7	10	5	Trace	9	11	1.7	—	.01	.08	1.8	—
Beef, dried or chipped ....2 ounces	57	48	115	19	4	2	Trace	0	11	2.9	—	.04	.18	2.2	—
Beef potpie, baked, 4¼-inch diam., weight before baking about 8 ounces. 1 pie	227	55	560	23	33	9	2	43	32	4.1	1,860	.25	.27	4.5	7
Chicken, cooked: Flesh only, broiled ....3 ounces	85	71	115	20	3	1	1	0	8	1.4	80	.05	.16	7.4	—
Chicken, canned, boneless ....3 ounces	85	65	170	18	10	3	2	0	18	1.3	200	.03	.11	3.7	3
Chicken potpie, baked 4¼-inch diam, weight before baking about 8 ounces. 1 pie	227	57	535	23	31	10	3	42	68	30	3,020	.25	.26	4.1	5
Heart, beef, lean, braised.3 ounces	85	61	160	27	5	—	—	1	5	5.0	20	.21	1.04	6.5	1
Kidney, braised beef ....3.5 ounces	100	53	252	33	12	—	—	.8	18	13.1	1,150	.51	4.82	10.7	—
Lamb, cooked: Chop, broiled ....4 ounces	112	47	400	25	33	18	1	0	10	1.5	—	.14	.25	5.6	—
Leg, roasted ....3 ounces	85	54	235	22	16	9	—	0	9	1.4	—	.13	.23	4.7	—
Shoulder, roasted ....3 ounces	85	50	285	18	23	13	1	0	9	1.0	—	.11	.20	4.0	—
Liver: Beef, sauteed ....3.5 ounces	100	56	229	26	11	—	—	5.3	11	8.8	53,400	.26	4.19	16.5	27
Calf, sauteed ....3.5 ounces	100	51	261	29	13	—	—	4	13	14.2	32,700	.24	4.17	16.5	37
Lamb, broiled ....3.5 ounces	100	50	261	32	12	—	—	2.8	11	17.9	74,500	.40	5.11	24.9	36
Chicken, simmered ....3.5 ounces	100	65	165	20	4	—	—	3.1	16	8.5	12,300	.17	2.69	11.7	16
Pork, cured, cooked: Ham, light cure, lean and fat, roasted ....3 ounces	85	54	245	18	19	7	2	0	8	2.2	0	.40	.16	3.1	—

Food, approximate measure, and weight (in grams)	Grams	Water Percent	Food energy Calories	Protein Grams	Fat Grams	Fatty acids Saturated (total) Grams	Unsaturated linoleic Grams	Carbohydrate Grams	Calcium Milligrams	Iron Milligrams	Vitamin A value International units	Thiamin Milligrams	Riboflavin Milligrams	Niacin Milligrams	Ascorbic acid Milligrams
Luncheon meat:															
Boiled ham, sliced ..2 ounces	57	59	135	11	10	4	1	0	6	1.6	0	.25	.09	1.5	—
Pork, fresh,[3] cooked:															
Chop, thick, with bone. 1 chop, 3.5 ounces	98	42	260	16	21	8	2	0	8	2.2	0	.63	.18	3.8	—
Roast, oven-cooked, no liquid added ....3 ounces	85	46	310	21	24	9	2	0	9	2.7	0	.78	.22	4.7	—
Cuts, simmered ......3 ounces	85	46	320	20	26	9	2	0	8	2.5	0	.46	.21	4.1	—
Sausage:															
Bologna, slice, 3-in. diam., x ¼-inch ....2 slices	26	56	80	3	7	—	—	Trace	2	.5	—	.04	.06	.7	—
Braunschweiger, slice 2-in. diam. x ¼ in. ....2 slices	20	53	65	3	5	—	—	Trace	2	1.2	1,310	.03	.29	1.6	—
Deviled ham, canned ..1 tablespoon	13	51	45	2	4	2	Trace	0	1	.3	—	.02	.01	.2	—
Frankfurter, heated (8 per lb. purchased pkg.) ....1 frank	56	57	170	7	15	—	—	1	3	.8	—	.08	.11	1.4	—
Salami, dry type ......1 ounce	28	30	130	7	11	—	—	Trace	4	1.0	—	.10	.07	1.5	—
Salami, cooked ......1 ounce	28	51	90	5	7	—	—	Trace	3	.7	—	.07	.07	1.2	—
Turkey, roasted flesh only..3.5 ounces	100	62	190	32	6	—	—	0	8	1.8	—	.05	.18	7.7	—
Veal, medium fat, cooked, bone removed:															
Cutlet ....3 ounces	85	60	185	23	9	5	Trace	—	9	2.7	—	.06	.21	4.6	—
Roast ....3 ounces	85	55	230	23	14	7	Trace	0	10	2.9	—	.11	.26	6.6	—
FISH AND SHELLFISH:															
Bluefish, baked with table fat ....3 ounces	85	68	135	22	4	—	—	0	25	.6	40	.09	.08	1.6	1

Cod, broiled	3.5 ounces	100	65	170	29	53	—	—	0	31	1.0	180	.08	.11	3.0	—
Crabmeat, canned	3 ounces	85	77	85	15	2	—	—	1	38	.7	—	.07	.07	1.6	—
Fish sticks, breaded, cooked	10 sticks or 8 ounce pkg.	227	66	400	38	20	5	10	15	25	0.9	—	.09	.16	3.6	—
Flounder, baked	3.5 ounces	100	58	202	30	8	—	—	0	23	1.4	—	.07	.08	2.5	0
Haddock, breaded, fried	3 ounces	85	66	140	17	5	1	Trace	5	34	1.0	—	0.3	.06	2.7	2
Halibut, broiled	3.5 ounces	100	67	171	25	7	—	—	0	16	.8	680	.05	.07	8.3	—
Ocean perch, breaded, fried	3 ounces	85	59	195	16	11	—	—	6	28	1.1	—	.08	.09	1.5	—
Salmon, pink, canned	3 ounces	85	71	120	17	5	1	Trace	0	[4]167	.7	60	.03	.16	6.8	—
Sardines, Atlantic, canned in oil, drained solids	3 ounces	85	62	175	20	9	—	—	0	372	2.5	190	.02	.17	4.6	—
Shad, baked with table fat and bacon	3 ounces	85	64	170	20	10	—	—	0	20	.5	20	.11	.22	7.3	—
Shrimp, canned, meat	3 ounces	85	70	100	21	1	—	—	1	98	2.6	50	.01	.03	1.5	—
Swordfish, broiled with butter or margarine	3 ounces	85	65	150	24	5	—	—	0	23	1.1	1,750	.03	.04	9.3	—
Tuna, canned in oil, drained solids	3 ounces	85	61	170	24	7	2	1	0	7	1.6	70	.04	.10	10.1	—
MATURE DRY BEANS AND PEAS, NUTS, PEANUTS; RELATED PRODUCTS																
Almonds, shelled, whole kernels	1 cup	142	5	850	26	77	6	15	28	332	6.7	0	.34	1.31	5.0	Trace
Beans, dry:																
Common varieties as Great Northern, navy, and others:																
Cooked, drained:																
Great Northern	1 cup	180	69	210	14	1	—	—	38	90	4.9	0	.25	.13	1.3	0
Navy (pea)	1 cup	190	69	225	15	1	—	—	40	95	5.1	0	.27	.13	1.3	0
Canned, solids and liquid:																
White with —																
Frankfurters (sliced)	1 cup	255	71	365	19	18	—	—	32	94	4.8	330	.18	.15	3.3	Trace

Food, approximate measure, and weight (in grams)	Grams	Water (Percent)	Food energy (Calories)	Protein (Grams)	Fat (Grams)	Fatty acids Saturated (total) (Grams)	Fatty acids Unsaturated linoleic (Grams)	Carbohydrate (Grams)	Calcium (Milligrams)	Iron (Milligrams)	Vitamin A value (International units)	Thiamin (Milligrams)	Riboflavin (Milligrams)	Niacin (Milligrams)	Ascorbic acid (Milligrams)
Pork and tomato sauce ....1 cup	255	71	310	16	7	2	1	49	138	4.6	330	.20	.08	1.5	5
Pork and sweet sauce .....1 cup	255	66	385	16	12	4	1	54	161	5.9	—	.15	.10	1.3	—
Red kidney ....1 cup	255	76	230	15	1	—	—	42	74	4.6	10	.13	.10	1.5	—
Lima, cooked, drained.1 cup ...	190	64	260	16	1	—	—	49	55	5.9	—	.25	.11	1.3	—
Cashew nuts, roasted ...1 cup ...	140	5	785	24	64	11	4	41	53	5.3	140	.60	.35	2.5	—
Coconut, fresh meat only:															
Shredded or grated, firmly packed ......1 cup	130	51	450	5	46	39	Trace	12	17	2.2	0	.07	.03	.7	4
Cowpeas or blackeye peas, dry, cooked ....1 cup ...	248	80	190	13	1	—	—	34	42	3.2	20	.41	.11	1.1	Trace
Lentils, cooked ....1 cup ...	200	72	212	16	Trace	—	—	38	50	4.2	40	.14	.12	1.2	0
Peanuts, roasted, salted, halves ....1 cup ...	144	2	840	37	72	16	21	27	107	3.0	—	.46	.19	24.7	0
Peanut butter ....1 tablespoon ...	16	2	95	4	8	2	2	3	9	.3	—	.02	.02	2.4	0
Peas, split, dry, cooked..1 cup ...	250	70	290	20	1	—	—	52	28	4.2	100	.37	.22	2.2	—
Pecans, halves ....1 cup ...	108	3	740	10	77	5	15	16	79	2.6	140	.93	.14	1.0	2
Soybeans, cooked ....1 cup ...	200	71	260	22	11.4	—	7	22	146	5.4	60	.42	.18	1.2	0
Walnuts, black or native, chopped ......1 cup ...	126	3	790	26	75	4	36	19	Trace	7.6	380	.28	.14	.9	—
VEGETABLES AND VEGETABLE PRODUCTS															
Asparagus, green:															
Cooked, drained:															
Spears, ½-in diam. at base ....4 spears.....	60	94	10	1	Trace	—	—	2	13	.4	540	.10	.11	.8	16
Pieces, 1½ to 2-in. lengths ....1 cup ...	145	94	30	3	Trace	—	—	5	30	.9	1,310	.23	.26	2.0	38

Food, approximate measure	Grams	Water (%)	Food energy	Protein	Fat			Carbohydrate	Calcium	Iron	Vitamin A	Thiamin	Riboflavin	Niacin	Ascorbic acid
Canned, solids and liquid ....1 cup	244	94	45	5	1	—	—	7	44	4.1	1,240	.15	.22	2.0	37
Beans:															
Lima, cooked, drained .1 cup	170	71	190	13	1	—	—	34	80	4.3	480	.31	.17	2.2	29
Snap:															
Green:															
Cooked, drained .1 cup	125	92	30	2	Trace	—	—	7	63	.8	680	.09	.11	.6	15
Canned, solids and liquid ....1 cup	239	94	45	2	Trace	—	—	10	81	2.9	690	.07	.10	.7	10
Yellow or wax:															
Cooked, drained..1 cup	125	93	30	2	Trace	—	—	6	63	0.8	290	.09	.11	.6	16
Canned, solids and liquid ....1 cup	239	94	45	2	1	—	—	10	81	2.9	140	.07	.10	.7	12
Sprouted mung beans, cooked, drained....1 cup	125	91	35	4	Trace	—	—	7	21	1.1	30	.11	.13	.9	8
Beets:															
Cooked, drained, peeled: Diced or sliced....1 cup	170	91	55	2	Trace	—	—	12	24	.9	30	.05	.07	.5	10
Canned, solids and liquid ....1 cup	246	90	85	2	Trace	—	—	19	34	1.5	20	.02	.05	.2	7
Beet greens, leaves and stems, cooked, drained ....1 cup	145	94	25	3	Trace	—	—	5	144	2.8	7,400	.10	.22	.4	22
Blackeye peas. See Cowpeas.															
Broccoli, cooked, drained: Stalks cut into ½-in. pieces ....1 cup	155	91	40	5	1	—	—	7	136	1.2	3,880	.14	.31	1.2	140
Chopped, yield from 10-oz frozen pkg....1⅓ cups	250	92	65	7	1	—	—	12	135	1.8	6,500	.15	.30	1.3	143
....1 cup	155	88	55	7	1	—	—	10	50	1.7	810	.12	.22	1.2	135
Brussels sprouts															
Cabbage, common: Raw, finely shredded or chopped ....1 cup	90	92	20	1	Trace	—	—	5	44	.4	120	.05	.05	.3	42
Cooked ....1 cup	145	94	30	2	Trace	—	—	6	64	.4	190	.06	.06	.4	48
Cabbage, celery or Chinese, raw, cut in 1-in. pieces ....1 cup	75	95	10	1	Trace	—	—	2	32	.5	110	.04	.03	.5	19

Food, approximate measure, and weight (in grams)		Water	Food energy	Protein	Fat	Fatty acids		Carbohydrate	Calcium	Iron	Vitamin A value	Thiamin	Riboflavin	Niacin	Ascorbic acid
						Saturated (total)	Unsaturated linoleic								
	Grams	Percent	Calories	Grams	Grams	Grams	Grams	Grams	Milligrams	Milligrams	International units	Milligrams	Milligrams	Milligrams	Milligrams
Carrots:															
Raw:															
Whole, 5½x1 inch.....1 carrot	50	88	20	1	Trace	—	—	5	18	.8	5,500	.03	.03	.3	4
Grated ....1 cup	110	88	45	1	Trace	—	—	11	41	.8	12,100	.06	.06	.7	9
Cooked, diced ....1 cup	145	91	45	1	Trace	—	—	10	48	.9	15,220	.08	.07	.7	9
Cauliflower, cooked, flowerbuds	120	93	25	3	Trace	—	—	5	25	.8	70	.11	.10	.7	66
Celery, raw:															
Stalk, large outer.....1 stalk	40	94	5	Trace	Trace	—	—	2	16	.1	100	.01	.01	.1	4
Pieces, diced ....1 cup	100	94	15	1	Trace	—	—	4	39	.3	240	.03	.03	.3	9
Collards, cooked ....1 cup	190	91	55	5	1	—	—	9	289	1.1	10,260	.27	.37	2.4	87
Corn, sweet															
Cooked ....1 ear	140	74	70	3	1	—	—	16	2	.5	⁶310	.09	.08	1.0	7
Canned, solids and liquid ....1 cup	256	81	170	5	2	—	—	40	10	1.0	⁶690	.07	.12	2.3	13
Cowpeas, cooked, immature seeds.....1 cup	160	72	175	13	1	—	—	29	38	3.4	560	.49	.18	2.3	28
Cucumbers, 10-ounce:															
Raw, pared ....1 cucumber ..	207	96	30	1	Trace	—	—	7	35	.6	Trace	.07	.09	.4	23
Dandelion greens, cooked ......1 cup	180	90	60	4	1	—	—	12	252	3.2	21,060	.24	.29	—	32
Endive, curly (including escarole) ....2 ounces	57	93	10	1	Trace	—	—	2	46	1.0	1,870	.04	.08	.3	6
Kale, leaves including stems, cooked ......1 cup	110	91	30	4	1	—	—	4	147	1.3	8,140	—	—	—	68
Lettuce, raw:															
Butterhead, as Boston types; head, 4-inch diameter ......1 head	220	95	30	3	Trace	—	—	6	77	4.4	2,130	.14	.13	.6	18
Crisphead, as Iceberg; head ....1 head	454	96	60	4	Trace	—	—	13	91	2.3	1,500	.29	.27	1.3	29

Food	Grams	Water (%)	Food energy	Protein	Fat	Saturated fatty acids	Unsaturated fatty acids	Carbohydrate	Calcium	Iron	Vitamin A	Thiamine	Riboflavin	Niacin	Ascorbic acid
Looseleaf, or bunching varieties, leaves ...2 large	50	94	10	1	Trace	—	—	2	34	.7	950	.03	.04	.2	9
Mushrooms, canned, solids and liquid .....1 cup	244	93	40	5	Trace	—	—	6	15	1.2	Trace	.04	.60	4.8	4
Mustard greens, cooked.....1 cup	140	93	35	3	1	—	—	6	193	2.5	8,120	.11	.19	.9	68
Okra, cooked.....8 pods	85	91	25	2	Trace	—	—	5	78	.4	420	.11	.15	.8	17
Onions: Cooked.....1 cup	210	92	60	3	Trace	—	—	14	50	.8	80	.06	.06	.4	14
Young green, small, without tops.....6 onions	50	88	20	1	Trace	—	—	5	20	.3	Trace	.02	.02	.2	12
Parsley, raw, chopped.....1 tablespoon	4	85	Trace	Trace	Trace	—	—	Trace	8	.2	340	Trace	.01	Trace	7
Parsnips, cooked.....1 cup	155	82	100	2	1	—	—	23	70	.9	50	.11	.12	.2	16
Peas, green: Cooked.....1 cup	160	82	115	9	1	—	—	19	37	2.9	860	.44	.17	3.7	33
Canned, solids and liquid.....1 cup	249	83	165	9	1	—	—	31	50	4.2	1,120	.23	.13	2.2	22
Peppers, sweet: Raw, about 5 per pound: Green pod without stem and seeds..1 pod	74	93	15	1	Trace	—	—	4	7	.5	310	.06	.06	.4	94
Cooked, boiled, drained.....1 pod	73	95	15	1	Trace	—	—	3	7	.4	310	.05	.05	.4	70
Potatoes, medium (about 3 per pound raw): Baked, peeled after baking.....1 potato	99	75	90	3	Trace	—	—	21	9	.7	Trace	.10	.04	1.7	20
Boiled, peeled after boiling.....1 potato	136	80	105	3	Trace	—	—	23	10	.8	Trace	.13	.05	2.0	22
French-fried, piece 2x½x½ inch: Cooked in deep fat...10 pieces	57	45	155	2	7	2	4	20	9	.7	Trace	.07	.04	1.8	12
Frozen, heated....10 pieces	57	53	125	2	5	1	2	19	5	1.0	Trace	.08	.01	1.5	12
Mashed: Milk added.....1 cup	195	83	125	4	1	—	—	25	47	.8	50	.16	.10	2.0	19
Pumpkin, canned.....1 cup	228	90	75	2	1	—	—	18	57	.9	14,590	.07	.12	1.3	12
Spinach: Cooked.....1 cup	180	92	40	5	1	—	—	6	167	4.0	14,580	.13	.25	1.0	50
Canned, drained solids.....1 cup	180	91	45	5	1	—	—	6	212	4.7	14,400	.03	.21	.6	24

| Food, approximate measure, and weight (in grams) | Water | Food energy | Pro-tein | Fat | Fatty acids | | Carbo-hy-drate | Cal-cium | Iron | Vita-min A value | Thia-min | Ribo-flavin | Niacin | Ascor-bic acid |
					Satu-rated (total)	Unsatu-rated lin-oleic								
	Per-cent	Calo-ries	Grams	Grams	Grams	Grams	Grams	Milli-grams	Milli-grams	Inter-national units	Milli-grams	Milli-grams	Milli-grams	Milli-grams
Squash:														
Cooked:														
Summer, diced ....1 cup........ 210	96	30	2	Trace	—	—	7	52	.8	820	.10	.16	1.6	21
Winter, baked, mashed ....1 cup........ 205	81	130	4	1	—	—	32	57	1.6	8,610	.10	.27	1.4	27
Sweet potatoes:														
Cooked, medium, 5x2 inches:														
Baked, peeled after baking ....1 sweet potato. 110	64	155	2	1	—	—	36	44	1.0	8,910	.10	.07	.7	24
Boiled, peeled after boiling ....1 sweet potato. 147	71	170	2	1	—	—	39	47	1.0	11,610	.13	.09	.9	25
Candied, 3½x2¼ inches .....1 sweet potato. 175	60	295	2	6	2	1	60	65	1.6	11,030	.10	.08	.8	17
Canned, vacuum or solid pack ....1 cup........ 218	72	235	4	Trace	—	—	54	54	1.7	17,000	.10	.10	1.4	30
Tomatoes:														
Raw, approx. 3-in. diam., 2⅜ in.high..1 tomato 200	94	40	2	Trace	—	—	9	24	.9	1,640	.11	.07	1.3	²42
Canned, solids and liquid ....1 cup........ 241	94	50	2	1	—	—	10	14	1.2	2,170	.12	.07	1.7	41
Tomato catsup:														
Tablespoon ....1 tablespoon . 15	69	15	Trace	Trace	—	—	4	3	.1	210	.01	.01	.2	2
Tomato juice, canned:														
Cup ....1 cup........ 243	94	45	2	Trace	—	—	10	17	2.2	1,940	.12	.07	1.9	39
Turnips, cooked, diced...1 cup........ 155	94	35	1	Trace	—	—	8	54	.6	Trace	.06	.08	.5	34
Turnip greens, cooked...1 cup........ 145	94	30	3	Trace	—	—	5	252	1.5	8,270	.15	.33	.7	68
FRUITS AND FRUIT PRODUCTS														
Apples, raw (about 3 per lb.)⁵ ....1 apple 150	85	70	Trace	Trace	—	—	18	8	.4	50	.04	.02	.1	3

Apple juice, bottled or canned ...... 1 cup	248	88	120	Trace	Trace	—	—	30	15	1.5	—	.02	.05	.2	2
Applesauce, canned: Sweetened ...... 1 cup	255	76	230	Trace	Trace	—	—	61	10	1.3	100	.05	.03	.1	3[2]
Unsweetened or artificially sweetened ... 1 cup	244	88	100	Trace	Trace	—	—	26	10	1.2	100	.05	.02	.1	2[2]
Apricots: Raw (about 12 per lb.)[3] 3 apricots	114	85	55	1	Trace	—	—	14	18	.5	2,890	.03	.04	.7	10
Canned in heavy syrup. 1 cup	259	77	220	2	Trace	—	—	57	28	.8	4,510	.05	.06	.9	10
Dried, uncooked (40 halves per cup) ... 1 cup	150	25	390	8	1	—	—	100	100	8.2	16,350	.02	.23	4.9	19
Cooked, unsweetened, fruit and liquid ... 1 cup	285	76	240	5	1	—	—	62	63	5.1	8,550	.01	.13	2.8	8
Apricot nectar, canned ... 1 cup	251	85	140	1	Trace	—	—	37	23	.5	2,380	.03	.03	.5	8[3]
Avocados, whole fruit, raw[5] California (mid- and late-winter) ... 1 avocado	284	74	370	5	37	5	7	13	22	1.3	630	.24	.43	3.5	30
Florida (late summer, fall) ... 1 avocado	454	78	390	4	33	4	7	27	30	1.8	880	.33	.61	4.9	43
Bananas, raw, medium size[5] ... 1 banana	175	76	100	1	Trace	—	—	26	10	.8	230	.06	.07	.8	12
Banana flakes ... 1 cup	100	3	340	4	1	—	—	89	32	2.8	760	.18	.24	2.8	7
Blackberries, raw ... 1 cup	144	84	85	2	1	—	—	19	46	1.3	290	.05	.06	.5	30
Blueberries, raw ... 1 cup	140	83	85	1	1	—	—	21	21	1.4	140	.04	.08	.6	20
Cantaloup, raw, medium, 5-inch diameter[6] ... ½ melon	385	91	60	1	Trace	—	—	14	27	.8	6,540[4]	.08	.06	1.2	63
Cherries, canned, red, sour, pitted, water pack ... 1 cup	244	88	105	2	Trace	—	—	26	37	.7	1,660	.07	.05	.5	12
Cranberry-juice cocktail, canned ... 1 cup	250	83	165	Trace	Trace	—	—	42	13	.8	Trace	.03	.03	.1	40[*]
Cranberry sauce, sweetened, canned, strained ... 1 cup	277	62	405	Trace	1	—	—	104	17	.6	60	.03	.03	.1	6
Dates, pitted, cut ... 1 cup	178	22	490	4	1	—	—	130	105	5.3	90	.16	.17	3.9	0
Figs, dried, large ... 1 fig	21	23	60	1	Trace	—	—	15	26	.6	20	.02	.02	.1	0

Food, approximate measure, and weight (in grams)	Grams	Water (Percent)	Food energy (Calories)	Protein (Grams)	Fat (Grams)	Fatty acids Saturated (total) (Grams)	Fatty acids Unsaturated linoleic (Grams)	Carbohydrate (Grams)	Calcium (Milligrams)	Iron (Milligrams)	Vitamin A value (International units)	Thiamin (Milligrams)	Riboflavin (Milligrams)	Niacin (Milligrams)	Ascorbic acid (Milligrams)
Fruit cocktail, canned, in heavy sirup ...... 1 cup	256	80	195	1	Trace	—	—	50	23	1.0	360	.05	.03	1.3	5
Grapefruit:															
Raw, medium, 3¾-in. diam.[5]															
White ...... ½ grapefruit ..	241	89	45	1	Trace	—	—	12	19	.5	10	.05	.02	.2	44
Pink or red ...... ½ grapefruit ..	241	89	50	1	Trace	—	—	13	20	.5	540	.05	.02	.2	44
Canned, sirup pack ... 1 cup	254	81	180	2	Trace	—	—	45	33	.8	30	.08	.05	.5	76
Grapefruit juice:															
Fresh ...... 1 cup	246	90	95	1	Trace	—	—	23	22	.5	(6)	.09	.04	.4	92
Canned, white:															
Unsweetened ...... 1 cup ..	247	89	100	1	Trace	—	—	24	20	1.0	20	.07	.04	.4	84
Sweetened ...... 1 cup ..	250	86	130	1	Trace	—	—	32	20	1.0	20	.07	.04	.4	78
Frozen, concentrate, unsweetened:															
Diluted with 3 parts water, by volume .. 1 cup ..	247	89	100	1	Trace	—	—	24	25	.2	20	.10	.04	.5	96
Dehydrated crystals prepared with water 1 cup ..	247	90	100	1	Trace	—	—	24	22	.2	20	.10	.05	.5	91
Grapes, raw[7] .... 1 cup ..	153	82	65	1	1	—	—	15	15	.4	100	.05	.03	.2	3
Grape juice:															
Canned or bottled .... 1 cup	253	83	165	1	Trace	—	—	42	28	.8	—	.10	.05	.5	Trace
Frozen concentrate, sweetened:															
Diluted with 3 parts water, by volume. 1 cup ..	250	86	135	1	Trace	—	—	33	8	.3	10	.05	.08	.5	(8)
Grape juice drink, canned .. 1 cup ..	250	86	135	Trace	Trace	—	—	35	8	.3	—	.03	.03	.3	(8)
Lemon juice, raw ... 1 cup ..	244	91	60	1	Trace	—	—	20	17	.5	50	.07	.02	.2	112
Lemonade concentrate:															
Diluted with 4⅓ parts water, by volume ... 1 cup	248	88	110	Trace	Trace	—	—	28	2	Trace	Trace	Trace	Trace	.2	17
Lime juice:															

Food	Measure	Grams															
Fresh	1 cup	246	90	65	1	Trace	—	—	—	22	22	.5	20	.05	.02	.2	79
Canned, unsweetened	1 cup	246	90	65	1	Trace	—	—	—	22	22	.5	20	.05	.02	.2	52
Limeade concentrate, frozen: Diluted with 4⅓ parts water, by volume	1 cup	247	90	100	Trace	Trace	—	—	—	27	2	Trace	Trace	Trace	Trace	Trace	5
Oranges, raw, 2⅝-in. diam., all commercial varieties[4]	1 orange	180	86	65	1	Trace	—	—	—	16	54	.5	260	.13	.05	.5	66
Orange juice, fresh, all varieties	1 cup	248	88	110	2	1	—	—	—	26	27	.5	500	.22	.07	1.0	124
Canned, unsweetened	1 cup	249	87	120	2	Trace	—	—	—	28	25	1.0	500	.17	.05	.7	100
Frozen concentrate: Diluted with 3 parts water, by volume	1 cup	249	87	120	2	Trace	—	—	—	29	25	.2	550	.22	.02	1.0	120
Dehydrated crystals, prepared with water	1 cup	248	88	115	1	1	—	—	—	27	25	.5	500	.20	.07	1.0	109
Orange-apricot juice drink	1 cup	249	87	125	1	Trace	—	—	—	32	12	.2	1,440	.05	.02	.5	[10]40
Orange and grapefruit juice: Frozen concentrate: Diluted with 3 parts water, by volume	1 cup	248	88	110	1	Trace	—	—	—	26	20	.2	270	.16	.02	.8	102
Papayas, raw, ½-inch cubes	1 cup	182	89	70	1	Trace	—	—	—	18	36	.5	3,190	.07	.08	.5	102
Peaches: Raw: Whole, medium, 2-inch diameter	1 peach	114	89	35	1	Trace	—	—	—	10	9	.5	[11]1,320	.02	.05	1.0	7
Sliced	1 cup	168	89	65	1	Trace	—	—	—	16	15	.8	[12]2,230	.03	.08	1.6	12
Canned, yellow-fleshed, solids and liquids: Sirup pack, heavy: Halves or slices	1 cup	257	79	200	1	Trace	—	—	—	52	10	.8	1,100	.02	.06	1.4	7
Water pack	1 cup	245	91	75	1	Trace	—	—	—	20	10	.7	1,100	.02	.06	1.4	7
Dried, uncooked	1 cup	160	25	420	5	1	—	—	—	109	77	9.6	6,240	.02	.31	8.5	28
Cooked, unsweetened, 10-12 halves and juice	1 cup	270	77	220	3	1	—	—	—	58	41	5.1	3,290	.01	.15	4.2	6

Food, approximate measure, and weight (in grams)		Water	Food energy	Protein	Fat	Fatty acids		Carbohydrate	Calcium	Iron	Vitamin A value	Thiamin	Riboflavin	Niacin	Ascorbic acid
						Saturated (total)	Unsaturated linoleic								
	Grams	Per cent	Calories	Grams	Grams	Grams	Grams	Grams	Milligrams	Milligrams	International units	Milligrams	Milligrams	Milligrams	Milligrams
Frozen:															
Carton, 12 ounces, not thawed .....1 carton 340		76	300	1	Trace	—	—	77	14	1.7	2,210	.03	.14	2.4	ʷ135
Pears:															
Raw, 3x2½-inch diameter³ .... 1 pear 182		83	100	1	1	—	—	25	13	.5	30	.04	.07	.2	7
Canned, solids and liquid: Sirup pack, heavy:															
Halves or slices..1 cup 255		80	195	1	1	—	—	50	13	.5	Trace	.03	.05	.3	4
Pineapple:															
Raw, diced ....1 cup 140		85	75	1	Trace	—	—	19	24	.7	100	.12	.04	.3	24
Canned, heavy sirup pack, solids and liquid:															
Crushed ....1 cup 260		80	195	1	Trace	—	—	50	29	.8	120	.20	.06	.5	17
Sliced, slices and juice ....2 small or 1 large	122	80	90	Trace	Trace	—	—	24	13	.4	50	.09	.03	.2	8
Pineapple juice, canned..1 cup 249		86	135	1	Trace	—	—	34	37	.7	120	.12	.04	.5	²22
Plums, all except prunes:															
Raw, 2-inch diameter, about 2 ounces² ...1 plum 60		87	25	Trace	Trace			7	7	.3	140	.02	.02	.3	3
Canned, sirup pack (Italian prunes): Plums (with pits):															
and juice³ ....1 cup 256		77	205	1	Trace	—	—	53	22	2.2	2,970	.05	.05	.9	4
Prunes, dried, "softenized" medium:															
Uncooked³ ....4 prunes 32		28	70	1	Trace			18	14	1.1	440	.02	.04	.4	1
Cooked, unsweetened .1 cup 270		66	295	2	1			78	60	4.5	1,860	.08	.18	1.7	2
Prune juice, canned or bottled ....1 cup 256		80	200	1	Trace			49	36	10.5	—	.03	.03	1.0	⁵5
Raisins, seedless, 1 cup 165		18	480	4	Trace			128	102	5.8	30	.18	.13	.8	2

Food	Approximate measure	Grams	Water (%)	Food energy (calories)	Protein (g)	Fat (g)	Saturated (g)	Oleic (g)	Linoleic (g)	Carbohydrate (g)	Calcium (mg)	Iron (mg)	Vitamin A (I.U.)	Thiamin (mg)	Riboflavin (mg)	Niacin (mg)	Ascorbic acid (mg)
Raspberries, red: Raw	1 cup	123	84	70	1	1	—	—	—	17	27	1.1	160	.04	.11	1.1	31
Frozen, 10-ounce carton, not thawed	1 carton	284	74	275	2	1	—	—	—	70	37	1.7	200	.06	.17	1.7	59
Rhubarb, cooked, sugar added	1 cup	272	63	385	1	Trace	—	—	—	98	212	1.6	220	.06	.15	.7	17
Strawberries: Raw	1 cup	149	90	55	1	1	—	—	—	13	31	1.5	90	.04	.10	1.0	88
Frozen, 10-ounce carton, not thawed	1 carton	284	71	310	1	1	—	—	—	79	40	2.0	90	.06	.17	1.5	150
Tangerines, raw, medium	1 tangerine	116	87	40	1	Trace	—	—	—	10	34	.3	360	.05	.02	.1	27
Tangerine juice, canned, sweetened	1 cup	249	87	125	1	1	—	—	—	30	45	.5	1,050	.15	.05	.2	55
Watermelon, raw, wedge	1 wedge	925	93	115	2	1	—	—	—	27	30	2.1	2,510	.13	.13	.7	30
GRAIN PRODUCTS																	
Bagel, 3-in. diam.	1 bagel	55	29	165	6	2	—	—	—	30	8	1.2	0	.15	.11	1.4	0
Barley, pearled, light, uncooked	1 cup	200	11	700	16	2	—	—	—	158	32	4.0	0	.24	.10	6.2	0
Biscuits, baking powder, from home recipe with enriched flour, 2-in. diam.	1 biscuit	28	27	105	2	5	1	2	1	13	34	.4	Trace	.06	.06	.1	Trace
Biscuits, baking powder, from mix, 2-in. diam.	1 biscuit	28	28	90	2	3	1	1	1	15	19	.6	Trace	.08	.07	.6	Trace
Bran flakes (40% bran), added thiamin and iron	1 cup	35	3	105	4	1	—	—	—	28	25	12.3	0	.14	.06	2.2	0
Bran flakes with raisins, added thiamin and iron	1 cup	50	7	145	4	1	—	—	—	40	28	13.5	Trace	.16	.07	2.7	0
Breads: Boston brown bread, slice 3x¾ in.	1 slice	48	45	100	3	1	—	—	—	22	43	.9	0	.05	.03	.6	0
Cracked-wheat bread: Slice	1 slice	25	35	65	2	1	—	—	—	13	22	.3	Trace	.03	.02	.3	Trace
French or vienna bread: Enriched, 1 lb. loaf	1 loaf	454	31	1,315	41	14	3	3	2	251	195	10.0	Trace	1.27	1.00	11.3	Trace

Food, approximate measure, and weight (in grams)		Water	Food energy	Protein	Fat	Fatty acids		Carbohydrate	Calcium	Iron	Vitamin A value	Thiamin	Riboflavin	Niacin	Ascorbic acid
						Saturated (total)	Unsaturated linoleic								
	Grams	Percent	Calories	Grams	Grams	Grams	Grams	Grams	Milligrams	Milligrams	International units	Milligrams	Milligrams	Milligrams	Milligrams
Italian bread:															
Enriched, 1 lb. loaf..1 loaf	454	32	1,250	41	4	Trace	2	256	77	10.0	0	1.32	.91	11.8	0
Raisin bread:															
Slice ....1 slice	25	35	65	2	1	—	—	13	18	.3	Trace	.01	.02	.2	Trace
Rye bread:															
American, light (⅓ rye, ⅔ wheat):															
Slice ....1 slice	25	36	60	2	Trace	—	—	13	19	.4	0	.05	.02	.4	0
Pumpernickel, loaf:															
1 lb. ....1 loaf	454	34	1,115	41	5	—	—	241	381	10.9	0	1.04	.64	5.4	0
White bread, enriched:															
Slice ....1 slice	25	36	70	2	1	—	—	13	21	.6	Trace	.06	.05	.6	Trace
Slice, toasted ......1 slice	22	25	70	2	1	—	—	13	21	.6	Trace	.06	.05	.6	Trace
Whole-wheat bread:															
Slice ....1 slice	28	36	65	3	1	—	—	14	24	.8	Trace	.09	.03	.8	Trace
Slice, toasted ......1 slice	24	24	65	3	1	—	—	14	24	.8	Trace	.09	.03	.8	Trace
Breadcrumbs, dry, grated.1 cup	100	6	390	13	5	1	1	73	122	3.6	Trace	.22	.30	3.5	Trace
Buckwheat flour, light, sifted ....1 cup	98	12	340	6	1	—	—	78	11	1.0	0	.08	.04	.4	0
Bulgur, canned, seasoned.1 cup	135	56	245	8	4	—	—	44	27	1.9	0	.08	.05	4.1	0
Cookies:															
Brownies with nuts:															
Made from home recipe with enriched flour ...1 brownie	20	10	95	1	6	1	1	10	8	.4	40	.04	.02	.1	Trace
Made from mix ....1 brownie	20	11	85	1	4	1	1	13	9	.4	20	.03	.02	.1	Trace
Chocolate chip:															
Made from home recipe with enriched flour ...1 cookie	10	3	50	1	3	1	1	6	4	.2	10	.01	.01	.1	Trace

Food	Weight (g)	Water (%)	Food energy (cal)	Protein (g)	Fat (g)	Saturated (g)	Unsaturated oleic (g)	Unsaturated linoleic (g)	Carbohydrate (g)	Calcium (mg)	Iron (mg)	Vitamin A (IU)	Thiamine (mg)	Riboflavin (mg)	Niacin (mg)	Ascorbic acid (mg)
Commercial ......1 cookie	10	3	50	1	2	1	Trace	—	7	4	.2	10	Trace	Trace	Trace	Trace
Fig bars, commercial ..1 cookie	14	14	50	1	1	—	—	—	11	11	.2	20	Trace	.1	.1	Trace
Corn flakes, added nutrients:																
Plain ....1 cup	25	4	100	2	Trace	—	—	—	21	4	.4	0	.11	.02	.5	0
Corn (hominy) grits, degermed, cooked:																
Enriched ....1 cup	245	87	125	3	Trace	—	—	—	27	2	.7	[13]150	.10	.07	1.0	0
Cornmeal:																
Whole-ground, unbolted, dry ...1 cup	122	12	435	11	5	2	1	2	90	24	2.9	[15]620	.46	.13	2.4	0
Degermed, enriched:																
Dry form ....1 cup	138	12	500	11	2	—	—	—	108	8	4.0	[15]610	.61	.36	4.8	0
Cooked ....1 cup	240	88	120	3	1	—	—	—	26	2	1.0	[15]140	.14	.10	1.2	0
Corn muffins, made with enriched degermed cornmeal and enriched flour; muffin 2⅜-in diam. ....1 muffin	40	33	125	3	4	1	2	Trace	19	42	.7	[15]120	.08	.09	.6	Trace
Crackers:																
Graham, 2½-in. square. 4 crackers	28	6	110	2	3	—	—	—	21	11	.4	0	.01	.06	.4	0
Saltines ....4 crackers	11	4	50	1	1	—	—	—	8	2	.1	0	Trace	Trace	.1	0
Doughnuts, cake type ...1 doughnut	32	24	125	1	6	1	4	Trace	16	13	[14].4	30	[16].05	[16].05	[14].4	Trace
Farina, quick-cooking, enriched, cooked ....1 cup	245	89	105	3	Trace	—	—	—	22	147	[17].7	0	[17].12	[17].07	[17]1.0	0
Macaroni, cooked:																
Enriched:																
Cooked, until tender.1 cup	140	72	155	5	1	—	—	—	32	8	[17]1.3	0	[17].20	[17].11	[17]1.5	0
Unenriched:																
Cooked, until tender ...1 cup	140	72	155	5	1	—	—	—	32	11	.6	0	.01	.01	.4	0
Macaroni (enriched) and cheese, baked ...1 cup	200	58	430	17	22	10	8	2	40	362	1.8	860	.20	.40	1.8	Trace
Canned ....1 cup	240	80	230	9	10	4	5	1	26	199	1.0	260	.12	.24	1.0	Trace
Muffins, with enriched white flour, muffin, 3-inch diam. ......1 muffin	40	38	120	3	4	1	2	1	17	42	.6	40	.07	.09	.6	Trace
Noodles (egg noodles), cooked:																
Enriched ....1 cup	160	70	200	7	2	Trace	Trace	Trace	37	16	[17]1.4	110	[17].22	[17].13	[17]1.9	0
Unenriched ......1 cup	160	70	200	7	2	Trace	Trace	Trace	37	16	1.0	110	.05	.03	.6	0

Food, approximate measure, and weight (in grams)	Water	Food energy	Protein	Fat	Fatty acids		Carbohydrate	Calcium	Iron	Vitamin A value	Thiamin	Riboflavin	Niacin	Ascorbic acid
					Saturated (total)	Unsaturated linoleic								
	Percent	Calories	Grams	Grams	Grams	Grams	Grams	Milligrams	Milligrams	International units	Milligrams	Milligrams	Milligrams	Milligrams
Oatmeal or rolled oats, cooked ....1 cup 240	87	130	5	2	—	1	23	22	1.4	0	.19	.05	.2	0
Pancakes, 4-inch diam.:														
Wheat, enriched flour (home recipe) .....1 cake 27	50	60	2	2	Trace	Trace	9	27	.4	30	.05	.06	.4	Trace
Buckwheat (made from mix with egg and milk) ......1 cake 27	58	55	2	2	1	Trace	6	59	.4	60	.03	.04	.2	Trace
Plain or buttermilk (made from mix with egg and milk) ......1 cake 27	51	60	2	2	1	Trace	9	58	.3	70	.04	.06	.2	Trace
Pizza (cheese) 5½-in. sector; ⅛ of 14-in. diam. pie ......1 sector 75	45	185	7	6	2	Trace	27	107	.7	290	.04	.12	.7	4
Popcorn, popped, plain ...1 cup 6	4	25	1	Trace	—	—	5	1	.2	—	—	.01	.1	0
Pretzels:														
Dutch, twisted ....1 pretzel 16	5	60	2	1	—	—	12	4	.2	0	Trace	Trace	.1	0
Thin, twisted ....1 pretzel 6	5	25	1	Trace	—	—	5	1	.1	0	Trace	Trace	Trace	0
Stick, regular, 3⅛ inches ......5 sticks 3	5	10	Trace	Trace	—	—	2	1	Trace	0	Trace	Trace	Trace	0
...ice, brown ....1 cup 205	70	238	5	1	—	—	51	24	1.0	0	.18	.04	2.8	0
Rice, white:														
Enriched:														
Raw ....1 cup 185	12	670	12	1	—	—	149	44	"5.4	0	".81	".06	"6.5	0
Cooked ....1 cup 205	73	225	4	Trace	—	—	50	21	"1.8	0	".23	".02	"2.1	0
Instant, ready-to-serve ...1 cup 165	73	180	4	Trace	—	—	40	5	"1.3	0	".21	—	"1.7	0
Unenriched, cooked ...1 cup 205	73	225	4	Trace	—	—	50	21	"1.4	0	".04	.02	".8	0
Parbolled, cooked ....1 cup 175	73	185	4	Trace	—	—	41	33	"1.4	0	".19	—	"2.1	0

Food	Weight (g)	Water	Food energy	Protein	Fat	(Sat. fat)	(Unsat. fat)	Carbohydrate	Calcium	Iron	Vitamin A	Thiamine	Riboflavin	Niacin	Ascorbic acid
Rice, puffed, added nutrients .... 1 cup	15	4	60	1	Trace	—	—	13	3	.3	0	.07	.01	.7	0
Rolls, enriched:															
Cloverleaf or pan:															
Home recipe ...... 1 roll	35	26	120	3	3	1	1	20	16	.7	30	.09	.09	.8	Trace
Commercial ...... 1 roll	28	31	85	2	2	Trace	Trace	15	21	.5	Trace	.08	.05	.6	Trace
Frankfurter or hamburger ...... 1 roll	40	31	120	3	2	1	1	21	30	.8	Trace	.11	.07	.9	Trace
Rye wafers, whole-grain, 1⅞x3½ inches ...... 2 wafers	13	6	45	2	Trace	—	—	10	7	.5	0	.04	.03	.2	0
Spaghetti, cooked, tender stage, enriched ...... 1 cup	140	72	155	5	1	—	—	32	11	[17]1.3	0	[17].20	[17].11	[17]1.5	0
Spaghetti with meat balls and tomato sauce:															
Home recipe ...... 1 cup	248	70	330	19	12	4	1	39	124	3.7	1,590	.25	.30	4.0	22
Canned ...... 1 cup	250	78	260	12	10	2	4	28	53	3.3	1,000	.15	.18	2.3	5
Waffles, with enriched flour, 7-in. diam. ...... 1 waffle	75	41	210	7	7	2	1	28	85	1.3	250	.13	.19	1.0	Trace
Waffles, made from mix, enriched, egg and milk added, 7-in. diam. ...... 1 waffle	75	42	205	7	8	3	1	27	179	1.0	170	.11	.17	.7	Trace
Wheat, puffed, added nutrients ...... 1 cup	15	3	55	2	Trace	—	—	12	4	.6	0	.08	.03	1.2	0
Wheat, shredded, plain ...... 1 biscuit	25	7	90	2	1	—	—	20	11	.9	0	.06	.03	1.1	0
Wheat flakes, added nutrients ...... 1 cup	30	4	105	3	Trace	—	—	24	12	1.3	0	.19	.04	1.5	0
Wheat flours:															
Whole-wheat, from hard wheats, stirred .... 1 cup	120	12	400	16	2	Trace	1	85	49	4.0	0	.66	.14	5.2	0
All-purpose or family flour, enriched:															
Sifted ...... 1 cup	115	12	420	12	1	—	—	88	18	[17]3.3	0	[17].51	[17].30	[17]4.0	0
Unsifted ...... 1 cup	125	12	455	13	1	—	—	95	20	[17]3.6	0	[17].55	[17].33	[17]4.4	0
Self-rising, enriched .... 1 cup	125	12	440	12	1	—	—	93	331	[17]3.6	0	[17].55	[17].33	[17]4.4	0
Cake or pastry flour, sifted .... 1 cup	96	12	350	7	1	—	—	76	16	.5	0	.03	.03	.7	0
Wheat germ, toasted .... 1 cup	65	3	260	20	8	3	3	33	31	6	74	1.1	.66	3.5	6.6

Food, approximate measure, and weight (in grams)	Grams	Water (Percent)	Food energy (Calories)	Protein (Grams)	Fat (Grams)	Fatty acids Saturated (total) (Grams)	Fatty acids Unsaturated linoleic (Grams)	Carbohydrate (Grams)	Calcium (Milligrams)	Iron (Milligrams)	Vitamin A value (International units)	Thiamin (Milligrams)	Riboflavin (Milligrams)	Niacin (Milligrams)	Ascorbic acid (Milligrams)
FATS, OILS															
Butter:															
Regular .... 1 tablespoon .	14	16	100	Trace	12	6	Trace	Trace	3	0	[12]470	—	—	—	0
Whipped, 6 sticks or 2, 8-oz. containers per pound .... 1 tablespoon .	9	16	65	Trace	8	4	Trace	Trace	2	0	[12]310	—	—	—	0
Fats, cooking:															
Lard .... 1 cup	205	0	1,850	0	205	78	20	0	0	0	0	0	0	0	0
1 tablespoon	13	0	115	0	13	5	1	0	0	0	0	0	0	0	0
Vegetable fats ... 1 cup	200	0	1,770	0	200	50	44	0	0	0	—	0	0	0	0
1 tablespoon	13	0	110	0	13	3	3	0	0	0	—	0	0	0	0
Margarine:															
Regular .... 1 tablespoon .	14	16	100	Trace	12	2	3	Trace	3	0	[20]470	—	—	—	0
Soft, 2, 8-oz. tubs per pound .... 1 tablespoon .	14	16	100	Trace	11	2	4	Trace	3	0	[20]470	—	—	—	0
Mayonnaise ..... 1 tablespoon .	14	15	100	Trace	11	2	6	Trace	3	.1	40	Trace	.01	Trace	—
Oils, salad or cooking:															
Corn .... 1 tablespoon .	14	0	125	0	14	1	7	0	0	0	—	0	0	0	0
Cottonseed ..... 1 tablespoon .	14	0	125	0	14	4	7	0	0	0	—	0	0	0	0
Olive .... 1 tablespoon .	14	0	125	0	14	2	1	0	0	0	—	0	0	0	0
Peanut .... 1 tablespoon .	14	0	125	0	14	3	4	0	0	0	—	0	0	0	0
Safflower .... 1 tablespoon .	14	0	125	0	14	1	10	0	0	0	—	0	0	0	0
Soybean .... 1 tablespoon .	14	0	125	0	14	2	7	0	0	0	—	0	0	0	0
SUGARS, SWEETS															
Honey, strained or extracted .... 1 tablespoon .	21	17	65	Trace	0	—	—	17	1	.1	0	Trace	.01	.1	Trace
Jams and preserves... 1 tablespoon .	20	29	55	Trace	Trace	—	—	14	4	.2	Trace	Trace	.01	Trace	Trace
Jellies .... 1 tablespoon .	18	29	50	Trace	Trace	—	—	13	4	.3	Trace	Trace	.01	Trace	1

Food																
Molasses, cane: Light (first extraction) . 1 tablespoon	20	24	50	—	—	—	—	—	13	33	.9	—	.01	.01	Trace	—
Blackstrap (third extraction) . . . . 1 tablespoon	20	24	45	—	—	—	—	—	11	137	3.2	—	.02	.04	.4	—
Sirups: Sorghum . . . . . 1 tablespoon	21	23	55	—	—	—	—	—	14	35	2.6	—	—	.02	Trace	—
Table blends, chiefly corn, light and dark. 1 tablespoon	21	24	60	0	0	—	—	—	15	9	.8	0	0	0	0	0
Sugars: Brown, firm packed . . . 1 cup	220	2	820	0	0	—	—	—	212	187	7.5	0	.02	.07	.4	0
White: Granulated . . . . . . 1 cup	200	Trace	770	0	0	—	—	—	199	0	.2	0	0	0	0	0
Granulated . . . . . 1 tablespoon	11	Trace	40	0	0	—	—	—	11	0	Trace	0	0	0	0	0
Powdered, stirred before measuring. 1 cup	120	Trace	460	0	0	—	—	—	119	0	.1	0	0	0	0	0
MISCELLANEOUS ITEMS																
Bouillon cubes, approx. ½ in. . . . 1 cube	4	4	5	1	Trace	—	—	—	Trace	—	—	—	—	—	—	—
Gelatin: Plain, dry powder in envelope . . . 1 envelope	7	13	25	6	Trace	—	—	—	0	—	—	—	—	—	—	—
Dessert powder, 3-oz package . . . 1 package	85	2	315	8	0	—	—	—	75	—	—	—	—	—	—	—
Gelatin dessert, prepared with water . . . 1 cup	240	84	140	4	0	—	—	—	34	—	—	—	—	—	—	—
Olives, pickled: Green . . . 4 medium or 3 extra large or 2 giant	16	78	15	Trace	2	—	—	—	Trace	8	.2	40	—	Trace	—	—
Ripe; Mission . . . 3 small or 2 large	10	73	15	Trace	2	—	—	—	Trace	9	.1	10	Trace	Trace	—	—
Pickles, cucumber: Dill, medium, whole, 3¾ in. long, 1¼ in. diam. . . . 1 pickle	65	93	10	1	Trace	—	—	—	1	17	.7	70	Trace	.01	Trace	4

Food, approximate measure, and weight (in grams)	Grams	Water Percent	Food energy Calories	Protein Grams	Fat Grams	Fatty acids Saturated (total) Grams	Unsaturated Linoleic Grams	Carbohydrate Grams	Calcium Milligrams	Iron Milligrams	Vitamin A value International units	Thiamin Milligrams	Riboflavin Milligrams	Niacin Milligrams	Ascorbic acid Milligrams
Fresh, sliced, 1½ in. diam., ¼ in. thick..2 slices	15	79	10	Trace	Trace	—	—	3	5	.3	20	Trace	Trace	Trace	1
Sweet, gherkin, small, whole, approx. 2½ in. long, ¾ in. diam...1 pickle	15	61	20	Trace	Trace	—	—	6	2	.2	10	Trace	Trace	Trace	1
Popcorn. See Grain Products.															
Pudding, home recipe with starch base:															
Vanilla (blanc mange).1 cup	255	76	285	9	10	5	Trace	41	298	Trace	410	.08	.41	.3	2
Pudding mix, dry form,															
4-oz. package ....1 package	113	2	410	3	2	1	Trace	103	23	1.8	Trace	.02	.08	.5	0
Sherbet ....1 cup	193	67	260	2	2	—	—	59	31	Trace	120	.02	.06	Trace	4
Soups:															
Canned, condensed, ready-to-serve:															
Prepared with an equal volume of milk:															
Cream of chicken.1 cup	245	85	180	7	10	3	3	15	172	.5	610	.05	.27	.7	2
Cream of mush-															
room ....1 cup	245	83	215	7	14	4	5	16	191	.5	250	.05	.34	.7	1
Tomato ....1 cup	250	84	175	7	7	3	1	23	168	.8	1,200	.10	.25	1.3	15
Prepared with an equal volume of water:															
Bean with pork..1 cup	250	84	170	8	6	1	2	22	63	2.3	650	.13	.08	1.0	3
Beef broth, bouil-															
lon consommé.1 cup	240	96	30	5	0	0	—	3	Trace	.5	Trace	Trace	.02	1.2	—
Beef noodle ......1 cup	240	93	70	4	3	1	1	7	7	1.0	50	.05	.07	1.0	Trace
Cream of chicken.1 cup	240	92	95	3	6	1	3	8	24	.5	410	.02	.05	.5	Trace
Cream of mush-															
room ....1 cup	240	90	135	2	10	1	5	10	41	.5	70	.02	.12	.7	Trace
Minestrone ....1 cup	245	90	105	5	3	1	—	14	37	1.0	2,350	.07	.05	1.0	—
Split pea ....1 cup	245	85	145	9	3	1	Trace	21	29	1.5	440	.25	.15	1.5	1
Tomato ....1 cup	245	90	90	2	3	Trace	1	16	15	.7	1,000	.05	.05	1.2	12

Food		Weight (g)	Water (%)	Food energy	Protein	Fat			Carbo-hydrate	Calcium	Iron	Vitamin A	Thiamin	Ribo-flavin	Niacin	Ascorbic acid
Vegetable beef	1 cup	245	92	80	5	2	—	—	10	12	.7	2,700	.05	.05	1.0	—
Vegetarian	1 cup	245	92	80	2	2	—	—	13	20	1.0	2,940	.05	.05	1.0	—
Dehydrated, dry form:																
Chicken noodle (2-oz. package)	1 package	57	6	220	8	6	2	1	33	34	1.4	190	.30	.15	2.4	3
Onion mix (1½-oz. package)	1 package	43	3	150	6	5	1	1	23	42	.6	30	.05	.03	.3	6
Tomato-vegetable with noodles (2½-oz. package)	1 package	71	4	245	6	6	2	1	45	33	1.4	1,700	.21	.13	1.8	18
Frozen, condensed:																
Cream of potato																
Prepared with equal volume of milk	1 cup	245	83	185	8	10	5	Trace	18	208	1.0	590	.10	.27	.5	Trace
Prepared with equal volume of water	1 cup	240	90	105	3	5	3	Trace	12	58	1.0	410	.05	.05	.5	—
Cream of shrimp:																
Prepared with equal volume of milk	1 cup	245	82	245	9	16	—	—	15	189	.5	290	.07	.27	.5	Trace
Prepared with equal volume of water	1 cup	240	88	160	5	12	—	—	8	38	.5	120	.05	.05	.5	—
Tapioca, dry, quick cooking	1 cup	152	13	535	1	Trace	—	—	131	15	.6	0	0	0	.5	—
Tapioca cream pudding	1 cup	165	72	220	8	8	4	Trace	28	173	.7	480	.07	.30	.2	0
White sauce, medium	1 cup	250	73	405	10	31	16	1	22	288	.5	1,150	.10	.43	.5	2
Yeast:																
Brewer's, dry	1 tablespoon	8	5	25	3	Trace	—	—	3	17	1.4	Trace	1.25	.34	3.0	Trace

Yoghurt. See Milk, Cheese, Cream, Imitation Cream.

[1]Value applies to unfortified product; value for fortified low-density product would be 1,500 I.U., and the fortified high-density product would be 2,290 I.U.

[2]Contributed largely from beta-carotene used for coloring.

[3]Outer layer of fat on the cut was removed to within approximately ½-inch of the lean. Deposits of fat within the cut were not removed.

[4]If bones are discarded, value will be greatly reduced.

[5]Measure and weight apply to entire vegetable or fruit including parts not usually eaten.

[6]Based on yellow varieties; white varieties contain only a trace of cryptoxanthin and carotenes, the pigments in corn that have biological activity.

[7]Year-round average. Samples marketed from November through May, average 29 milligrams per 200-gram tomato; from June through October, around 52 milligrams.

[8]This is the amount from the fruit. Additional ascorbic acid may be added by the manufacturer. Refer to the label for this information.

[9]Value for varieties with orange-colored flesh; value for varieties with green flesh would be about 540 I.U.

[10]Value listed is based on products with label stating 30 milligrams per 6 fl. oz. serving.

[11]For white-fleshed varieties value is about 20 I.U. per cup; for red-fleshed varieties, 1,080 I.U. per cup.

[12]Present only if added by the manufacturer. Refer to the label for this information.

[13]Based on yellow-fleshed varieties; for white-fleshed varieties value is about 50 I.U. per 114-gram peach and 80 I.U. per cup of sliced peaches.

[14]This value includes ascorbic acid added by manufacturer.

[15]This value is based on product made from yellow varieties of corn; white varieties contain only a trace.

[16]Based on product made with enriched flour. With unenriched flour, approximate values per doughnut are: Iron, 0.2 milligram; thiamin, 0.01 milligram; riboflavin, 0.03 milligram; niacin, 0.2 milligram.

[17]Iron, thiamin, riboflavin, and niacin are based on the minimum levels of enrichment specified in standards of identity promulgated under the Federal Food, Drug, and Cosmetic Act.

[18]Iron, thiamin, and niacin are based on the minimum levels of enrichment specified in standards of identity promulgated under the Federal Food, Drug, and Cosmetic Act. Riboflavin is based on unenriched rice. When the minimum level of enrichment for riboflavin specified in the standards of identity becomes effective the value will be 0.12 milligram per cup of parboiled rice and white rice.

[19]Year-round average.

[20]Based on the average vitamin A content of fortified margarine. Federal specifications for fortified margarine require a minimum of 15,000 I.U. of vitamin A per pound.

Appendix B
Personal Feeding Chart

Please use the following pages to note the foods you introduce and your baby's reaction to them. In case of allergic reactions, this record will be very useful to your doctor, to baby sitters, and for your own quick reference in selecting foods.

PERSONAL FEEDING CHART

DATE	AGE GIVEN	BEVERAGES	CEREAL	FRUIT	VEGETABLE	DAIRY	PROTEIN	LIKE	DISLIKE	ALLERGY	COMMENTS

REACTION

PERSONAL FEEDING CHART

DATE	AGE GIVEN	BEVERAGES	CEREAL	FRUIT	VEGETABLE	DAIRY	PROTEIN	REACTION			COMMENTS
								LIKE	DISLIKE	ALLERGY	

Bibliography

The United States Government publishes many informative booklets on food purchasing, preparation, and storage. They are available either free or at minimal cost by writing to:

Consumer Information Center
Pueblo, Colorado 81009

When ordering, indicate the name and item number and enclose any amount due in either check or money order made payable to the Superintendent of Documents (do not send stamps). You may also request a free issue of *The Consumer Information Catalog*.

If all the booklets are free, write FREE on the envelope. The following selection from the catalog offers many booklets that are especially useful in the economical and nutritious preparation of baby foods.

FOOD

PURCHASE
Consumer's Guide to Food Labels, 519K. Free. 4 pp. 1981. Discusses ingredient and nutrient listing, open dating, metric units, and symbols used on food labels.

How To Buy Economically: A Food Buyer's Guide. 521K. Free. 28 pp. 1981. How to cut costs on meat, poultry, eggs, milk, fruits, and vegetables; months during which you can get the best buys.

PREPARATION AND STORAGE

Home Freezing of Fruits and Vegetables. 212K. $3.50 48 pp. 1981. Equipment needed; tips on selection, preparation, and processing of fruits and vegetables; includes glossary of terms.

Can Your Kitchen Pass the Food Storage Test? 532K. Free. 6 pp. 1980. Checklist of food storage hazards and how to correct them.

Freezing Combination Main Dishes. 133K. $2.25 22 pp. 1978. Selection of ingredients; recipes and instructions for preparation, packaging, freezing, and reheating.

Microwave Oven Radiation. 582K. Free. 6 pp. 1979. How microwave ovens work; federal safety standards; and tips for proper use.

DIET AND NUTRITION

The Confusing World of Health Foods. 518K. Free. 4 pp. 1981. Discusses the claims for "health," "organic," and "natural" foods; compares cost and nutritional value of health foods versus conventional.

Food Is More Than Just Something to Eat. 651K. Free. 32 pp. 1976. Simple guide to nutrition; includes a daily food guide.

Roughage. 526K. Free. 2 pp. 1980. Claims and facts about high fiber diets; the effects of fiber on health; and best food sources for fiber.

Myths about Vitamins. 529K. Free. 4 pp. 1981. Discusses claims made about various vitamins; includes a chart of U.S.

Recommended Daily Allowances and a list of the best vitamin sources.

A Primer on Dietary Minerals. 524K. Free. 4 pp. 1981. Describes necessary minerals and lists best food sources.

The following organizations also publish useful booklets and newsletters:

La Leche League, 9616 Minneapolis Avenue, Franklin Park, Illinois 60131

Consumer Action Now, Inc., Park Avenue, New York, New York 10021

The Federation of Homemakers, 922 N. Stuart Street, Arlington, Virginia 22203

Consumers Reports, **Consumers Union** (at newsstands)

INDEX

Acetic acid, 28
Acorn squash, 250
Additives, 23, 27–30
Agar-agar, 29
Allergies, 35, 43, 52
All-purpose croquettes,
    268–69
All-purpose fruit juice,
    243–44
All-purpose meat stew, 195
All-purpose omelet, 267
All-purpose raw-vegetable
    juice, 244–45
Almond flavor, 29
Alpha-tocopherol (vitamin E),
    13
Aluminum foil, 58, 117, 144
    baking in, 117, 144
    steaming in, 58
American Academy of
    Pediatricians, 13
American cheese, 220
Amino acids, 4, 30

lysine, 30
    methionine, 30
    threonine, 30
    tryptophan, 30
Annato, 29
Antibodies, 34
Antioxidants, 28
Anything custard, 216
Apple/carrot purée, raw,
    120
Apple/grapefruit purée, 131
Apple/orange purée, 131
Apples, 119–21, 230, 249,
    263, 264
    baked, 250
    baked with sweet potatoes,
        179–80
    dried, 118
    stewed dried, 121
    storing, 119
    sugar source, 5
    varieties, 119

Applesauce, 125, 249
　raw, 119
Apricot nectar, 240
Apricots, 121–23, 226, 228,
　　249, 250, 263, 264
　baked, 122
　dried, 118
　raw purée, 121–22
　stewed, 122
　stewed dried, 123
　storing, 121
　vitamin A source, 8
Apricot whip, 230–31
Arrowroot cookies, 106
Artichokes, 148
Artificial colors, 29
Artificial flavors, 29
Artificial ingredients, 25
Ascorbic acid, (vitamin C),
　　7, 11–12, 30
Asparagus, 148–49, 183, 266
　vitamin A source, 8
Atherosclerosis, 235
Avocados, 123–24, 249, 263

Baby Familia cereal, 102
Baby-food system, 86–98
Bacon, 192, 271
Bacteria, temperature for
　　multiplication, 73
Bacterial illnesses, 71
Baked apple/parsnips, 171
Baked apples, 250
　with sweet potatoes,
　　179–80
Baked custard, 215–16
Baked fish, 207
Baked goods, 100
Balanced menu, 45–47
Banana bread sticks, 259
Banana/grapefruit purée, 131
Banana/orange purée, 131
Bananas, 29, 124–26, 226,
　　228, 249, 263, 264

　baked, 125–26
　broiled, 126
　raw, 125
　sautéed, 126
　starch source, 5
　storing, 125
　sugar source, 5
　vitamin B source, 10
Barley, 99, 100
Beans, baked, 250, 266
　kidney, 250
Beans, green and wax. See
　　Green beans
Beans, lima, See Lima
　　beans
Beef, 188, 222
　braising timetable, 194
　freezer storage, 193
　roast (precooked), 192
Beet greens, 161
Beets, 5, 151–52
Benzoic acid, 28
Benzoldehyde, 29
Berries, 126–28, 226, 263
Betain, 29
Beverages, 232–46
　fruit and vegetable juices,
　　239–46
　milk. See Milk
BHA (butylated
　　hydroxyanisole), 28
BHT (butylated hydroxy-
　　toluene), 28, 106, 172
Bib, 48
　plastic catchall, 256–57
Biotin (B complex vitamin),
　　7
Blackberries, 126
Blueberries, 126, 230
Bottle feeding, 33, 35–39
Bottles, disposable, 37–38
Botulism, 71
Brains, 188, 197, 199–200
Braising, 202
　time table, 194

Bran, 99
Brand names, 22
Breads, 104
Bread sticks
  banana, 259
  carrot, 259
  date, 259
  fruit, 259
Breast feeding, 33–35
Breast milk, 235
  mineral content, 34
  vitamin content, 8, 10, 11,
    13, 34
Brewer's yeast, 10, 30
  vitamin B source, 10
British Food Standards
    Committee, 28
Broccoli, 152–53, 183, 266
  calcium source, 15
  vitamin A source, 8
  vitamin C source, 11
Broccoli leaves, 161
Brookhaven National
    Laboratory, Research
    Medical Service, 94
Brown rice, 4, 100, 110
  incomplete protein
    source, 5
  phosphorus source, 17
  vitamin B source, 10
Brown sugar, 95–96
Brussels sprouts, 153
Buckwheat, 99
Burping, 53
Butter, 94
  saturated fat source, 7
  vitamin A source, 9
Buttermilk, 237
Butternut squash, 250

Cabbage, 154–55
  carrot/cabbage, 155
  lemon/cabbage, 155
  vitamin K source, 13

Calcium, 14, 15–16
Calcium propionate, 28
Calories, 2–3
Cane sugar, 30, 96
Canned foods
  botulism, 71
  fruits, 117–18, 249–50
  home canning, 84–85
  prepared dishes, 252
  signs of spoilage, 72
  storage, 83–85
  vegetables, 146–47, 250,
    265
Cantaloupe, 132–34, 249,
    263
  vitamin A source, 8
  vitamin C source, 11
Cantaloupe purée, 133–34
Caramel, 29
Carbohydrates, 2, 4–6, 99
Carboxymethyl cellulose, 29
Carotene, 8, 126
  starch source, 5
  sugar source, 5
Carrot/apple purée, 120
Carrot bread sticks, 259
Carrot/cabbage, 155
Carrot juice
  boiled, 246
  fresh, 245–46
Carrot/orange purée, 131
Carrots, 19, 142, 155–56,
    183, 266
  carrot/cabbage, 155
  celery/carrots, 158
  sugar source, 5
  vitamin A source, 8
Carrot tops, 13
Cauliflower, 156–57, 183, 266
  vitamin K source, 13
Celery, 157–58
  celery/carrots, 158
  celery/peas, 158
Celiac disease, 52–53
Cellulose compounds, 29

Central nervous system, 4
Cereal grains, 99–114
 bran, 99
 finger foods, 257–62
 germ, 99
 instant baby food, 248
 labeling, 100
 stone-ground, 100
 whole, 99, 101
Cereals, 100–104, 226
 dry infant, 248
 enriched, 10, 14, 102
 instant, 248
 precooked dry, 101
 preparing, 103–104
 purée, 106
 refined enriched, 102
 starch source, 5
 storing, 102
 whole-grain, 102
Chard, 161
 vitamin A source, 8
Cheddar cheese, 220
Cheese, 219–20
 American, 220
 calcium source, 15–16
 Cheddar, 220
 complete protein source, 4
 cottage, 220, 253
 finger food, 273
 grade seal, 220
 grating, 220
 label information, 220
 macaroni and, 108
 noodle and, pudding, 107
 phosphorus source, 17
 spread, 23
 Swiss, 220
 using, 220–21
 vitamin A source, 8
 vitamin B source, 10
Cheese spread, 23
Cheese whey, 30
Cheesing, 53, 235
Cherries, 29, 128–29, 263

Chicken
 fatty acids source, 7
 steamed drumsticks, 270–71
 See also Poultry
Chicken/turkey purée,
  202–203
Chick peas (garbanzo beans),
  166, 224
Children's Cancer Research
  Foundation, 28
Chile con carne, 252
Chinese bamboo steam
  basket, 57
Chlorophyll, 29
Chocolate milk, 237
Cholesterol, 6, 7, 235
Choline (B complex vitamin),
  7
Citral, 29
Citric acid, 28
Citrus fruit purée, 131
Citrus fruits, 129–31
 vitamin C source, 129
Citrus fruit sherbet, 227–28
Coal-tar dyes, 29
Coconut oil, 6, 7, 95
Cod-liver oil
 iodine source, 16
 vitamin D source, 12
Cold food, 54, 248
Colic (gas pain), 52, 70
Collard greens, 11, 19, 161
 calcium source, 15
Commercial formulas,
  36–37
Complementary protein
  proportions, 223–24
Complete protein. See
  Protein
Constipation, 53
Converted rice, 110
 incomplete protein
  source, 4
Cookies
 oatmeal, 261–62

Cookies (*cont*.)
  peanut butter, 260–61
Cooking equipment, 55–69
Copper, 14
Corn, 29, 99, 158–59, 266
  phosphorus source, 17
  starch source, 5
Cornmeal, 99, 100, 223, 224
Corn oil, 6, 7, 95
Cornstarch, 29, 105
Corn syrup, 30
Cottonseed oil, 6, 95
Cottage cheese, 221, 253
Count, label information,
  22–23
Crabs, 205
Cracked wheat, 100
Crackers, 104
Cranberries, 126
Cranberry sauce, 127–28
  jellied, 250
Crayfish, 205
Cream of wheat cereal,
  enriched, 102
Crockpot, electric, 57–58
Cucumbers, 160
Cured meats, 193
Cuisinart ® food processor, 65
Custard
  anything, 216
  baked, 215–16
  easy vegetable, 216
  fruit, 216, 228–29
  fruit/egg yolk, 228
  peanut butter, 223, 229
  stirred, 216
  vegetable, 216
  vegetable/egg yolk, 216
  wheat germ, 216
Cyclamates, 30

Dahl, Lewis K., 94
Dairy foods, 226, 252–54
Dandelion greens, 161

Date bread sticks, 259
Date-oatmeal bread, 260
Dating codes, 25–26
Department of Agriculture,
  20, 21
  See also U.S. government
    standards
Desserts, 226–31
  apricot whip, 230–31
  citrus fruit sherbert, 227–28
  fruit crunch, 229–30
  fruit custard, 228–29
  fruit/egg yolk custard, 228
  fruit milk sherbert, 226–27
  gelatin desserts, 231
  peanut butter custard, 229
Deviled chicken spread,
  251
Deviled ham spread, 251
Deviled liver spread, 251
Dextrose, 30˙
Diarrhea, 52, 70
Diet for a Small Planet
  (Lappé), 20
Digestive difficulties,
  51–53, 70
Diglycerides, 28
Disodium phosphate, 29
Double boiler, 57–58
Dried apricots, 118, 123,
  230
Dried beans (black,
  cranberry, kidney, lima,
  navy, pinto), 19, 164,
  166
  incomplete protein
    source, 4
  iron source, 14
  phosphorus source, 17
  starch source, 5
  vitamin B source, 9
Dried fruits, 118, 231
  finger foods, 263
  iron source, 14

Dried lentils, 19, 164, 166
  incomplete protein
    source, 14
  iron source, 14
  phosphorus source, 17
  vitamin B source, 9
Dried peaches, 118, 231
Dried pears, 118
Dried peas (black-eyed, split,
    whole), 19, 164, 166
  incomplete protein source,
    4
  iron source, 14
  phosphorus source, 17
  starch source, 5
  vitamin B source, 9
Drumsticks, steamed, 270–71
Dry infant cereals, 248

Eggplant, 160–61
Eggs, 188, 210–16, 233
  combined with incomplete
    proteins, 212
  complete protein source, 4
  freezer storage, 211–12
  finger foods, 266–68
  instant baby food, 251
  omelets, 267–68
  recipes, 213–16
  refrigerator storage, 211
  scrambled, 214, 215
  smooth, 215
  USDA grades A and B,
    210
  white, 30, 210, 211
  yolk. See Egg yolk
Egg-white solids, 30
Egg yolk, 12, 19, 29, 210,
    211, 212, 213, 251
  iron source, 14
  phosphorus source, 17
  saturated fat source, 7
  vitamin A source, 8
Egg yolk purée, 213

Egg yolk/wheat germ
    purée, 213
Electric blender, 59–64, 89
  repairing, 63–64
  selecting, 60–61
  using, 61–63
Electric crockpot, 57–58
Electric warming dishes,
    47–48, 73
Empty-nutrition sources, 5–6
Emulsifiers, 28–29
Enriched bread, iron source,
    14
Enriched cereals, 102
  iron source, 14
  vitamin B source, 10
Enriched cream of rice
    cereal, 102
Enriched cream of wheat
    cereal, 102
Enriched foods, 23–24
Enriched pastas, incomplete
    protein source, 4
Epstein, Samuel, 28
Ewald, Ellen B.
  Recipes for a Small Planet
    by, 20
Evaporated milk, 3, 36, 234

Family dishes, puréed for
    baby, 223
Fats, 2, 4, 5, 6–7
  oils, 6–7. See also Oils
  saturated, 94
  solid, 6–7
  unsaturated, 94
Fatty acids, 7, 95
Federal Trade Commission,
    24
Federation of Homemakers, 31
Feeding, 33–54
  away from home, 53–54
  baby's refusal to eat,
    49–50

Feeding (*cont.*)
  balanced diet, 45–47
  bottle, 33, 35–38
  breast, 33–35
  introducing new foods, 41–45
  self-feeding, 50–51
  schedules, 39–40
Feeding chair, 48
Feeding equipment, 47–49
Fillers, 23
Finger foods, 255–74
Flavored food, 23
Fish, 188, 204–208, 222
  baked, 207
  complete protein source, 4
  fatty, 204, 205
  finger foods, 272–73
  fresh, 205
  frozen, 205, 206
  grades, 205–206
  lean, 204–205
  phosphorus source, 17
  poached, 207
  puréeing, 208
  shellfish, 205
  stew, 208
  storage, 206
  thawing, 206
  vitamin A source, 8
  vitamin B source, 9
Fish-liver oil
  vitamin A source, 8
Fish-protein concentrate, 30
Fish sticks, steamed, 272–73
Flour, 29, 104–106
  enriched, 101, 104
  oat, 100
  refined, 104
  rye, 100
  soy, 30, 104
  stone ground, 100
  storing, 105

  unbleached, 100, 104
  using, 105–106
  whole-grain, 100, 104, 105
Folic acid (B complex vitamin), 7
Fomon, Samuel, 2, 9, 11, 15, 36, 235
Food and Nutrition Board, National Research Council, 26
Food combination guide, 92–93
Food cubes, 48, 54, 82
Food handling and storage, 72–73, 74.
  See also Storage
Food mill, 66–67, 90
Food processor, 64–66, 89–90
  repairing, 66
  selecting, 65
  using, 65–66
Food starches, 29
Food storage. *See* Storage
Fork and spoon, 68, 91
Formulas, 13
  evaporated milk, 36
  goat's milk, 37
  preparation, 36–37
  soybean-based, 37
  temperature, 38
  whole milk, 36
Fortifiers, 28, 30–31
Frankfurters, 272
Freezer storage, 78–82
  eggs, 211
  meats, 193
  poultry, 201
  vegetables, 147
  what and how to freeze, 79–81
Frozen food
  fruits, 117
  prepared dishes, 252
  vegetables, 145–46, 265

Fruit bread sticks, 259
Fruit crunch, 229–30
Fruit custard, 228–29
Fruit drinks, 23, 24, 26, 241
Fruit/egg yolk custard, 228
Fruit juices, 239–44
  signs of spoilage, 72
Fruit leather, 264
Fruit/milk sherbet, 226–27
Fruits, 115–41, 226
  canned, 117–18
  dried, 118
  finger foods, 263
  fresh, 115–16
  frozen, 117
  instant baby food, 248–59
  raw, 116
  recipes, 119–41
  ripe, 116
  steaming, 117
  stewing, 117
Fruit/vegetable omelet, 268

Garbanzo beans (chick peas),
    166, 224
Gas pain (colic), 52, 70
Gelatin, 29
Gelatin desserts, 231
Germ, cereal, 99–100
Goat's milk, 237
  formula, 37
Government publications
  bacterial illnesses, 71
  freezer storage, 80–81
  home canning, 85
  "Infant Care," 35
Graham crackers, 106, 248
Granolas, 102
Grapefruit, 130, 263
  purée combinations, 131
  vitamin C source, 11, 129
Grapefruit juice, 11
  fresh, 243

Grape juice
  sugar source, 5
Grapes, 131–32, 263
  sugar source, 5
Grater, 67
Green beans, 149–50, 266
  calcium source, 15
  vitamin A source, 9
Green peppers
  vitamin C source, 11
Greens. See Leafy greens
Grits, 99
Guava, 141, 249
  juice, 240
  vitamin C source, 11
Gum arabic, 29
Gum tragacanth, 29

Halibut-liver oil
  vitamin D source, 12
Ham, 192, 193
  baked, 192
  boiled, 192
  deviled spread, 251
Hamburgers, 272
High chair, 48
Hives, 52
Home canning, 84–85
Honey, 96
How to check freezer
    temperature, 78
How to introduce new food,
    41–44
How to plan ahead, 86–87
How to prepare a formula,
    36–38
How to purée, 89–93
  food combination guide,
    92–93
  thickeners, 29, 91
  thinners, 91
How to read labels. See
    Labels/labeling
How to save cleanup time,
    88

How to save time, 87–88
How to use and modify
    recipes, 93–98
  cooking methods and times,
    93
  fats and oils, 94–95
  measurements, 96–97
  salt, 94
  substitutions, 97–98
  sweeteners, 95–96
How to use leftovers, 88
Hummos, 224
Hydrogenated fats, 29
Hydrogenated oils, 6, 95
Hydrolyzed milk protein, 30
Hydrolyzed plant protein, 29

Ice cream, 253
  calcium source, 15
  saturated fat source, 7
Ice milk, 253
Imitation food, 23
Incomplete protein. See
    Protein "Infant Care,"
    government publication,
    35
Infection, 34
Ingredients listed on label.
    See List of ingredients
Inspection shields, 21–22
Instant baby food, 247–54
  canned fruit, 259
  cereals, 248
  cold food, 248
  dairy foods, 252–54
  eggs, 251
  fresh fruit, 248–49
  meats, 251
  stewed fruit, 249
  vegetables, 250
Instant breakfast drink
    powders, 237, 241
Instant cereals, 248
Iodine, 14, 16, 31

Iodized salt, 14, 94
Iron, 14, 15, 23, 30, 34, 35,
    36, 101, 110, 115

Jellied cranberry sauce, 250
Jellied vegetables/fruit, 163,
    185–86
Juices, fruit and vegetable,
    239–46
  beverages not legally juices,
    241
  federal standards,
    240–41
  storing canned, 242
  straining, 242

Kale, 11, 19, 161
  calcium source, 15
Kasha, 100, 102
Kidney/carrot stew, 199
Kidneys, 19, 188, 197
  iron source, 14
  vitamin A source, 8
Kohlrabi, 11, 164

Labels/labeling
  baked goods, 106
  brand names, 22
  canned and frozen prepared
    dishes, 252
  canned fruit, 117–18
  cheese products, 220–21
  dating codes, 25–26
  description of food, 23–24
  enriched cereal products,
    101, 102
  enriched flour, 104
  fruit and vegetable juices
    and beverages, 240–41
  ingredients. See List of
    ingredients
  peanut butter, 172

processing, 25
refined flour, 104
RDA information, 26
USDA/USFDA grades.
    See U.S. government
    standards
weight, measure, and count
    information, 26
whole-grain flour, 100, 104
Lactic acid, 28
La Leche League, 35
Lamb, 188, 222
    braising timetable, 194
    freezer storage, 193
    liver, 197
Lappé, Frances Moore
    Diet for a Small Planet by,
    20
Leafy greens, 20, 162–63,
    183, 266
    iron source, 14
    scrambled, 163
    vitamin A source, 8
    vitamin B source, 9–10
Lecithin, 29
Leeks. See Onions
Leftovers
    how to use, 88
    meal-in-one purée, 88–89
Legumes, dried (peas,
    beans, lentils), 164–66
    complementary protein
    proportions, 223, 224
    cooking times, 166
    pea/bean/lentil purée, 166
Lemon/cabbage, 155
Lemon flavor, 29
Lemon juice, 11
    fresh, 243
Lemons, 130
    vitamin C source, 11, 31,
    129
Lettuce, 167
Lima beans, 150, 266

Limes, 130
    vitamin C source, 129
Linoleic acid, 7, 34, 95, 236,
    239
Liquid vegetable oils, 6, 7, 95
List of ingredients, 24–25,
    26–31
    additives, 27–30
    antioxidants, 28
    artificial colors, 29
    artificial flavors, 29
    emulsifiers, 28–29
    fortifiers, 30
    fruit and vegetable juices
    and beverages, 251
    preservatives, 28
    stabilizers (thickeners), 29,
    91
    sweeteners, 30
Liver, 12, 19, 188, 197
    deviled spread, 251
    finger food, 270
    iron source, 15
    phosphorus source, 17
    vitamin A source, 9
    vitamin B source, 9
Liver purée, 198
Lobster, 205
Lysine, 30

Macaroni and cheese, 108,
    223, 252
Magnesium, 14
Mango, 141, 249, 263
    juice, 240
    vitamin A source, 8
Margarine, 95
Mayonnaise, 95, 186
Meal-in-one eggs, 214.
Meal-in-one fish stew, 208
Meal-in-one leftover purée,
    88–89
Meal-in-one poultry stew,
    203–204

Measurements, 96–97
Measures, label information, 23
Meatballs, 269
Meat purée, 193–94
Meats, 188–93
  all-purpose meat stew, 195
  braising timetable, 194
  complete protein source, 4
  cost per serving chart, 190–91
  cured, 193
  deviled spreads, 251
  finger foods, 268–69
  frankfurters, 272
  freezer storage, 193
  ground, 192, 195–96
  inspection seal, 21, 189
  instant baby food, 252
  iodine source, 16
  iron source, 14
  organ. See Organ meats
  precooked, 192, 252
  puréeing, 196–97
  refrigerator storage, 193
  saturated fat source, 7
  spoilage, 71, 72
  stewing, 195
  U.S. government standards, 21, 189, 192
  See also Beef; Lamb; Pork; Veal
Medium white sauce, 186
Melon/cantaloupe, 132–33
Menu planning guide, 47
Methionine, 30
Methyl cellulose, 29
Microwave ovens, 59
Milk, 232–39
  breast, 9, 10, 11, 13, 34, 235
  calcium source, 15
  certified raw, 236
  complete protein source, 4
  condensed, 236
  evaporated, 3, 36, 233
  fortified, 9, 12, 238–39
  goat, 37, 237
  homogenized, 36, 233
  nonfat dry, 3, 9, 19, 30, 105, 221, 234
  skim, 3, 9, 233, 235
  U.S. government standards, 233, 234
  whole. See Whole milk
Mineral oil, 6
Minerals, 2, 14–17, 30, 115, 140
  calcium, 14, 16–17
  copper, 14
  iodine, 14, 16
  iron, 14–15, 23, 31, 34, 35, 36, 101, 110, 115
  lost in cooking, 55–56
  magnesium, 14
  overconsumption of supplements, 2, 9, 12, 39
  phosphorus, 14, 17, 115
  potassium, 14, 30
  sodium, 14, 16
  supplements, 39
Mini-Blend jar, 60, 61, 172
Modified food starch, 105
Molasses, 30, 95, 96
  iron source, 14
Monoglycerides, 28
Monosodium glutamate (MSG), 27, 29
Mushrooms, 167–68, 183
Mustard greens, 162

National Research Council, Food and Nutrition Board, 26
Natural foods, 24–25
Nectarines/peaches, 134–35, 230, 249, 263

Niacin (B complex vitamin), 7, 9, 10, 23, 30, 34, 36, 101, 110

Nonfat dry milk, 3, 9, 19, 30, 234
  complete protein source, 4
  protein supplement, 105
  U.S. government standards, 221

Noodle and cheese pudding, 107, 221, 223

Noodles, 104
  starch source, 5

Nut bread sticks, 259

Nut butters. See Peanut butter

Nutritional cost, 18–32

Nutritional requirement, 1–17

Nuts
  essential fatty acids source, 7
  incomplete protein source, 4
  saturated fat source, 7
  vitamin E source, 13

Oat flour, 100

Oatmeal, 100, 102

Oatmeal cookies, 261–62

Oats, 99

Oils, 6, 94–95
  coconut, 6, 7, 95
  cod liver, 16
  corn, 6, 7, 95
  cottonseed, 6, 95
  halibut liver, 12
  hydrogenated, 6, 95
  liquid vegetable, 6, 7, 95
  mineral, 6
  palm, 6, 95
  peanut, 6, 7, 13, 95
  polyunsaturated, 6

  safflower, 6, 7, 13, 95
  soybean, 6, 7, 13, 95
  wheat germ, 6, 7, 13

Okra, 168–69

Omelets
  all-purpose, 267
  finger foods, 266
  wheat germ, 267

Onions, 169–70

Orange juice, 23
  dehydrated juice crystals, 242
  fresh, 242–43
  frozen concentrate, 240
  imitation, 241
  orangeade, 241
  sugar source, 5
  U.S. government standards, 240
  vitamin C source, 11, 31, 129

Oranges, 19, 130, 263
  navel (seedless), 130
  purée combinations, 131
  vitamin C source, 11, 30, 129

Organic foods, 24

Organ meats, 188, 197–200
  vitamin B source, 9–10
  See also Kidneys; Liver

Oster blender, Mini-Blend jar, 60, 61

Overcooking, 93–94

Palm oil, 6, 95

Pancake/bread cereal, 106

Pantothenic acid (B complex vitamin), 7

Pantry storage, 74–75

Papaya, 141, 249, 263
  juice, 240
  vitamin C source, 11

Parsley, 161
  vitamin C source, 11
Parsnips, 170–71
Pasta, 100, 104, 106–107
  enriched, 4
  finger foods, 258
Pea/bean/lentil purée, 223
Peaches, 226, 228, 230,
    249, 250, 263, 264
  dried, 118
  stewed dried, 135
  See also Nectarine/peaches
Peanut butter, 19, 250
  essential fatty acid
    source, 7
  incomplete protein
    source, 4
  phosphorus source, 17
  saturated fat source, 7
  vitamin B source, 9
Peanut butter clay, 172, 274
Peanut butter cookies, 172,
    260–61
Peanut butter custard, 172,
    223, 229
Peanut butter pancake,
    224–25
Peanut oil, 6, 7, 95
  vitamin E source, 13
Peanuts, 171–72
  complementary protein
    portions, 224
Pears, 135–36, 226, 228, 249,
    250
  dried, 118
Peas, 173, 183, 250,
    266
  celery/peas, 158
  starch source, 5
  sugar source, 5
Pectin, 29
Peppers, 174
Perfringens poisoning, 71
Phosphorus, 14, 115
Pineapple, 137–38, 250

Pineapple juice, canned,
    240–41
Planning a balanced menu,
    45–47
Plums/prunes, 138–39, 226,
    228, 230, 249, 263
  See also Prunes
Polyunsaturated oils, 6
Pork, 188, 222
  braising timetable,
    194
  freezer storage, 193
  liver, 197
  vitamin B source, 9
Potassium, 14, 30
Potatoes, sweet. See Sweet
    Potatoes
Potatoes, white, 174–76
  mashed, 175–76
  starch source, 5
  stewed apples and
    potatoes, 176
Poultry, 19, 188, 200–204, 222
  canned and frozen
    prepared dishes, 251–52
  chicken/turkey purée,
    202–203
  complete protein source,
    4
  economy buying, 201
  finger foods, 270
  freezer storage, 201
  instant baby food, 252
  liver, 197
  meal-in-one poultry stew,
    203
  precooked meals, 252
  puréeing, 203–204
  refrigerator storage, 201
  spoilage, 72, 201
  thawing, 201
  U.S. government
    standards, 200
  vitamin B source, 9–10

Precooked dry infant cereals, 101
  sweetened, 101
Precooked meals, 252
Preservatives, 28
Pressure cooker, 57
Processing, 25
Propyl gallate, 28
Protein/protein foods, 3–4, 105, 188–225, 226
  animal, 30
  complementary proportions, 223–24
  complete, 4, 222
  economy, 222–25
  eggs. See Eggs
  fortifiers, 30
  incomplete, 4, 99, 222
  inexpensive, 19–20
  instant baby food, 251
  meats. See Meats
  milk. See Milk
  poultry. See Poultry
  recipes, 188–225
  supplementing, 222–23
  vegetable, 30
Prune juice, canned, 240–41
Prunes, 118, 138–40, 250, 264. See also Plums/prunes
Puréeing. See How to purée
Puréeing equipment, 55–69
Puréeing fish, 208
Puréeing meat, 196–97
Puréeing poultry, 203–4
Purée storage, 73–74
Pyrodoxin (B₆ vitamin), 7, 9

Raisins, 118
Ralston cereal, 102
Rashes, 52
Raspberries, 126
Raw apple/carrot purée, 120

Raw (turbinado) sugar, 96
RDA (Recommended Dietary Allowance), 26
Recipe for a Small Planet (Ewald), 20
Recliner, 48
Refreezing, 81–82
Refrigerator storage, 75–77
  eggs, 211–12
  meats, 193
  poultry, 201
  vegetables, 147
Refusal to eat, 49–50
Research Medical Service, Brookhaven National Laboratory, 94
Rhubarb, 140–41, 230
Riboflavin (B₂ vitamin), 7, 9, 10, 23, 30, 101, 110
Rice, 99, 110
  basic purée, 111
  brown (natural), 4, 5, 10, 17, 100, 110
  complementary protein proportions, 223, 224
  converted, 4, 110
  cooking, 111
  enriched cream of, 102
  enriched polished, 110
  enrichment levels, 110
  and meat dishes, 113–14
  polished white, 110
  sautéed, 114, 223
Rice and wheat germ purée, 112, 223
Rice cheese, 223
Rice pudding, 112–13, 223, 248
  double boiler method, 113
  oven method, 113
  with fruit purée, 17
Rice purée, 111
  using leftover rice, 112

Rice purée, (cont.)
  with cheese, 112
  with wheat germ, 112
Rice/soybean purée, 112,
  223
Rice starch, 29, 105
Rutabagas. See Turnips
Rye flour, 100

Saccharin, 30
Safflower oil, 6, 7, 95
Saffron, 29
Salmon, 12
Salmonella, 211
Salmonellosis, 71
Salt, 94
  iodized, 16, 94
Salt-water fish
  iodine source, 16
Sautéed rice, 114, 223
Scallops, 205
Scrambled eggs, 214, 251
Scurvy, 12
Self-feeding, 50–51
Sesame crackers, 262
Sesame seeds, 223, 224
Shellfish, 205
  crab, 205
  crayfish, 205
  iodine source, 16
  lobster, 205
  scallops, 205
  shrimp, 205
Sherbets
  citrus fruit, 227–28
  fruit milk, 226–27
Shopping checklist, 31–32
Shortening
  liquid vegetable oil, 6
  solid, 95
Shrimp, 205
Skim milk, 3, 9, 233–34,
  235–36
  fortified, 234

Smoked meats. See Cured
  meats
Smooth eggs, 215
Sodium, 14, 16
Sodium caseinate, 30
Sodium nitrite, 28
Sodiums, various, as
    preservatives, 28
Solid fats, 6–7
Solid shortening, 95
Sorbic acid, 28
Soufflés, 216
Soybean oil, 6, 7, 95
  vitamin E source, 13
Soybean purée, 209
Soybean/rice purée, 112,
  223
Soybeans, 19, 29, 188,
    208–09, 222, 223, 266
  complete protein source,
    4, 30
  fatty acids source, 7
  formula based on, 37
  phosphorus source, 17
  vitamin B source, 9–10
Soy flour, 30, 104
Spaghetti, 104
Spaghetti and meatballs,
  252
Spareribs, 270
Spinach, 11, 19, 142, 161
  vitamin K source, 13
Spoon, 48
Squash. See Summer
    squash, Winter squash
Stabilizers (thickeners), 29
Standards of identity, 22, 23,
  25
Staph poisoning, 71
Starch/starches, 24, 105
  sources, 5, 29
Steam baskets, 56–57
Steam cooking, 55–59, 94, 117
Steamed drumsticks, 270–71
Steamed fish sticks, 272–73

Steamer blancher, 56
Sterilization, formula bottles, 37
Stewing
  fruit, 117
  meat, 195
  poultry, 203
Stirred custard, 216
Storage, 70–84
  canned food, 83
  freezing, 78–82
  pantry, 74–75
  refrigerator, 75–77
Strainers, 67–68, 90
Strawberries, 126
  vitamin C source, 11
Substitutions, 97–98
Sucrose, 30
Sugar, 24, 30
  brown, 95, 96
  forms, 30
  raw, 96
  sources, 5
Sugar syrup, 30
Sulfur dioxide, 28
Summer squash, 176–77, 266
  crookneck, 176
  Italian marrow, 176
  patty pan, 176
  straightneck, 176
  zucchini, 176
Sunflower seeds, 223
Sweetbreads, 188, 197, 199–200
Sweeteners, 30, 95–96
  brown sugar, 95–96
  cane sugar, 30, 95, 96
  corn syrup, 30
  dextrose, 30
  honey, 96
  molasses, 15, 30, 95, 96
  raw sugar (turbinado), 96
  sucrose, 30
  sugar syrup, 30

Sweet potatoes, 179–80, 183, 250
  baked with apples, 179–80
  sugar source, 5
  vitamin A source, 8
  vitamin B source, 9–10
Swiss cheese, 220
Synthetic ingredients, 25

Tangerines, 130
  vitamin C source, 129
Tapioca, 29, 105
Tartaric acid, 28
Teething, 52
Temperature
  bacteria multiplication danger zone, 73
  formulas, 38
  freezer storage, 78–82
  milk, 38, 54
  refrigerator storage, 75–77
Thiamine (B_1 vitamin), 7, 9, 10, 23, 30, 101, 110
Thickeners, 29, 91
Thinners, 91
Time saving
  cleanup, 88
  food cooking and preparation, 87
Tocopherols, 28
Tomato juice, canned, 11, 240–41
Tomatoes, 11, 181–83, 250, 266
  vitamin A source, 9
  vitamin K source, 13
Travel, 53–54
Tropical fruits, 141
Tryptophan, 30
Tuna fish, 12
Turbinado sugar, 96

Turkey, 222. *See also* Poultry
Turnip greens, 161
  vitamin K source, 13
Turnips, 19, 180
TV dinners, 252

Underwriters Laboratory seal, 58
United Nations FAO/WHO Export Committee on Food Additives, 27
Unit pricing, 23
U.S. Department of Agriculture, 20, 22. *See also* USDA Grades
U.S. Food and Drug Administration, 10, 20, 36, 240
U.S. government standards, 20, 21
  canned fruit, 118
  cheese, 220
  eggs, A and B, 210–11
  fish, 205–6
  flour enrichment, 100
  fruit, 115
  fruit and vegetable juices, 240–41
  labels/labeling, 21–22
  meats, 21, 189, 192
  meat inspection shields, 21–22, 189, 192
  milk, Grade A, 233
  nonfat dry milk, 221, 235
  poultry, 200
  rich enrichment, 110
  vegetables, 143

Veal, 188, 222
  braising timetable, 194
  freezer storage, 194
  liver, 197
Vegetable custard, 163, 184
  easy, 184
Vegetable/egg yolk custard, 163, 185
Vegetable gums, 29
Vegetable oil. *See* Liquid vegetable oil
Vegetables
  baked, 144
  boiled, 144–45
  canned, 145–46, 250, 265
  dark green, 142
  deep yellow, 142
  finger foods, 265
  freezer storage, 147
  fresh, 143–44
  frozen, 145–46, 265
  instant baby food, 250
  leafy green, 161
  mineral sources, 14–17, 30
  orange, 142
  raw, 265
  steamed, 144
  storage, 147
  USDA grade, 143
  vitamin sources, 9, 10, 11, 13, 30
Vegetable soufflé, 163, 183
Vitamins, 2, 7–13, 30–31
  A, 6, 8–9, 30
  B complex, (B_1, B_2, B_6, B_{12}), 7, 9–10, 99, 100, 239
  C, 7, 11–12, 30, 31, 115, 124, 129, 132, 135, 141, 145
  D, 6, 8, 12, 30, 34, 36
  E, 6, 8, 13, 34, 36, 100, 239
  fat soluble, 6, 7–8, 12
  K, 6, 8, 13, 239
  lost in cooking, 56

overconsumption of
supplements, 2, 9, 12,
39
supplements, 39
water soluble, 7, 10–11
Vomiting, 53

Watercress, 11, 161
Weights, label information,
22–23
Wheat, 99
Wheatena cereal, 102
Wheat-germ, 100, 108–9,
213–14, 216
fatty acids source, 7
incomplete protein
source, 4
vitamin B source, 9–10,
30
vitamin E source, 13,
30
Wheat-germ custard, 216
Wheat-germ oil, 6, 7
vitamin E source, 13
Wheat-germ omelet, 267
When to introduce a food,
42–44
Whey solids, 30
Whole foods, 24–25
Whole-grain bread, 4

Whole-grain cereals, 99,
100
incomplete protein source,
4
phosphorus source, 17
vitamin E source, 13
Whole-grain flour, 100
Whole milk, 3, 4, 9, 10, 13,
15, 17, 232–33, 235
homogenized, 36, 233
Whole-wheat cereals, 101
Whole-wheat flour, 100
Winter squash, 177–78, 183,
250
acorn, 177
banana, 177
butternut, 177
delicious, 177
Hubbard, 177
starch source, 5
vitamin A source, 8

Yams. See Sweet potatoes
Yogurt, 217–19, 253
complete protein source,
4
homemade, 217–19
yogurt cheese, 219

Zucchini, 176

ABOUT THE AUTHOR

SUE CASTLE worked as a computer systems analyst and a designer before she began raising a family, experience that taught her the clear, methodical approach found in her books. She lives in Briarcliff Manor, N.Y., with her family, who served happily as guinea pigs as she developed her recipes. Mrs. Castle is also the author of *Face Talk, Hand Talk, Body Talk* and co-author of *Our Child's Medical History*.